Western Muslims and Conflicts Abroad

This book explains why reactive conflict spillovers (political violence in response to conflicts abroad) occur in some migrant-background communities in the West. Based on survey data, statistical datasets, more than sixty interviews with Muslim community leaders and activists, ethnographic research in London and Detroit, and open-source data, this book develops a theoretical explanation for how both differences in government policies (immigration context) and features of migrant-background communities interact to influence the nature of foreign policy-focused activism in migrant communities. Utilizing rigorous, mixed-methods case study analysis, the author comparatively analyses the reactions of the Pakistani community in London and the Arab Muslim community in Detroit to the wars in Afghanistan and Iraq during the decade following 9/11. Both communities are politically mobilized and active. However, while London has experienced reactive conflict spillover, Detroit has remained largely peaceful.

The key findings show that, with regards to activism in response to foreign policy events, Western Muslim communities primarily politically mobilize on the basis of their ethnic divisions. Nevertheless, one notable exception is the Arab-Israeli conflict, which is viewed through the Islamic lenses; and the common Islamic identity is important in driving mobilization domestically in response to Islamophobia, and counterterrorism policies and practices perceived to be discriminatory. Certain organizational arrangements involving minority community leaders, law enforcement, and government officials help to effectively contain some unsettled youth who may otherwise engage in deviant behavior. Overall, the following factors contribute to the creation of an environment where reactive conflict spillover is more likely to occur: policies allowing immigration of violent radicals, poor economic integration without extensive civil society inter-group ties, the presence of radical groups, and connections with radical networks abroad.

Juris Pupcenoks is Assistant Professor of Political Science at Marist College, NY, USA and Associate Fellow at the Securitization of Migrant Integration (SoMI) Network.

Routledge Advances in International Relations and Global Politics

Western Muslims and Conflicts Abroad

Conflict Spillovers to Diasporas

Juris Pupcenoks

Routledge
Taylor & Francis Group

LONDON AND NEW YORK

First published 2016 by Routledge

2 Park Square, Milton Park, Abingdon, Oxfordshire, OX14 4RN
711 Third Avenue, New York, NY 10017

*Routledge is an imprint of the Taylor & Francis Group, an
informa business*

First issued in paperback 2017

Library of Congress Cataloging-in-Publication Data
A catalog record for this book has been requested

ISBN: 978-1-138-91552-7 (hbk)
ISBN: 978-0-8153-7068-0 (pbk)

Typeset in Sabon
by Apex CoVantage, LLC

For Nan-Chun, my dragon lady

Contents

Illustrations

Abbreviations

AAPAC	Arab American Political Action Committee
ACCESS	Arab Community Center for Economic and Social Services
ADC	American-Arab Anti-Discrimination Committee
AMC	American Muslim Council
BRIDGES	Building Respect in Diverse Groups to Enhance Sensitivity
CAAO	Congress of Arab American Organizations
CABU	Council for Arab-British Understanding
CAIR	Council on American-Islamic Relations
CIOM	Council of Islamic Organizations of Michigan
EDL	English Defence League
GIA	Armed Islamic Group of Algeria
Hizb, HT	Hizb ut-Tahrir
ICSR	International Centre for the Study of Radicalization
IIIT	International Institute of Islamic Thought
IONA	Islamic Organization of North America
ISB	Islamic Society of Britain
ISNA	Islamic Society of North America
ISPU	Institute for Social Policy and Understanding
LTTE	Tamil Tigers
MAB	Muslim Association of Britain
MAS	Muslim American Society
MCB	Muslim Council of Britain
MECAWI	Michigan Emergency Committee against War and Injustice
MPAC	Muslim Public Affairs Committee
PKK	Kurdistan Workers Party
TUC	Trades Union Congress (UK)

Foreign Terms

Allah	God
Asabiyyah	Social and ethnic solidarity
Banlieues	Often impoverished residential areas on the outer edge of a city
Barelvi	A form of Sunni Islam often practiced by natives of the Indian subcontinent
Fatwa	A religious opinion concerning Islamic law issues issued by an Islamic authority
Hadith	A body of narrations concerning the words and deeds of the Prophet Muhammad
Hijabi	Muslim woman wearing a headscarf
Imam	Islamic leader, often the worship leader of a mosque or a Muslim community
Jihadi	A term occasionally used to refer to a violent Muslim extremist
Khilafah	An Islamic caliphate
Koran	The main religious text of Islam
Masjid	Mosque, Muslim house of worship
Mujahideen	Term used to refer to Islamic guerilla fighters
Ramadan	The Islamic month of fasting, the ninth month of the Islamic calendar
Salafi(s)	A movement of Sunni Muslims that places great emphasis on literal interpretation of the Koran and Hadith
Sharia	The Islamic laws derived from the holy texts
Shia(s)	The second largest Muslim denomination after Sunni Islam
Sunni(s)	The largest Muslim denomination
Ummah	The worldwide Muslim community

Acknowledgments

This manuscript is a result of more than seven years of research. Parts of this manuscript have been previously presented at more than ten conferences and other forums held at the International Studies Association Meetings, the University of Delaware, Marist College, Washington College, and Westminster College (MO). I particularly want to thank my friend and mentor Mark J. Miller, who has taught me much about diasporas, migration, and security. Much useful feedback on various aspects of this research project has been received from Stuart J. Kaufman, M. A. Muqtedar Khan, Emek Uçarer, Farid Senzai, Nabeel Abraham, Sally Howell, Andrew Shryrock, Onur Tanay, Ryan McCabe, Alynna Lyon, Nabeel Abraham, Sally Howell, Andrew Shryock, Ted Gurr, Fiona Adamson, Peter Neuman, Ed Husain, Barak Mendelsohn, Michael Grillo, Pam Jackson, and Peter Doerschler. At Marist College, I particularly thank Josh Heath, Christina Cottone, and Kristen O'Brien for their capable research and editorial support. Finally, a special thanks is due to Natalja Mortensen and Lillian Rand at Routledge for their assistance all along the way; and to the anonymous reviewers for their outstanding criticisms and comments on this monograph.

This project could not have been possible without support, encouragement from my family and friends, including my parents Irēna Pupčenoka and Juris Pupčenoks, Jānis Pupčenoks, Bill and Nancy Gratz, Ryan Burson and Jane Smith, Sara Chehab, Iñaki Esnaola, Iñaki Iglesias Iruretagoyena, and Julien Couret.

Several institutions provided research assistance for this research. A generous University of Delaware Office of Graduate and Professional Education and the Center for International Studies' Fellowship for International Research sponsored the six-week fieldwork in London during the summer of 2009; and a Dissertation Fellowship from the University of Delaware Graduate Office funded early stages of this research during 2009–10. Partial assistance for another six-week field research stint in Detroit was granted by the University of Delaware Alumni Enrichment Award during the fall of 2009. Finally, Marist College, and the

International Studies Association provided additional financial support for this research and conference travel.

Field research for this project took me to London and Detroit, and I am grateful to numerous individuals for the received help in each of these locations. I would like to particularly thank the following individuals in London for their noteworthy help with recruitment of interviewees: Anas Al-Shaikh Ali and the International Institute of Islamic Thought-United Kingdom and Tehmina Kazi. In Detroit, the following individuals were indispensable with help in recruitment of interviewees: Muzammil Ahmed and the Institute for Social Policy and Understanding, Khadigah Alasry, and Eide Alawan. Finally, some material from early versions of chapters five and seven served as the basis for the article "Religion or Ethnicity?: Middle Eastern Conflicts and American Arab-Muslim Protest Politics," *Nationalism and Ethic Politics* 18(2): 170–192, 2012.

Juris Pupcenoks
Marist College
Mid-Hudson Valley, NY, USA
December 2015

1 Introduction

The most notorious terrorist acts committed in Europe since 9/11 was the London Underground bombing, consisting of a series of coordinated suicide bombings in the London public transport system on July 7, 2005. The explosions were conducted by several British-born yet migrant-background Muslims: three of Pakistani descent, and one Jamaican. These acts of terror killed 52 people and injured 700. The perpetrators claimed the attack to be a protest against the British military presence in Iraq. They also saw themselves as participants in a broader conflict between the West and extreme Islam.

This appalling act is just one instance of reactive conflict spillover to migrant-background communities. In this instance, a terrorist cell—seemingly enraged by the American-led war in Iraq—retaliated. However, not all Western Muslims disliked the War. Across the Atlantic, segments of American Muslims have celebrated the War in Iraq. In numerous instances, top officials in George W. Bush's administration traveled to Detroit, Michigan to seek endorsement for the Iraq War from local Muslim leaders. In Detroit and the Middle East, a picture featuring President Bush kissing the cheek of a prominent Detroit Shia Imam, Sayid Hassan Al-Qazwini, in March 2003 has since been widely circulated. Additionally, the decade following 9/11 showed that Detroit Muslim community had no involvement with any terrorist activities. How does one account for such diverse responses in Western Muslim communities? Why do conflicts from particular locales creep into diasporic communities in some parts of the world, but not others?

This book explains what causes "reactive conflict spillover"[1] in certain ethnic, migrant-background Muslim communities in the UK and the US. It develops a typology and theory of reactive transnational mobilization and reactive conflict spillover, while providing detailed case studies of Pakistani political mobilization in London and Arab Muslim political mobilization in Detroit. Both communities have been politically active in reaction to the so-called War on Terror conflicts[2] and the wars in Afghanistan and Iraq. Muslim leaders in both the UK and US condemned terrorism, yet notable transnational political violence occurred only in London.

Lessons learned from these communities should be applicable to other diasporic communities in the West. However, what at are reactive conflict spillovers and how do they start?

What are Reactive Conflict Spillovers?

Reactive conflict spillover is an episode of protracted violence within a diasporic community in a response to conflicts abroad. Frequently, spillovers occur following trigger events, which can be either violent (e.g. the beginning of the Second Intifada in Palestinian territories in 2000) or non-violent (e.g. the publication of Prophet Muhammad caricatures in 2005). In instances of planned terrorist acts and other cases of premeditated hostilities, violent acts can occur without an immediate preceding specific trigger event. However, more frequently, spillovers happen spontaneously following a vivid triggering event, such as news reports of horrifying crimes committed by a perceived adversary. Thus, spillovers can involve radicalization and acts taken by national liberation or ideological movements—as long as such behavior involves violent actions and is committed in response to an event taking place in another country.

Outside the Western world, conflict spillovers due to migration have been more common—and they have had grave implications. Common and obvious types of direct conflict spillover include conflict imported by different incoming refugee groups, or conflict begun by violent groups in one state resonating to another. Examples include the Israeli-Palestinian conflict spillover in Lebanon's Palestinian refugee camps and in the 1980s and conflict spillovers from the Rwandan civil war to refugee communities in neighboring states in the 1990s. In both instances, reactive spillovers of violence from home countries to refugee camps in other countries lead to infighting within the migrant populations abroad. In fact, Zolberg, Suhrke, and Aguayo (1989) coined the term "refugee-warrior communities" to describe certain migrant settlements consisting of armed fighters escaping ethnic wars in their homelands.

The situation in the Western advanced democracies is different, as Western states, for the most part, are better equipped to provide internal security and to deal with crime.[3] Western states are characterized by a well-established rule of law, and better law enforcement capacity. Compared to the developing world, such Western democracies possess greater capacity to either prevent or manage internal violence, if it were to arise.

Nevertheless, the potential of spillover from the Syrian conflict—or other conflicts ongoing in the Middle East—and possible impacts on the broader region and even the West provide just some examples of the importance of this question. US government officials in the past have warned of potential security risks associated with admitting refugees from countries experiencing internal strife.[4] At the same time, the causal process behind spillover violence has been little understood, even though such acts constitute threats to national security. A better comprehension of what causes migrant-background individuals' political mobilization to escalate into violence will also be able to suggest policy prescriptions of how to promote further migrant integrations in order to forestall such violence.

For example, during the summer of 2007, tensions between India and Pakistan escalated. Many were concerned about potential spillover of hostilities to global diasporas of the two countries. New York City mayor Mike Bloomberg dispatched his emissaries to NYC's Queens Borough to monitor Pakistanis and Indians residing there. Despite the concerns, relations between New York's South Asians remained cordial in 2007. This example illustrates just one instance where better understanding of the dynamics of peaceful and violent mobilization in response to foreign policy events would aid policy-makers in predicting when to expect political violence.

Reactive conflict spillover in the West generally is not a grave danger to state survival. Frequently, policing can solve potential hostilities. Nevertheless, spillovers can cause significant national security implications in extreme forms such as terrorism. Better understanding of the dynamics of spillovers would provide additional insights into "second image reversed" processes that explain how events abroad influence domestic politics.[5] Such an analytic framework would be highly useful to policy-makers who need to assess the second- and third-order consequences of conflict (and foreign policy events), which often are inadequately factored into national security decision-making.

This book explains how and why varied reactive conflict spillovers occur in localities in the Western world characterized by different immigration contexts and characteristics of migrant communities themselves. It is beyond the scope of this manuscript to explain why Western Muslims join and partake in operations of terrorist groups (such as Al-Qaeda and ISIS) abroad—because both the immigration context and characteristics of migrant communities in locations abroad are likely to be different. However, the findings of this research do point to the importance of structural conditions, state policies, and features of migrant communities in engendering discontent and mobilization by groups and individuals in other countries and localities.

Additionally, due to projected steady levels of sizeable immigration to the West, it is likely that concerns about spillovers will remain at the forefront of scholarly and public attention for the foreseeable future. The United Nations estimates that to prevent the aging of the population, the EU should accept 1.4 million migrants annually (six to eight times the projected intake), whereas migration to the US must continue at its projected annual rate of 750,000.[6] Some, including senior British diplomat and researcher Robert Cooper (2003), go as far as to argue that the chief threat to the West comes from chaos spillover from the developing world.

News media has widely reported on several episodes of reactive conflict spillover in diasporic communities. However, except for just a few recent studies (e.g. see Harff and Gurr 2004; Lyon and Lyon and Uçarer 2001; Miller 2000), academic work on this phenomenon is yet to be done.

Research Design

This project uses a structured and focused case study research approach and most-different systems design. The cases provide a systematic comparison and are focused on those aspects of historic instances which help to further understand the dynamics of reactive conflict spillover.[7] The study purposefully compares two communities, which are different in many aspects (ethnic complexion, location, etc.), yet have in common high levels of political activism. Furthermore, although both case studies are geographically focused on two specific areas, this study makes several important contributions to the broader understanding about political mobilization in other diasporic communities, as it places this inquiry within the broader social sciences literature. For these reasons, this study should yield insights useful for understanding other diasporic communities.

The purpose of this book is to explore the broad spectrum of political mobilization that conflicts abroad can generate in domestic migrant communities. Such activities can range from lobbying and orderly protests to violence. I am also particularly interested in understanding why some communities engage in risky political activism and violence whereas others do not. In other words, why do similar communities react differently to conflicts abroad?

The following chapter reviews key historical instances of conflict spillover through time and develops conceptual and theoretical frameworks for case study research. The rest of the manuscript investigates transnational mobilization and spillover by studying two politically active Muslim communities that have reacted quite differently to foreign policy events, with a particular focus on wars in Afghanistan (2001) and Iraq (2003). One of these communities—the Pakistani community in London—has experienced both peaceful mobilization and reactive conflict spillover. The other—Arab Muslims in Detroit—has remained passionate and mobilized, yet their activism has been largely contained.

From the first glance, the compositions of these two communities seem obviously very different. One is predominately Pakistani, the other, Arab-background. Most of London's Pakistanis are Sunnis, whereas half of Detroit's Arabs are Christians (mostly Chaldeans) and the remaining half are roughly evenly divided between Sunnis and Shias. The scale of communities is different, too, as there are over 200,000 Muslims in the Metro Detroit Area, and nearly a million Muslims in Greater London. Detroit is now a struggling regional city of less than one million, whereas over eight million live in the global city of London. These different backgrounds likely contributed to the way the communities viewed conflicts in Afghanistan and Iraq. However, consistent with the most different systems approach, an analytic comparison of such different communities—different in many other ways, but similar with regards to their high level of political mobilization—allows to search for common factors explaining the observed common patterns of high political mobilization within the divergent cases.

Indeed, these communities are similarly very politically active. London and Detroit are at the forefront of Muslim activism in England and the US in general, and Pakistani and Arab Muslim political activism in particular. Both cities have well-established, active Muslim communes and organizations, and sizeable minority populations. Furthermore, both of these communities are commonly perceived to be among the most important Muslim ethnic communities in the UK and US (for more, see Chapter 3). Thus, a comparative study of the two communities should be able to elucidate general patterns that lead to transnational mobilization and the spillover of violence. Various conflicts abroad have spurred political activism in both London and Detroit, yet—in contrast to London—only a single instance of political violence occurred in Detroit. In sum, political mobilization in response to foreign conflicts abroad have included activities such as voting at the ballot box, street protests, and terrorist acts.

During the decade following 9/11, London experienced numerous protests, marches, and rallies critiquing and opposing British foreign policy, the country's attempts to fight terrorism, and British policy towards the Middle East. The city also experienced foiled and successful reactive conflict spillovers, including the 2005 (London) metro bombing. Not all reactive conflict spillover in London involves Pakistani Londoners. In several instances, the perpetrators of violent acts were converts. In others, they traveled from other localities to commit attacks in London (e.g. the metro bombing). Yet London's Pakistanis have played a large role in inciting numerous instances of spillover, including the foiled 2006 Heathrow Airport bomb plot. These episodes of reactive conflict spillover are of particular interest to this study.

As London is the center of Muslim and Arab Muslim political activism in the UK, so too is Detroit the center of this activism in the US. The Arabs who migrated to the area in the first half of the twentieth century were generally Christians. About half of Detroit's Arabs are Muslims. After Paris, Dearborn, Michigan, has the largest Arab and Muslim communities of any city outside the Middle East.[8] The community has contributed to many domestic and foreign policy causes, yet except for one instance such activism has remained nonviolent. In recent years, more than 10,000 Arabs and Muslims marched in the streets, protesting Israel's bombardment of Lebanon in 2006. However, the community has remained relatively quiescent concerning Afghanistan and Iraq.

Tensions between the different groups of Muslims and Arabs in Detroit have escalated, as has peaceful protest in responses to conflicts abroad. In one instance, Arab Muslims experienced some hostilities in December 2006. After some Shias celebrated the execution of the former Sunni dictator Saddam Hussein in Iraq, several stores owned by Shia Muslims in Dearborn were attacked. However, the damage was minor and the violence short-lived.

Some Detroit Arab Muslims have been accused of monetarily supporting terrorist organizations abroad, and some have been indicted on charges of supporting Hezbollah. Yet political activism in Arab Detroit has been generally peaceful. For example, Detroit Muslims organized protests and marched in the streets to support Lebanon during Israel's 2006 attack on Hezbollah in southern Lebanon. On numerous occasions, the community has taken to the streets to support the Palestinian cause. Thus, despite reappearing concerns and occasional religiously motivated tensions, the city has experienced only this one instance of reactive conflict spillover, during the fall of 2006. More interestingly, Detroit Arabs' relative inactivity regarding Afghanistan and Iraq appears surprising in light of their otherwise heightened mobilization and activism. The key empirical puzzle that this research aims to address is this: What are the causes for the different patterns of mobilization in London and Detroit?

Overall, this study provides evidence that (with a few exceptions, such as the long-lasting the Arab-Israeli conflict) when responding to foreign policy events, the London and Detroit migrant-background communities commonly mobilize based on their ethnic divisions, reflecting established social networks and *selective* attention to the foreign policy issues and conflicts of the day.[9] Global and domestic triggers frequently galvanize communities into action—and communities tend to react to those conflicts that are framed as important—while some other major conflicts are overlooked.

Because this study covers a broad range of reactions to conflicts abroad, it also looks at relevant instances of violent radicalization that leads to terrorism. However, it is too simplistic to assume that terrorist radicalization is simply a form of political mobilization for at least two main reasons. First, Western Muslim political activism (including mobilization through Islamist groups), in the vast majority of cases, leads to neither political violence nor extremism. Second, terrorist violence is usually perpetrated by a handful of misguided individuals, frequently with connections to radical networks abroad. Moreover, Islamic radicalization is an individual process, "it is not something specific of derived from the quality of being Muslim," and is affected by many factors.[10] This study identifies the conditions under which such radicalization in response to foreign policy events may be more likely to occur, yet cautions against seeing it simply as a form of political mobilization. The evolving research on Muslim radicalization generally suggests that it is rather a complex, individual process.[11]

In sum, reactive conflict spillover occurs in migrant-background communities with strong identities. In such communities, the following three factors can create an environment conducive to transnational violence in response for conflicts abroad: policies allowing inflow of violent radicals, the presence of radical groups, and connections with radical groups abroad. The evidence on how poor integration affects this process appears inconclusive. However, there is evidence that some individuals in communities that experience high levels of structural economic discrimination are more likely to engage in radical politics, if the negative effects of the lack of integration are not abated by extensive inter-group ties. Indeed, certain organizational arrangements in Western Muslim communities help to effectively contain excitable youths who may otherwise engage in deviant behavior following a foreign policy calamity.

The empirical evidence derives from surveys and public opinion polls, statistical data about the two communities, open-source information, primary and secondary sources, analysis of government migration and security policies, and field research. This manuscript aims to provide conclusions representative of opinions of average Muslim individuals in each of the communities studied, and thus its primary sources of information are other than interview data with predominately community leaders and activists. Overall, analyses of governmental policy and contextual variables defining migration context were combined with information about the features of the diasporic communities studied. Field research and in-depth interviews provided further insights into individual and community motivations that could not be adequately captured by quantitative measures.

Public opinion polls and statistical data developed or consulted include Gallup, Pew, other public opinion polls, US Census data, and information from the British Government. LexisNexis Academic database data and internet research was used to develop descriptive datasets about the protests in the two cities through time, as well as some qualitative description of some of them. Gallup and Pew polls provided useful information on the two Muslim communities, such as their views on identity, international conflict issues, and support for violence. The government data (e.g. the US Census and the British Change Institute data on Muslim communities) provided useful background information. Furthermore, primary and secondary documents, analysis of governmental migration and security policies, and statistical data about political mobilization in the two communities, were used to develop different aspects of the case studies. Some of the primary sources consulted include Muslim press and publications such as the British Muslim Human Rights Commission's brochures.

Open source information includes descriptive information available from the media (including TV, websites, newspapers, magazines, radio, and blogs). While writing the London case study, I often consulted *The New York Times International, The Guardian,* and the *BBC.* The websites of the Muslim Council of Britain, the Muslim Association of Britain, Hizb ut-Tahrir, and other key groups also provided much valuable information. I also used information issued by the British government and its affiliate, The Change Institute. Some of the newspapers consulted for the Detroit case study include: *The New York Times, USA Today, CNN, Arab American News,* and *Watan.* Two smaller, left-leaning sources (*Workers World, World Socialist Website*) provided detailed descriptive information about some anti-war protests not available elsewhere. Various Arab and Muslim websites (e.g. Arab Detroit, Congress of Arab American Organizations, and American-Arab Anti-Discrimination Committee) were also consulted.

Furthermore, this study utilizes interviews with 66 respondents consisting of Muslim community leaders, activists, and experts—as well as a number of additional, less-structured, "street interviews." In addition, a handful of scholars were also consulted in each of the cities. The overarching goal was to choose a sample representative of diverse views of the community, consisting of key minority community leaders and their followers (including leaders and activists from both religious and secular groups, mainstream organizations, fringe groups, and the nonaffiliated).

Interviewees were selected through a two-way process. First, after conducting background research on the communities, I identified a number of community leaders and reached out to them via email prior to arriving to London and Detroit. A number of interviews were scheduled this way. I aimed to interview a broad range of community leaders and activists (both religious and secular/ethnic) representing a broad range of views (from Islamists to atheists). I also sought out and interviewed in both communities local Muslim researchers knowledgeable of the local minority community political activism. Second, additional interviewees were selected through a purposeful snowball sampling aimed at finding individuals (both leaders and activists) who were politically active regarding foreign policy events. Finally, in addition to interviewing Muslims, I met with several non-Muslim scholars of Muslims in both locations (these interviews are not included in the total number of interviews) and conversed informally (or through email) with a number of members of the minority communities.

From the total of 66 respondents, 32 were interviewed in London and 34 in Detroit.[12] Out of 32 respondents in London, 59 percent represented Muslim organizations,[13] 22 percent represented secular/ethnic organizations, and 19 percent were unaffiliated; furthermore, 50 percent were community leaders, 37 percent youths, and 13 percent researchers. Out of 34 respondents in Detroit, 41 percent represented

Muslim organizations, 24 percent represented secular/ethnic organizations, and 35 percent were unaffiliated; furthermore, 53 percent were leaders, 38 percent youths, and 9 percent researchers. Street interviews and meetings with scholars are excluded from the total sample of 66 respondents, but 26 of them wished to be identified in the research output. In addition to formal interviews, I obtained data through informal meetings and personal communication, telephone calls, and emails in London, Detroit, and beyond. Overall, the interview data is mainly used to supplement—and further elucidate—the insights provided by other sources of descriptive and quantitative data about the communities and their foreign policy-influenced political activism.

Overall, in order to obtain a representative sample from each community, a diverse array of individuals were interviewed. Interviewees included leaders and activists from key secular and religious organizations, activists and public intellectuals form Muslim communities, and local non-Muslim experts of the communities. In London, I interviewed a wide variety of leaders and representatives from mainstream groups and institutions such as the Muslim Council of Britain, the Muslim Public Affair Committee, and mosques, as well as from more radical and fringe groups, including Islam4UK. In Detroit, I met with a similar range of religious and secular leaders and activists, including Imams and individuals involved with major Arab and Muslim groups (including the American-Arab Anti-Discrimination Committee and the Council of American-Islamic Relations) and activists.

Interviews were conducted in various locales, including organization offices, mosques, coffee shops, personal residences, and public locations. In London, multiple interviewees preferred to meet in coffee shops or other public places, whereas in Detroit, most interviews took place in offices or mosques. Some of the meetings lasted less than half an hour, whereas others continued for up to four hours. Some of the interviews took place in the early morning, whereas others commenced as late as nine in the evening.

Additionally, measures were taken to minimize bias, and increase reliability of data obtained from field interviews. Conducting interviews in Western Muslim communities in the post-9/11 period creates challenges because these communities have been under intensive scrutiny by the government, media, and the public. Therefore, it is not surprising that many researchers conducting fieldwork on sensitive issues in minority communities have noted that some of their Muslim respondents were suspicious.[14] Ronald Stockton (2009), a Detroit-area scholar of local Muslims, warns that Muslims are likely to tell researchers whatever they want to hear during interviews. Aware of such problems, I did my best to make the interviewees more comfortable. I empathized with the respondents—even when I gravely disagreed with their positions—and highlighted my connections with Muslim communities in each area.

Summary of the Chapters

Chapter 2 provides a selective historic overview of reactive conflict spillovers to the West, as well as a few instances of situations when spillovers were feared but did not occur. The chapter also develops a typology of spillovers and a theoretical framework explaining both transnational mobilization in response to and reactive conflict spillover of conflicts abroad. It outlines the importance of trigger events and ethnic identities in transnational mobilization; and looks at an interaction of contextual variables (namely, the nature of migration and security policies allowing inflow of radicals, and the extent of integration) and migrant community-specific factors (namely, the presence of radical groups, and connections with radical networks abroad) to explain the likelihood of reactive conflict spillovers. The chapter concludes by outlining how this framework helps with understanding two different kinds of spillovers: Mobilized Violence Spillover (e.g. a terrorist attack) and Street Violence Spillover (e.g. a violent protest). Meanwhile, Chapter 3 provides a more thorough introduction to migrant and Muslim communities in Europe and the US, examines studies of Muslims in the UK and London and in the US and Detroit, and provides more specific information about the evolution of the Pakistani community in London and Arab Muslims in Detroit, while particularly outlining the said communities' views and actions in political activism.

Chapters 4 and 5 look at transnational mobilization in Muslim and Pakistani communities in London and Muslim and Arab communities in Detroit. Chapter 4 draws on data from public opinion polls, studies of Muslims in the West, and interviews with Muslim leaders and activists to outline key foreign policy events of interest for Western Muslims. It identifies some of the key global and domestic triggers for political mobilization, and argues that conflicts in Africa tend to be overlooked, while conflicts in the Middle East are of particular interest to Western Muslims. Chapter 5 looks at the roles that Islamic and ethnic identities have in political mobilization in the two communities. It argues that common Islamic identity is important for galvanizing political mobilization in response to certain domestic issues (including perceived Islamophobia and counter-terrorism policies seen as unfair), as well as long-lasting conflicts involving a Muslim country and a non-Muslim country (e.g. the Arab-Israeli conflict), but ethnic identities largely influence mobilization to foreign policy events to a larger extent than religious commonalities do.

The last three chapters discuss the dynamics of reactive conflict spillovers. First, both Chapters 6 and 7, the two main empirical chapters, present detailed case studies of London's Pakistani and Detroit's Arab Muslim reactions to wars in Afghanistan and Iraq. Additionally, the Detroit chapter also seeks to explain why there has been very little community activism in response to these conflicts, and provides information on Detroit Arab Muslim reactions to two additional conflicts: the

Israel-Hezbollah War of 2006, and the Gaza War of winter 2009. The key reason for the inclusion of these two additional conflicts in the Detroit chapter is that they show that, under certain conditions, the community is capable of noteworthy activism in response to conflicts abroad—even if there has been little activism regarding Afghanistan and Iraq. These two chapters seek to explain the different patterns of mobilization in the two communities. Chapter 6 outlines the key factors that contributed to the spillover of violence to London: presence of violent radicals, presence of radical groups, and connection to radical networks abroad. The lack of economic integration—as well as discrimination and inadequate political representation—contributed to the creation of an environment where some British Muslims became more susceptible to radical politics. Meanwhile, Chapter 7 shows that the largely peaceful nature of Detroit's Muslims mobilization in response to the war in Iraq is largely due to absence of violent radicals in the community, extensive inter-group ties which helped to mediate the negative effects of economic deprivation, an absence of radical groups in the community, and an absence of connections to radical networks abroad.

Finally, the conclusion summarizes the key findings, outlines factors that influence the dynamics of community reactions to conflicts abroad, and explains this study's implications migration, security, studies on Muslims in the West and global diasporas; and literatures on comparative politics, international relations, and sociology. It provides policy recommendations regarding what Muslim community leaders and government officials can do to increase expressions of peaceful protest, prevent instances of reactive conflict spillover, and promote integration. The study concludes with an assessment of the future of migrant political mobilization and reactive conflict spillovers in the West.

Notes

1 The author would like to thank Dr. Ted Gurr for helping to coin this term during the 2009 International Studies Association's Annual Convention in New York City.
2 The concept of the War on Terror has been highly controversial. Critics have argued that certain governments, to reduce civil liberties and to infringe upon human rights, have exploited the conflict. Others have insisted that it is impossible to wage a war on terrorism, a concept. The UK, the US, and many other governments have officially discontinued use of this term.
3 Adamson 2006; Cooper 2003.
4 Banta 2008.
5 Gourevitch 1978; Keohane and Milner 1996; Rosenau 1997.
6 Hatton and Williamson 2005, 374–6; United Nations 2000.
7 See George and Bennett 2005, 67.
8 Belton 2003.
9 With regards to domestic issues, a pan-Muslim, *ummah*-based understanding of identity frequently determines the nature of political activism. However, when it comes to conflicts and other issues abroad, ethnically based political

mobilization patterns dominate considerations of which conflicts abroad will receive attention (for more, please see Chapters 4–5).

10 Pisoiu 2014, 796.

11 Pisoiu 2014.

12 London's sample includes 29 regular interviews and a single focus group meeting with three people; Detroit's sample includes 29 regular interviews and a single focus group meeting with five people. In addition, in both locations I communicated (either in person, over the telephone or electronically) with a number of local scholars who study local Muslim communities in general and Muslim scholars of Muslims in the West in particular (three in London and two in Detroit); attended events taking place in each Muslim community; and gathered a number of informal street interviews, predominately with Muslim youths. These additional, more informal, meetings are excluded from the total interview count in Detroit and London.

13 Muslim organization here is defined as an organization that caters to Muslims (including Mosques) and aims to represent Muslims on the basis of their religion.

14 Cainkar 2009; Gest 2010; Wiktorowicz 2005.

2   Reactive Mobilization and Conflict Spillover

This chapter provides a selective, historical overview of episodes of reactive conflict spillover in the Western world and develops a conceptual and theoretical framework for this study. First, it provides examples of both conflict spillovers and instances when such acts were expected but did not occur. Next, it develops a typology of spillovers, reviews a broad array of social science scholarship, and develops a theoretical framework outlining factors that influence reactive transnational mobilization and spillovers. When mobilization does happen, does it occur in response to grave conflicts abroad or in response to a leaders' strategic framing of conflicts? Do communities react based on one dominant community identity, or their ethnic differences?

Once communities are mobilized in response to foreign conflicts, it is likely that different immigration contexts and migrant characteristics and actions largely determine whether such mobilization leads to political violence. What roles do the contextual variables, such as asylum, migration, and security policies, and the level of integration (especially measured in terms of the unemployment rate, income level, level of education obtained, and levels of political representation) play? To what extent are reactions influenced by migrant-background community characteristics and actions, such as presence of radical groups or connections with radical networks abroad?

Conflicts with Spillover Effects

Spillovers have occurred in many places over several centuries. This section describes selectively some more recent instances in which, often following a triggering event, a conflict abroad generates violent reactions in diasporic communities in the transatlantic area. This overview shows that spillovers are not just a contemporary or first-generation issue. They can involve migrants and minorities from Western and non-Western countries and can manifest themselves in many different forms.

Conflict spillovers are not just a contemporary or first-generation migrant issue. In response to the Irish struggle for independence from Britain in the 1820s and 1830s, Irish Americans mounted attacks on

British targets in Canada. American political openness and international rivalry with Britain allowed for an effective Irish transatlantic mobilization in the US.[1] America allowed a transnational Irish nationalist movement to emerge because leading policy-makers believed that it would not threaten US domestic security and weaken a key US competitor: Britain. As late as the 1830s, the British feared a US invasion of Canada, where the British created the defensive Wellington system of fortification.[2] Overall, Irish nationalist movements of the 1850s bore a striking resemblance to the Irish movements of the late 1900s—at the core, they consisted of durable personal networks.

Meanwhile, former homeland religious tensions spilled over to the American Irish settlements. Tensions between Catholic and Protestant Irish led to the Philadelphia riots of 1844 and the New York City Orange Riots in 1871 and 1872. Irish communities were notorious for ferocious gang activity in New York City in the early 1800s.[3] Irish separatist groups fundraised among Irish Americans. Until the 1980s, the British feared that the Irish Republican Army was collecting funds in the US.[4]

Furthermore, reactions to conflicts in diasporic communities can be both violent and peaceful. One of the most notorious terrorist attacks in Europe since 9/11, the Madrid train bombings, consisted of a series of coordinated bombings against the Madrid commuter train system on March 11, 2004. The bombings killed 191 people and wounded some 1,800. The subsequent government investigation determined that the bombing was conducted by an Al Qaeda-inspired violent extremist terrorist cell. The cell consisted of a loose group of Moroccan, Syrian, and Algerian (mainly immigrant) Muslims who committed these violent acts to force Spanish withdrawal from Iraq.

In another instance, in the 1980s, Sikh diaspora demands for Khalistan turned hostile in Europe.[5] The Sikh separatist movement in India, demanding an independent Sikh homeland (Khalistan) in the Indian Punjab region, gained a particular momentum following the Indian government assault on the Golden Temple during Operation Blue Star in June 1984. Another cause of this momentum was popular backlash against Sikhs after a Sikh bodyguard assassinated Indian Prime Minister Indira Gandhi in October 1984.[6] The movement for Khalistan reached its zenith in the 1970s and 1980s.

The Sikh diaspora in the West was actively involved with awareness raising, fundraising, violent protests, and several terrorist plots. The US estimates that the global Sikh population ranges between 18 and 30 million.[7] The Sikh diaspora kept strong ties with Sikhs in India—and many Western Sikhs were recent refugees who aimed to escape prosecution in India. Sikh organizations, including Khalistan Council, Dal Khalsa, Babbar Khalsa, International Sikh Youth Federation, World Sikh Organization, and Council of Khalistan, organized demonstrations in Britain, the US, Canada, and West Germany.

Following the 1984 Operation Blue Star in India, violent Sikh extremism spread quickly to Canada.[8] Canadian Sikh radicals publically pledged to kill Hindus and violently confronted members of the Canadian Sikh community twice in 1985.[9] The Canadian government alleged that Sikh separatists were responsible for the 1985 bombing of Air India Flight 182 off the coast of Ireland. The bombing resulted in 329 deaths—280 of them Canadian citizens, many of a South Asian background.[10] This attack constitutes the largest mass murder in modern Canadian history. Alleged perpetrators were members of the Sikh organization Babbar Khalsa, and other separatist groups. In the early 2000s, several Sikh individuals were charged with orchestrating the attack after an investigation lasting almost 20 years. However, due to the lack of credible evidence, only a single individual (Inderjit Singh Reyat) was convicted.

Similarly, the Turkish-Kurdish conflict has led to both peaceful and violent activism in Western-European Turkish communities since the 1990s. In 1978, the Kurdistan Workers Party (PKK) was founded in Turkey. Initially, the group called for the creation of a Kurdish state within the boundaries of the Kurdish areas in Turkey, Iran, Iraq, and Syria. Later, it demanded Kurdish autonomy in Turkey. By the mid-1980s, a full-scale insurgency raged in Turkey. The group reached its peak in the late 1980s and the early 1990s. The number of rebels declined precipitously between 1994 and 1996, and then stabilized to around 5,000 or 6,000 fighters.[11] Following the 1998 arrest of the PKK's leader, Abdullah Öcalan, many more left the group. Nevertheless, in the decade following Öcalan's arrest, around 3,000 men and women, predominantly based in northern Iraqi mountain camps, remained loyal PKK members.[12] During the conflict, tens of thousands of guerillas, Turkish soldiers, and civilians died.[13] According to the Turkish military, from 1984 to 2008, 14,000 PKK members were captured, and 32,000 guerillas were killed.[14]

Early in its existence, the PKK recognized the importance of cultivating support in Europe. In 1981, during the PKK's first conference in Lebanon, the group decided to intensify operations among Kurds in Europe to help re-launch its campaign there.[15] By 1981, there were already some two million Turkish workers in Europe, half of those in Germany.[16] As the conflict intensified in Turkey, Western Europe witnessed a surge in PKK-linked demonstrations and marches. PKK leaders quickly recognized that it was notably easier to organize, fundraise, and operate in a democratic, European environment.[17] In Europe, centers of PKK activity were often cultural clubs, cafes, reading rooms, debating centers, and social welfare offices.[18]

By the early 1990s, PKK activities in Germany and Western Europe became increasingly hostile.[19] The PKK started to launch coordinated attacks against Turkish targets in Europe—including consulates, banks, and airline offices.[20] Police repression of the group led to more violence. In the early 1990s, German government security specialists estimated that, in the Kurdish population of roughly 500,000, there were 7,500 suspected PKK members and 50,000 sympathizers in the country.[21] Germany banned the PKK in 1993, and other European countries took similar measures against the group and its affiliates.

In some instances, violence escalates after a significant trigger event abroad. In other cases, spillovers occur following symbolic actions by respective parties. Fighting erupted between Turkish- and Greek Americans in certain American factories and on city streets at the end of World War I. The diasporic tensions escalated as the Allies occupied Ottoman Turkey's capital, Istanbul, and the Greeks annexed the city of Izmir. Although Greek-Turkish confrontation dates back hundreds of years, the Allied invasion of Turkey was the trigger event that spurred violence among co-ethnics in the US. Afterwards, close to a half of the Turkish American community returned to Turkey to participate in the Turkish War of Independence.

In another case involving a paramilitary Turkish group, both the escalation of the conflict in Turkey and certain actions by the US government triggered reactions. Principally in the 1970s and 1980s, the Grey Wolves—the youth wing of the Turkish, far-right Milliyetci Hareket Partisi (MHP)—were implicated in numerous violent engagements in Europe.[22] In the 1990s, the group was accused of inciting further violence within Turkish expatriate communities in Cyprus, Germany and the United Kingdom.

In Turkey, fighting between leftists and the Grey Wolves resulted in more than 5,000 deaths. The Grey Wolves attacked leftist events and property, and groups were sent to incite riots in the countryside.[23] This violence resurfaced following the increasing electoral successes of the resurgent MHP in Turkish elections. In the 2007 legislative elections, the party won 14.3 percent of the national vote and 71 seats in the national parliament.

On a global scale, the Grey Wolves are suspected of plotting numerous political assassinations and disappearances of Turkish and Kurdish human rights activists. The group has known ties to the Turkish mafia and has raised funds for Chechen guerilla separatists. In the late 1970s, the Grey Wolves were involved in deadly confrontations with Turkish leftists in Germany. A former member of the group attempted to assassinate Pope John Paul II in 1981. In 1996, the Grey Wolves organized an attack on a Greek Cypriot protest against Turkish occupation of part of Cyprus, beating one of the protesters to death.

As recently as 2007, the group held violent rallies across Europe. In one instance, a protest-turned-riot led to an attack on an Armenian coffee shop in Brussels.[24] The protesters demanded an end to an ongoing Turkish military operation in Northern Iraq against the Kurdistan Workers Party (PKK). They also denounced the resolution passed by the US Congressional Committee on Foreign Affairs, which labeled the destruction of the Armenian peoples following World War I as Ottoman "genocide." Thus, in the Grey Wolves' case, triggers for reactive conflict spillover range from an intensifying conflict in Turkey to a widely publicized decision to endorse a pro-Armenian resolution.

However, spillovers do not solely begin with migrants from non-Western countries in the West. In the mid-1920s, Italians scared the Paris police more than any other community—with the exception of North Africans.[25] After the Italian Fascist leader Benito Mussolini crushed the far-left opposition in 1919 and 1920, many defeated radicals sought refuge in Paris, where they joined established migrant-worker communities.[26]

Mussolini's Fascist gangs, which operated between the World War I and II, *squadristi*, chased thousands of the defeated radicals into France. In 1919, French police drew up a list of 160 Italian revolutionaries in France, most of them in Paris.[27] By the mid-1920s, competing anti-Fascist leaders in France started to plan an overthrow of the Italian government. From 1923 to 1929, some 60 Italians were wounded and a dozen assassinated in skirmishes between Fascists and anti-Fascists in Paris.[28]

Occasionally, spillovers may involve internal conflicts among migrants from the same country. After World War II, the ideologically divided Cuban diaspora experienced infighting. Many Cubans came to the US after Fidel Castro's Communist forces won the civil war of the 1950s and gained control of the island. For decades, the Cuban American community has been deeply divided between those who support and those who oppose the Cuban communist government.

The most important example of émigré terrorism in modern America was a campaign waged by anti-Castro Cubans against suspected traitors.[29] From the 1960s to the 1980s, Cuban American terrorist groups Acción Cubana, El Poder Cubano, Frente de Liberación Nacional de Cuba, Omega7, and Secret Cuban Government conducted numerous bombings, shootings, and killings of their opponents.[30] Cuban groups in America actively fundraised to support anti-Castro activism in Cuba. Such groups were heavily supported by the Central Intelligence Agency, which commonly used émigré and migrant populations to further its interests.[31]

A decade later, in the 1990s, Canada struggled to contain Sri Lankan separatist-linked gang violence. From 1976 to 2009, the Tamil Tigers (also known as the LTTE) fought the Sri Lankan government for the right to establish an independent Tamil state in northern and eastern Sri Lanka. Canadian police reported that by the late 1990s, some 8,000 Tamil guerillas were in the Toronto area alone.[32] Additionally, in the late 1990s, Toronto battled escalating Tamil gang violence, ongoing weapons smuggling, and LTTE intimidation of the Tamil diaspora for extortion purposes. Although the links are hard to establish, some reports have alleged connections between Canadian Sri Lankan street gangs and the LTTE.[33] It was not until 2006, three years before the Tamil Tigers' military defeat in Sri Lanka, that Canada proscribed the LTTE under the country's anti-terrorism laws. However, spillovers do not exclusively involve homeland conflicts.

International and even cultural conflicts can resonate in certain communities. Following the start of the Second Intifada (2000–2005) in the Palestinian Territories, Muslim-Jewish violence spiked in France in 2000 and 2001. In the Middle East, Arab-Israeli conflict has arguably been the main cause of instability since the end of the Cold War. The Second Intifada, also known as the Al-Aqsa Intifada, was a period of intensified Palestinian-Israeli violence. The Intifada is believed to have evolved from riots caused by Israeli Prime Minister Ariel Sharon's visit to Temple Mount, a holy Muslim shrine, on September 28, 2000. The resulting hostilities claimed lives of an estimated 5,500 Palestinians and over 1,000 Israelis.[34]

The ongoing Arab-Israeli conflict has greatly influenced the continuously strained relationship between European Muslims and Jews. Following the beginning of the Second Intifada, anti-Semitic attacks in France steeply increased.[35] In 2001, Muslim youth initiated most of the roughly 400 anti-Semitic incidents across France.[36] However, it is also important to note that a 2006 Pew poll found that—in a difference of opinion of Jews in many Muslim-majority countries, European Muslims tend to have a generally positive view of Jews. Nevertheless, anti-Semitic incidents in France spiked again following Israel's incursion into the West Bank in 2002, and in response to the Gaza War of 2008–09.[37] These incidents were triggers for hostile mobilization.

More recently, violent Muslim protests erupted in European cities following the 2005 Muhammad cartoons controversy. The controversy began when the Danish newspaper *Jyllands-Posten* published twelve Prophet Muhammad cartoons on September 30, 2005. The newspaper claimed that it published the cartoons to support the right to criticize Islam, and to forego self-censorship, even if it meant slandering the religion. However, the cartoons offended many Muslims, causing numerous protests to break out globally.

The controversy was exacerbated after a group of hardline Danish Imams collected and publicized a dossier at an event in Egypt.[38] The dossier contained several particularly offensive cartoons that were submitted to the newspaper, but never published. However, it was hard to distinguish which of the cartoons were printed and which were not. Thus, much Muslim anger largely resulted from the misconception that the more offensive cartoons were published.[39]

Whereas often-violent protests raged across the Middle East and Pakistan, the majority of European demonstrations were peaceful. More sizable, orderly events occurred in Paris and Brussels. At times, radical leaders hijacked protests in London and Denmark, with some protests becoming violent. While the offensive cartoons were a trigger for activism, many of the protests opposed perceived-European, cultural imperialism; the perceived clash between European and Muslim civilizations; and the targeting of Muslims in the War on Terror.

Finally, states have before expressed exaggerated fears about possible violent spillovers. During the early 1990s, the Algerian Civil War resonated in France. The War erupted following a 1992 decision to rescind Algerian national election results, results which would have given the Islamic Salvation Front the majority of seats in parliament. After intense fighting and numerous deaths, the Algerian government managed to defeat Islamist forces by the late 1990s. At the beginning of the fighting, concerns were expressed about a potential spillover in Western-European Algerian communities, particularly in France.[40] Fears were further increased because France had provided economic and military assistance to the Algerian regime.

Although the worst of French fears were not realized, the conflict did result in reactive conflict spillover. Initially, Algerian Islamists solicited money for the War from the Algerian diaspora in France. Militants harassed and killed French Algerians who did not support them. The most notorious episode occurred in 1995, when the Armed Islamic Group launched a bombing campaign in France.[41] French police eventually arrested or killed the guerillas who disrupted French cities using bomb threats. France embraced draconian counterterrorism and conducted tens of thousands of identity checks. By 1998, several thousand alleged activists and sympathizers were detained.[42]

Overall, this brief section describes some well-known instances of reactive conflict spillover in the transatlantic area during the last two centuries. It shows how spillovers, whether involving street clashes or radicalization and terrorism, frequently occur following triggering events. It also shows that it is often not well-understood when and why spillovers occur. In addition, it is rather perplexing why certain intense conflicts do not spill over to sizeable and politically mobilized diasporas. It is also puzzling why, in some cases, the same conflicts spill over sporadically, affecting certain communities while avoiding others.

When Spillovers Are Feared but Do Not Happen

In many instances, migrant-background communities live in peace despite significant, escalating conflicts abroad. As the following examples demonstrate, continued, friendly cohabitation of potentially hostile communities in both the US and Europe has surprised many outsiders.

Populations from hostile nations can live side by side even while military conflicts exist in their home states. For generations, Pakistanis and Indians have peacefully coexisted in Queens, New York—even when relations between Pakistan and India, two nations which have fought against each other several times since the end of World War II, deteriorated. This amicable, diasporic relationship in the US is particularly perplexing because the same two South-Asian diasporas in London have clashed violently, especially during the turbulent 1960s. New York City officials sent their emissaries to local Pakistani and Indian communities to assess the likelihood of reactive conflict spillover when the two countries were at war, or when tensions between the countries were strained. The emissaries tended to receive the same answer time after time: Pakistanis and Indians in New York City coexist peacefully regardless of tensions in South Asia. Indeed, according to the 2000 U.S. Census, more than 200,000 Pakistanis and Indians lived in New York City, yet, local police chiefs reported that no conflicts existed between the two groups.[43]

Similarly, politically, ideologically, and religiously fragmented populations can peacefully coexist. Detroit Muslims exhibit numerous cleavages, most notably, their countries of origin (mainly Lebanon, Yemen, Iraq, and Palestine) and religious sects (Sunnis and Shias). The community is politically mobilized, but political activism in response to the Lebanese Civil War, the American-led wars in Afghanistan and Iraq, and broader Sunni-Shia tensions has resulted only in minor hostility. Following 9/11, Detroit Muslims have not been convicted of involvement with terrorist activities. Another example concerns ideologically divided Vietnamese and Chinese diasporic communities. During turbulent times in their respective states, the two groups have managed to cohabitate in close proximity to each other in American cities. Moreover, the peaceful coexistence of certain diasporic communities despite the conflicts in their homelands is not unique to the US.

In many instances, relatively agreeable cohabitation is possible between the titular group and minority populations—even when relations are tense between receiving and sending states. The breakup of the Soviet Union left over 25 million Russians, mostly of immigrant background, outside the Russian Federation and within the territories of the Former Soviet Republics. In the newly independent Eastern European nations of Ukraine, Estonia, and Latvia, relations between the sizeable Russian minorities and the titular nations themselves displayed almost non-existent communal violence.[44] This relative lack of violence endured even though diplomatic relations and rhetoric between Estonia and Latvia and their former occupier, the Russian Federation, were quite hostile during the 1990s. Meanwhile, a very different outcome occurred in the Republic of Moldova. In 1990, an ethnic war broke out between the government of Moldova and ethnic, Russian-supported Transdniestrian separatists.

In other instances, diasporas may provide financial support for parties involved in ethnic conflict, but the actual fighting does not spread to the diaspora itself. In the 1990s, widespread fears emerged that the Yugoslav Wars of Succession could have spread to other countries in South Europe and to diasporas elsewhere. Ethnic violence spread from Kosovo to Macedonia in the early 2000s, creating a major security challenge.[45] However, contrary to popular belief, the Yugoslav conflicts only minimally strained the already tense relationship between Greece and Turkey and did not spread to diasporas.[46] For example, although "conditions were ripe" for conflict between Croat and Serb diasporas in Australia and the US, the spillover did not happen in either of those countries.[47] Nevertheless, Serb and Croat diasporas in Europe and the US helped to escalate conflicts in their former homelands. They provided financial support, military equipment, and even, some volunteers for the fighting.[48]

As these different cases show, the conflict resonance in diasporic communities is varied. An obvious explanation does not exist as to why such violence only spread across certain migrant communities. Why do some conflicts spill over, while others do not? Why do hostilities occur in some diasporas, but not in other, similar communities?

Towards a Typology of Reactive Conflict Spillover

Reactive conflict spillovers happen when violence in domestic migrant-background communities occurs in response to conflicts abroad. Such conflicts can be national or international, but they must generate much reactive political activism in diasporic communities. Triggers are significant, galvanizing, and, frequently, symbolic events involving intense fighting, provocative statements, rumored atrocities, or similar events.

Hostilities in diasporic communities can take different forms, including the destruction of property or an increase in sectarian tensions. This study defines reactive conflict spillover as a violent response in diaspora to a trigger event, which is followed by: (A) several incidents involving the destruction of property and assaults on individuals, or (B) sizable destruction of property and/or numerous assaults against individuals at one time.

Reactive political activism occurs on a continuum where spillovers are extreme political action. Spillovers can consist of riots, violent protests, sustained campaigns to destroy property, and/or the imposition of bodily harm. Such actions can manifest in arson, assault, bombing, hijacking, lynching, occupation, hostage-taking, kidnapping, raids, the firing of rockets, sabotage, vandalism, property destruction, or shootings. The study is also interested in instances where conflict spillovers did not occur despite notable potential for hostilities. Such negative cases are likely to provide valuable insights concerning the conditions that deter spillovers.[49]

Furthermore, it is important not to conflate violence in response to conflicts abroad with inter-communal hostility or criminal action. For example, a bar fight between individuals of two different nationalities is not reactive conflict spillover. With each spillover, one should be able to identify a broader conflict (e.g. the Israeli-Palestinian conflict), and, frequently, a more specific trigger event (e.g. the beginning of the Second Intifada in 2000) that leads to a reactive spillover (e.g. the escalation of Muslim violence against Jews in France).[50] The suggested reactive spillover conceptualization includes different kinds of reactive political violence and excludes minor frictions.

Overall, reactive conflict spillover can occur as a response to a national or an international conflict (see Figure 2.1). As described in Table 2.1, spillovers can erupt due to the importation of a homeland conflict to a host state (e.g. the Turkish-Kurdish conflict to Western Europe since the 1990s); migrant reaction to a host-state conflict (e.g. terrorist acts in response to Spain's involvement in the Iraq War of 2003); in response to a third-state conflict (such as violent demands by diaspora Sikhs of the creation of Khalistan in India); or from an international conflict (e.g. Muslim-migrant reactions to the War on Terror in Western Europe since 2001).

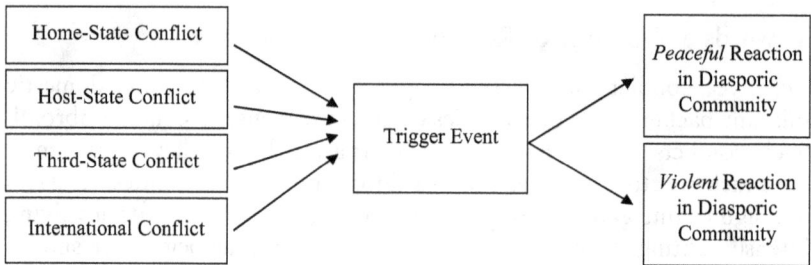

Figure 2.1 Conflicts, Triggers and Reactions in Minority Communities

Table 2.1 Examples of Reactive Conflict Spillovers in Diasporas

Conflict Type	Location	Specific Conflict	Trigger	Spillover
Home-State Conflict	West European Countries	Turkish-Kurdish Conflict, 1990s	Intensification of the conflict	PKK Activities in Western Europe, esp. Germany
Host-State Conflict	Spain	Spanish Presence in Iraq War of 2003	Escalation of the Iraq War	Madrid Train Bombing, 2004
Third-State Conflict	Britain, US, Canada, W. Germany	Sikh demands for Khalistan in India	Indian Government's assault on Sikh Temple in India, 1984	Violent protests in West Europe; instances of terrorism in Canada
International Conflict	West European Countries	War on Terror, 2001-	*Jyllands-Posten* publishes Prophet Muhammad caricatures, 2005	Violent responses in several Muslim communities in the West

Theorizing Reactive Conflict Spillover

Freeman (2005) has criticized the existing scholarship on migration-related topics because it either: (1) celebrates immigration and the immigrant experience (as opposed to being objective), or (2) draws insufficiently on related studies in other disciplines. This research will not attempt to study reactive conflict spillover as unique. Instead, it will assess scholarship on conflict spillover and contagion to identify gaps in the literature, seek points of convergence and departure, and prepare the groundwork for an original theory of reactive conflict spillover.

The scarce literature addressing conflict spillover and contagion tends to discuss the importation of former-homeland conflicts to diasporic communities in predominately developing countries. These studies tend to be largely descriptive and frequently explain how political violence from one country spills over to another. The literature also frequently investigates spillovers of wars and ethnic conflicts.

However, migrant-community violence in response to conflicts abroad, or reactive conflict spillover, is addressed only in passing. Virtually none of these studies investigates reactive conflict spillover in Western states. Nor do any explain why violent conflict spills over into some communities while sparing other, similar communities.

Several migration scholars mention the possibility of homeland conflict spillover, yet largely in an atheoretical, descriptive approach. Some migration studies argue that migrant-background communities can threaten the internal security of states where they live, and that radical groups in European migrant communities can replicate former-homeland violence.[51] Mark J. Miller (2000) coins the term "conflict spillover" to illustrate how fighting from internal conflicts in Algeria and Turkey partially reached European migrant communities. Weiner (1993, 9) argues that immigration can influence security in three ways: armed refugees can attack host state, migrants can threaten state political stability, and migrants can cause major societal value shifts in host countries. Civil wars sometimes spread as violent radicals migrate to other places during refugee flows and when violent radicalization occurs near conflict zones.[52]

Leo Lucassen (2005) shows that immigrants have historically been seen as threatening due to the perceived differences in immigrant religion, loyalty to another country, or social practices. Irish migrants arriving in England in the 19th century were perceived as a religious threat, ethnic Polish migrants within Germany's Eastern region after the 1870s were perceived as a nationalist threat (as it was thought that they desired an independent Poland and might have asked for this region to become a part of it), and Italians arriving in pre-World War I France were perceived as a social threat.[53] The author insists that threats arising from social differences (e.g., Italian-worker refusal to participate in French strikes) are generally seen as less serious than threats emerging from nationalism and religion. European Muslims, according to the author, are seen as constituting social and religious threats. Muslims in Europe tend to be of different ethnicities and religions, providing potential sources of social concern, like criminality, poverty, and ghettoization. The latter is especially associated with second-generation Muslims.[54]

Wæver et al. (1993) argue that societal security is now the most effective way for understanding the new European security agenda in the post-Cold War world. Securitization theory assumes that any actor can securitize any issue. Thus, as actors are attempting to securitize the issue of migration, they will increasingly talk of security implications of immigration (e.g., some immigrant association with crime or terrorism) until they convince the public that concerns about immigration are now a part of the broader national security agenda. The securitization of an issue is successful if the actor has convinced the majority that the issue must be perceived and handled as a national security issue.

Abiri (2000) argues that securitization of migration happens as governments and "native" populations realize the economic, social, and cultural challenges that integration of refugees and other migrants represent. Securitization of migration also happens when organizations handling refugee issues shift their discourse from human rights to human security—including migrants' own security.[55] Chebel d'Appollonia and Reich's (2008) edited volume concludes that there are four threats that link immigration and security in the transatlantic area: (1) enlarged EU borders, (2) threats to political and civil rights posed by numerous noncitizen residents, (3) potential "enemies inside" within immigrant-background communities, and (4) host-country inability to produce enough material benefits for second-generation migrants.[56]

Overall, the migration-and-security literature tends to remain mostly descriptive and does not seek causal mechanisms, necessary and sufficient conditions, or family-resemblance criteria[57] in explaining the migration-and-security nexus. The process through which different migration and security threats are constructed and perceived is still poorly understood and undertheorized.[58] Thus, more work needs to be done to understand the international repercussions of migrants: Under what conditions will migration-related challenges lead to increased international tensions? What will be the intensity of such tensions, e.g., when will such tensions lead to specific kinds of political violence, such as militarized interstate disputes or wars?

On the other hand, a few have cautioned against securitization of migration. Some insist that migrants in European political discourse have been increasingly defined as real and imagined threats, or as scapegoats for many social ills, such as unemployment and crime. Buzan and Wæver (2003, 359) and Faist 2006 assert that links between immigration and security are inconclusive and empirically difficult to establish. Alexseev (2005), Bigo (2001, 121) and Koser 2011 claim that because the migration-security nexus is inconclusive, migration issues tend to become securitized—largely due to exaggerated media reports. For example, Hopkins (2010) offers a "politicized places hypothesis." Hopkins argues that hostile political reactions to nearby immigrant populations are most likely to happen when communities undergo sudden influxes of immigrants and when salient national rhetoric reinforces the threat. Moreover, securitization of migration can urge states to adopt discriminatory immigration policies, which may lure common, law-abiding citizens into criminal activities.[59] Finally, Chebel d'Appollonia argues that excessive securitization of migration has been harmful on virtually all levels, as "the excesses of securitization have been detrimental to both migrants and immigration policies, generating in turn further insecurity both in the United States and Europe."[60] Excessively securitized immigration and integration policies create additional obstacles to migrant integration, yet political activism by the targeted population can be one successful desecuritization strategy.[61]

Migration-and-security scholarship argues how and why migrants should or should not be connected to security, but it does not address why only some foreign conflicts are imported, and why some migrant communities are more prone to conflict spillover than others. Thus, migration-and-security literature provides rich, descriptive, and, often, historical information about the relationship between migrants and state security, and occasional theoretical insights by frequently building on securitization theory. These insights are valuable in recognizing the immigration and institutional contexts in which reactive conflict spillovers can occur.

Meanwhile, diasporic-activism studies highlight how diasporas can mobilize and become intertwined with national or transnational activism. Horowitz elaborates on several ways that diasporas can relate to communal conflict.[62] A diaspora can be a participant to a communal conflict for the benefit of a homeland (e.g. German minorities in Czechoslovakia and Poland during in the post-World War I period). A migrant group can be party to a communal conflict in a host country (e.g. Chinese in Malaysia or Palestinians in Lebanon). Finally, diasporas may provide resources and political support to troubled communities in their former home countries.[63]

Regardless of how one conceptualizes "diaspora," several studies have shown that homeland conflicts tend to manifest in large communities of expatriates living abroad. Such communities also sometimes tend to be more forceful regarding homeland conflicts, compared to their co-ethnics in home states. In some cases, the evidence shows that "diasporas harbor grievance for much longer than resident populations; since they "do not themselves suffer any of the costs of conflict, [they] have a greater incentive to seek vengeance than the resident populations," a pattern shown by the Irish in North America and Jews worldwide.[64] In other words, homeland conflicts are important to diasporas. However, it is less clear what causes such conflicts to spillover to diasporic and migrant communities.

A seminal article in diasporic studies is Armstrong's 1976 "Mobilized and Proletarian Diasporas." The author places diasporas into two simple categories. "Proletarian" (disadvantaged) diasporas consist of largely poorly educated and equipped individuals. "Mobilized" diasporas are communities that do not have a general status advantage, yet enjoy many material and cultural advantages compared to other groups in multiethnic societies. The study shows that, in many instances, powerful, mobilized diasporas in the Russian and Ottoman Empires were inclined to become involved with their homeland issues. Armstrong's analysis seems germane to the post-Cold War era realities, where diasporas, such as those of the Jews, Sri-Lankans, and Chinese, have gained notable political power in their receiving states without losing interest in their home states.[65]

Several studies examine conflict spillover from one country or city to another. They tend to emphasize how violent-radical ideas can circulate among similar communities with competent leadership and developed group identities. Ted Gurr, a pioneer of conflict spillover among scholars of ethnic conflict, provides one of the more thorough conceptualizations of conflict spillover, which he sees as either conflict contagion or conflict communication. Contagion and communication refer to processes by which one group's actions inspire and guide groups elsewhere, both strategically and tactically.[66] Gurr identifies two conditions for conflict spillover. The first, empowering ideas and victories by like-minded groups elsewhere can become contagious to communities with collective identities and common interests. The second, for such contagion to occur, the given community must have a solid leadership, which is able to effectively communicate with members.[67] Strong contagion occurs within networks of similar groups, often because of thickening webs of connections. Another study articulates that conflict diffusion in ethnic communities can occur in two ways. First, outside conflicts can spread if migrant flows or a break-up of multiethnic states greatly changes a locality's ethnic composition. Conflict diffusion can also happen if the intensification of a conflict abroad encourages domestic groups to embrace radicalism.[68]

Indeed, many studies show that conflicts tend to spill over to similar trans-border communities, and that violent political disobedience may spread from one migrant community to another trans-border community.[69] Hill and Rothchild also argue that conflict spillover can occur by example.[70] Thus, if a large diasporic group witnesses successful violence against a neighboring state, it may attempt to do the same. The authors' suggestions are more pertinent to large diasporic minorities living in relatively weaker developing-world states. However, the possible power of example should not be overlooked in instances such as the spread of violence and rioting among European diasporas following the 2005 Prophet Muhammad cartoon controversy.[71] Such descriptive studies allow for a better understanding of spillovers, or for broad, conceptual understandings of how spillovers may occur. Yet they only offer a few tools that could bolster a comprehensive theory. The most promising research used to better understand conflict spillovers is influenced by mobilization scholarship.

Many studies that explain spillover of violence to migrant communities are influenced by mobilization theories, which tend to argue that a certain combination of opportunities and threats leads to mobilization. For example, one of the best-known mobilization theorists, Doug McAdam, argues that the convergence of cognitive liberation, organizational resources, and political-opportunity structures create an environment in which mobilization is likely to occur.[72] In a revised model, McAdam, Tarrow, and Tilly show that varied mobilization patterns result from interactions between threats and opportunities and organizational and social group activities. These interactions lead to innovative group action.[73]

Similarly, Hanagan (2002) finds that the Irish-nationalist movement in the US was able to mobilize and flourish largely because the US government tolerated such movement, and provided opportunities for it to emerge and thrive. The study finds that Irish-nationalist movements beginning in the 1850s developed similarly to Irish-nationalist movements of the late 1900s. At their very core, both of these movements involved personal networks. Thus, according to this study of Irish movements, transnational political activism can best be explained by understanding political opportunities for mobilization provided by host states (such as the US). Meanwhile, some historical examples of Irish mobilization question the applicability of Hanagan's thesis. For example, in the early 1800s, violent Irish gangs actively operated in New York City, even though the opportunity structure did not favor such activism (during that time period, local authorities actively took measures to curtail the activism of such gangs[74]).

Some studies have applied mobilization theories in their analysis of European Islamic movements. Quintin Wiktorowicz's (2005) seminal study finds that radical Islamic movements are identity movements similar to other social movements. According to Wiktorowicz, individuals join radical Islamic movements if they become convinced of the authenticity of radical interpretations during a "cognitive opening," when their previously held beliefs are shattered. Next, those who join the movements socialize to engage in risky activism. Eventually, high-risk Islamic activism becomes "at once the pursuit of a value and self-interest."[75]

Next, Lyon and Uçarer (2001) develop a "transnational mobilization model" (used to explain the spillover of the Turkish-PKK conflict from Turkey to Germany in the 1990s). This model insists that separatist-movement mobilization abroad is a product of: (1) consolidated and politicized identity, (2) operational resources, and (3) political opportunity.[76]

Lyon and Uçarer's model conceptualizes how the old mobilization theory can be applied to phenomenon such as violent separatist mobilization outside of the country of origin. It is likely that several variables identified by the model, especially the importance of consolidated-and-politicized identity, will be relevant in explaining migrant political activism and violence. Nevertheless, common drawbacks of such studies include their relative theoretical simplicity, lack of methodological rigor, and case-selection based on the dependent variable (the instance where spillover has occurred). It is hard to understand why spillovers do not occur if we only study cases where they have happened.

Generally, the existing studies of conflict spillover overwhelmingly tend to look at conflict spillover from one location to another. Several studies are descriptive, while more theoretically grounded scholarship suggests that personal networks, group identity, available resources, leadership, and political opportunities may play important causal roles in spillover. Contagion studies show that conflict is more likely to spill over into similar communities, and that when one community experiences violence, it can influence another. Additionally, this study will also aim to synthesize insights from several relatively similar disciplines and make them "talk" to each other.[77]

An unfortunate lack of engagement exists among scholars studying matters pertinent to migration and/or security within the subfields of political science and sociology. For example, a division remains between migration scholars studying security and ethnic-conflict scholars studying migration.[78] Migration scholars of security issues could learn from ethnic-conflict scholars why migrants would be more likely to engage in ethnic conflict. On the other hand, ethnic conflict scholars could learn from migration scholars about the importance of migrants' pasts and immigration context in migrant mobilization.

In other words, more thorough accounts with more extensive analytical leverage could result from security scholars' emphasis on discovering the root causes of political contention, combined with the migration scholars' focus on historically rich narratives. Such accounts could generalize, deriving from rich narratives. Additionally, a few recent studies suggest that political mobilization theory can help to develop frameworks for mobilization in migrant communities. Indeed, this study draws on newer versions of the mobilization theory initially developed by McAdam, Tarrow, and Tilly (2001) as it looks at the environment in which migrants arrive, characteristics of evolving diasporic communities, and how actions that both state and minorities take affect patterns of transnational mobilization.

Meanwhile, the existing social science literature allows for the creation of more sophisticated frameworks. Future research should similarly focus on synthesizing and building upon existing, relevant insights across the subfields. The contributions of this study include a theoretically and methodologically sophisticated framework for understanding reactive conflict spillover, and an analysis of how homeland and *international* conflicts resonate in certain migrant-background communities.

Moving forward, it is important to understand how and why diasporic communities mobilize, and why only sometimes such mobilization leads to violence in similar communities. The existing studies, at times, explain well why spillovers have occurred following political violence, yet they do not satisfactorily address why conflict spillovers occur in some places but not in others. This chapter will next discuss patterns of transnational mobilization. After all, in many instances, communities must already be mobilized if political violence is to occur. Social science literature suggests that triggers and cohesive community identity are crucial pre-requisites for such mobilization.

Transnational Mobilization

This research project, at first, questions whether triggers are important to the political mobilization of migrant-background communities. Then, it seeks to specify the kind of identity important in political mobilization. Prevalent mobilization theories state that events often galvanize mobilizations, and this book questions whether the same process is present during reactive political activism. Moreover, are all triggers equally significant? Does the framing of triggers influence response to a given conflict—or does the level of violence abroad primarily influence activism?

Furthermore, mobilization theories and theories of diasporic political activism emphasize identity in mobilization. This study seeks to further clarify whether religion, ethnicity, or another characteristic constitutes such identity. Based on previous studies, triggers and identity seem to inspire political mobilization in response to events abroad. Furthermore, why do different triggers conjure activism, and what kind of community identity is essential for activism?

Triggers: Grave Conflicts or Strategic Framing?

Triggers frequently occur prior to spontaneous reactions to conflicts abroad. However, why do triggers galvanize communities? Numerous studies demonstrate the importance of conflicts abroad to migrant-background communities and highlight certain significant events as triggers for political activism. Literature on ethnic conflicts and riots underlines the importance of a "galvanizing event," "rumor," or "precipitating event" prior to political violence.[79] Stuart J. Kaufman (2006, 37) suggests that events such as highly publicized murders of important leaders are particularly galvanizing.

The seminal book *Deadly Ethnic Riot* finds that riots have different trajectories, but they share one commonality: the proliferation of rumors before an outbreak of ethnic violence.[80] During riots following a precipitating event, violence escalates if a hostile atmosphere exists in the community. The existing studies agree that broad socioeconomic-change processes, galvanizing events, or other triggers matter in outbreaks of political activism. However, the studies do not specify the underlying, causal mechanisms. This book seeks to clarify these mechanisms.[81]

On one hand, we can argue that conflicts and triggers abroad do not have intrinsic value. In her study of the deadly global protests following the publication of the Prophet Muhammad cartoons in the *Jyllands-Posten* newspaper in Denmark, Jytte Klausen (2009b) finds that the protests occurred *after* conservative Danish-Muslim leaders mentioned the caricatures while attending a highly publicized event in Egypt. In addition, leaders promoting violence are likely to have incentives for their tactics. For example, one such incentive could be a shared belief that uses of force generate more grassroots support. Therefore, community leaders ascribe importance to certain triggers and legitimatize certain means of action; the masses are more likely to use violence if it seems legitimate. On the other hand, it is possible that highly publicized conflicts leading to major humanitarian crises generate reactions in migrant-background communities.

Indeed, this study shows that political mobilization occurs in those instances when community leaders emphasize the significance of the given triggers through their actions and public statements. [82] Ultimately, the inherent magnitude of conflict (e.g. high number of casualties or the severity of the humanitarian catastrophe) is less important.

Dominant Identity or Fragmentation?

The scholarship on diasporic activism and mobilization commonly identifies cohesiveness and group identity as prerequisites for diasporic-community action. These studies also suggest that whereas first-generation migrant communities are interested in home-state politics, subsequent generations predominately care about local issues. Nevertheless, studies by Leiken (2012, 2009, 2005) and Lucassen (2005) show that second-generation minority individuals are particularly contentious and dissatisfied with their treatment by the government. The literature suggests that migrant-background individuals can be contentious regardless of how long they have been in a country (e.g. first- or second-generation). Therefore, we could expect that only those communities that retain strong, distinct religious or ethnic identities would likely to react to conflicts abroad. A threat to a strong identity is likely to spur the community into action, and leaders are likely to play a major role in directing its activism.

An overarching theme derived from the scholarship on diasporas suggests that a common identity is required for a diasporic community to become active.[83] Mobilization theories frequently state that an existing group identity is a prerequisite for community mobilization. However, it is less clear what such identity entails (Ethnicity? Religion? Something else?). Cohen (1997) insists that groups united by world religions, borderland cultures, and stranded minorities are not to be confused with diasporas. Thus, according to this view, Eastern-European Russians are not a diaspora but a stranded minority, and Mexicans in the US border region are a borderland culture. Nevertheless, various Western-Muslim communities are frequently studied based on their religion, or studied as "Muslims,"[84] even though diasporic communities also commonly maintain multiple layers of identity; thus, it is unclear whether one dominant identity exists.[85] This study will show that a variety of ethnic identity markers (especially nationality, sectarian cleavages, and race) guide diasporic community mobilization to conflicts abroad; and Muslim ethnic identities frequently determine the focus of their foreign policy interests.

Reactive Conflict Spillover

Context: Opportunities and Threats

Once reactive transnational mobilization has occurred, it is likely that a combination of mobilization opportunities offered by countries and cities where minority communities live—and the characteristics of the given community—will determine whether the mobilization remains peaceful or escalates into violence. The migration context is largely determined by national migration and security policies, and structural variables influencing the ease and level of migrant integration.

Overall, the studies of whether second-generation minorities are better integrated than first-generation migrants provide inconclusive evidence.[86] However, some evidence suggests that second- and third-generation European minorities could be particularly drawn to terrorism because of ethnic and economic oppression.[87]

Additionally, some argue that Western foreign policy has the potential to cause political violence in local migrant-background communities. This argument is rather weak. Those Western Muslims who dislike Western foreign policy are most likely to be democratic in expressing their dissent and to influence government policy.[88] Islamist groups like Hizb ut-Tahrir (HT) tend to blame Muslim radicalization on Western intervention in the Muslim world. Such groups argue that European-Muslim radicalization is a direct outcome of the American-led wars in Afghanistan and Iraq or of the Israel-Palestine conflict.[89] The Iraq War, in particular, significantly motivated would-be terrorists in Europe, but also attracted more recruits.[90] However, such studies fail to explain why some communities radicalize, but others do not—even when they live in the same country and are affected by the same foreign policy. In attempt to find some answers to these questions, this study selects two cases from Western countries with similar foreign policies and compares them. Could it be particular domestic policies—not foreign policy—that prompt violence?

Indeed, differing approaches regarding national asylum and refugee policies create opportunity structures conducive to either peaceful or violent mobilization. Numerous studies show that states' policies concerning migrants can either promote or stifle integration (e.g., see Adamson 2006; Hammar 1985; Reitz 2002.) Others argue that immigration and asylum policies can have unexpected externalities (e.g., see Boswell 2000; Lavenex and Uçarer 2003). Some even contest that refugees from war zones contribute to civil wars.[91] These examples stipulate that indiscriminate acceptance of migrant groups (e.g., refugees from war zones) may cause political violence in these communities or create migrant populations opposed to the host state. Indeed, state policy decisions can greatly regulate the migrants entering countries and the actions of minority communities.[92] Thus, a country with policies allowing immigration of violent radicals would accept hundreds, or even thousands, of said radicals, as opposed to denying their admission because of national security concerns.

Furthermore, the level of integration, the availability of jobs, community education levels, the strength of representative organizations, and ties with other community organizations determine city-level political mobilization.[93] It is possibly even more important to what extent various migrant and ethnic groups perceive their level of integration to be deprived according to their own socioeconomic expectations. Crul and Vermeulen's (2003) study of second-generation migrant integration in six European countries (Belgium, France, the Netherlands, Austria, Germany, and Sweden) found varied levels of integration among predominately Moroccan- and Turkish-background populations. The study showed that certain immigration contexts largely determined the level of integration by different migrant-background populations. For example, due to the apprenticeship system in Austria and Germany, Turkish-background individuals were relatively better employed than their counterparts in France, Belgium, and the Netherlands.

Crul and Schneider (2010, 1) states that the level of integration in European cities is strongly dependent on the "integration context," which consists of "institutional arrangements in education, the labor market, housing, religion and legislation." As a whole, studies about how state policies influence migrant integration suggest that in countries and cities where governments enact policies aimed at assisting immigrants with overcoming inequalities, integration occurs at a greater rate. Thus, poor integration—described in terms of low employment rates, low income, little education, and weak political representation—are likely indicators that more radical politics appeal to the local minority community.

Moreover, studies in relative deprivation and social psychology suggest that if individuals (or groups) perceive that there exists a large difference between what is deserved and what is received, it can lead to anger, collective action and (in extreme cases) riots, terrorism and internal conflicts.[94] For example, Zagefka and Brown (2002) and Navas et al. (2005) emphasize the importance of mutually aligning perceptions as these studies argue that in order for migrant integration strategies to work, both migrants and host society need to have similar expectations of what integration entails. Frameworks grounded in relative deprivation theory have been used to explain intergroup prejudice,[95] Western migrant participation in protest politics,[96] the discontent of European Muslim youth,[97] and violent radicalization in Western Muslim communities.[98] Chebel d'Appollonia (2015, 11) builds on the work of social psychologists to show that people who feel that they are subjectively discriminated against and excluded (such as immigrants and minorities targeted via security measures) have more negative attitudes towards their host society, are more critical of the society they now live in, and have less trust in national institutions. Gest (2010, 65) explains that individual Western Muslims display anti-system behavior and alienation when there is "large discrepancy between expectation of the political system and perceived levels of fulfillment." Taken as a whole, it can be deducted that spillovers will be more likely to erupt in those minority communities where there are more individuals who perceive that they are significantly relatively socioeconomically deprived.

Furthermore, poor economic integration is frequently accompanied by alienation, which can lead to terrorism. Laqueur (1999) notes that the second and third generations of guest workers in Europe could be particularly attracted to terrorism because of their experience with ethnic and economic discrimination. In addition to socioeconomic considerations, political and policy issues also heavily influence communal perceptions. Due to the lack of intermediaries for political expression—accompanied by the institutionalization of radical, but currently usually non-violent, Islamic groups such as the Muslim Brotherhood—have inspired some of the said radical groups to attempt to become the community advocates on these issues.[99]

In many terrorist attacks in Europe and elsewhere, the perpetrators were isolated Muslims. Some belonged to online, would-be terrorist communities.[100] Other such loners typically feel alienated from their ethnic communities and broader national societies, and their participation in violent Islamic terrorist groups finally gives them a sense of belonging.[101]

For example, police analyst Mehmood Naqshbandi (2008) suggests a "silent pinball" route to terrorism to explain how migrant-background individuals become violent radicals. Naqshbandi (2008) explains that Muslim groups with different views approach Muslims new to the UK.

While interacting with these groups, some of the newcomers will feel inclined to take action in name of the faith. Numerous individuals are likely to become dedicated Sufis or Tablighis.[102] Other, more radically inclined individuals may reject other groups, and such a person "might join the *jihad* in Chechnya or might take a train to Kings Cross [one of the locations of the 7/7 London bombings]."[103] Similarly, in the American context, a study by the New York Police Department (Silber and Bhatt 2007) observes that radicalization contains four distinct phases: (1) pre-radicalization, (2) self-identification, (3) indoctrination, and (4) Jihadization. However, such individualized, "lone-wolf" radicalization that happens outside of a group framework (e.g., via the Internet) generally prompts unsophisticated terrorism (e.g., small and often, foiled, attacks), rather than catastrophes, like 9/11.[104] Rioting scholarship provides additional insights about the causes of violent mobilization.

Ashutosh Varshney's (2002) seminal study focuses on communal riots in India and finds that, in cities with strong institutionalized relationships between Hindus and Muslims, communal riots have been almost always absent. In such cities, associational civic engagement prompts emergence of "institutionalized peace systems." These "systems" are present within peaceful cities in India in forms of trade unions, associations of businessmen, traders, teachers, doctors, and lawyers, film clubs for poorer people, and at least a few cadre-based, integrated political parties.[105] Violent cities, where often strategically implanted rumors and skirmishes create riots, lack "such relationships of synergy [which] in peaceful cities nip rumors, small clashes, and tensions in the bud."[106] Building on these insights, it can be expected that minority communities that have institutionalized social relationships with each other will not engage in mutual conflict. Also, migrant-background communities that have institutional social relationships with local community members will not experience conflict spillover.

Meanwhile, institutionalized relationships between radical leaders and local government officials create opportunities for political violence. Paul Brass introduced the famous concept of "institutionalized riot systems," defined in India as "a network of actors, groups and connections involving persons from different social categories whose effect, leaving aside intentions for the moment, is to keep a town or city in a permanent state of awareness of Hindu-Muslim relationship."[107] In cities with such riot systems, "riot specialists" are at the core, "specializing" in converting incidents between two communities into riots. These people report incidents to popular or public authorities, such as professors or government officials, potentially creating communal violence, most commonly rioting. Riots are likely during mobilization or election times, when politicians act as "protector[s] of one community against the alleged threats of the other."[108] Thus, political and movement leaders spur violence. When large-scale disturbances are needed, students, hooligans, low-caste slum-dwellers, criminals, and trained activists are brought into cities.[109] Thus, Brass finds that riots erupt in those locales where there are institutionalized relationships aimed at promoting riots between malignant politicians on one side and radical leaders of an ethnic group on the other.

Overall, this study finds that policies allowing influx of violent radicals increase the likelihood of reactive conflict spillover. Such radicals can both participate in violent activities in response to foreign policy events as well as radicalize others (especially, excitable youth). However, poorly economically integrated migrant and minority communities (especially those "poorly integrated" in terms of high unemployment rate, low income level, little education, and low levels of political representation) only increase the possibility of spillovers if there is not a Varshneyesque, institutionalized peace system (or extensive civil society inter-group ties) involving the Muslim community and the broader community. Poverty itself does not lead to willingness to conduct criminal acts, yet it may create environments where some find radical politics more appealing; this is likely to particularly be the case in areas where numerous individuals and groups perceive that they experience relative socioeconomic deprivation. Nevertheless, even in economically deprived communities, extensive inter-group ties promote certain inter-group trust and can minimize the appeal of radicalism.

Migrant Communities: Characteristics and Actions

In addition to immigration context, characteristics and actions of local diasporic communities will influence whether the reactions to conflicts abroad are peaceful or violent. In particular, local radical groups—and connections with violent, radical networks abroad—can lead to reactive transnational violence.

Violent individuals and groups need few financial and social resources to create organizational support structures. Most cases of reactive conflict spillover are likely to be executed by small or even, amateurish, violent groups, including sleeper cells (e.g., the organizers of the Madrid and London train attacks in 2004 and 2005) or relatively weak or previously non-violent branches of homeland resistance movements (e.g., the PKK in Germany).

Compared to major groups that utilize violent tactics, smaller groups need not maintain significant support from those they claim to represent. Sageman observes that recent Muslim-extremist terrorist operations in Europe have been inexpensive and are often funded via welfare payments to unemployed would-be terrorists.[110] Due to the limited resource needs of radical movements, social appropriation of resources is not expected to be significant in explaining reactive conflict spillover. However, connections with radical networks may be significant.

Some such connections may involve transnational connections with violent, homeland or local radical Islamist groups. Former-homeland politics can play a key role in radicalization and terrorism across three dimensions: the appeal of homeland politics as a competitor to transnational Islam; the power of symbolic attachments to the homeland; and pragmatism that depends on the effectiveness of tactics that can lead groups to attack either former homelands or countries of current residence.

Alison Pargeter's (2006) study of radical, militant North African-background minorities in Europe found that such militants are as much interested in national politics as in transnational Islamist politics.[111] At times, homeland violence is replicated within European-Muslim communities.[112] In other instances, host states are targeted because homeland governments are too powerful and a conflict exists between the host state and the country of a migrant community. For example, the Algerian Civil War spilled over to France in the 1990s, the Turkish-Kurdish conflict spilled over to Turkish communities in Western Europe, and the Kurdish PKK executed many terrorist attacks in Germany in the 1990s.[113]

Some evidence suggests that symbolism particularly influences diasporic involvement with homeland issues.[114] Another set of explanations labels radical Islam as a major cause of violent radicalization.

Some blame radicalization on radical Islamist groups among Muslim communities. Zeno Baran famously labeled Hizb ut-Tahrir (HT) as a "conveyor belt for radicalism and terrorism."[115] She further explained that "while HT as an organization does not engage in terrorist activities, it has become the vanguard of the radical Islamist ideology that encourages its followers to commit terrorist acts."[116] Many other studies have similarly suggested that the radical, yet peaceful, Muslim groups in Europe can lead to violence and terrorism (e.g., see Cruickshank 2010; Husain 2007; Roy 2003). Moreover, some individuals (Muslim preachers, scholars, or intellectuals) may greatly influence Muslim communities, even though they do not belong to any official Muslim movement(s).[117]

Cynthia Irvin (1999) reveals that internal discourse and the environment influence the internal composition of militant, nationalist movements and their interactions with each other. Discourse and environment offer opportunities and impose limitations for collective mobilization on behalf of aggravated minorities.[118] Thus, within nationalist movements, regime responsiveness, organizational resources, and internal competition influence the strategies used to achieve movement goals. In closed regimes (characterized by undemocratic government and repression of minorities), groups adopt terrorism to compensate for reduced support and internal security demands.[119] Overall, a militant, nationalist movement's strategy and structures result from debate and coalition building among three types of movement leaders.[120]

Several works insist that ideology strongly determines the level of group violence. For example, Hoffman (2006, 237) finds that secular terrorist organizations in Europe chose less violent strategies than more recent Islamic terrorist groups because their ideology did not justify radicalism. Similarly, Weinberg (1992) gives evidence that an ideology justifying violence played the main role in (the) Russian Party of Socialist Revolutionaries' terrorist attacks in the early 20th century. Additionally, preoccupation with ideology about cosmic war and apocalyptical violence is common in Judeo-Christianity, Buddhism (specifically, Aum Shinrikyo, an extremist Buddhist cult), and Islam. Through selective interpretations of the holy texts, these themes have influenced some radical groups.[121] Neumann insists that modernity and globalization have profoundly impacted the "new" terrorism, which is often characterized by transnational networks and excessive violence.[122]

Multiple studies state that the presence of many delinquents can potentially promote violence. John Mueller argues that small groups of "opportunistic marauders recruited by political leaders and operating under their general guidance"[123] incite much violence during ethnic conflicts. Most of these "thugs" are either released prisoners, gang members, or soccer hooligans. Horowitz insists that communities with more gangs will most likely become violent and riot.[124] Guirdandon and Joppke (2001) suggest that the crime rate among more recent migrant-background communities in Western and Northern Europe is higher than that among natives.[125] They argue that it is largely because police disproportionately target immigrant communities and because communities consist of many young, crime-prone males.[126] Thus, if the data were controlled according to the frequency of police intervention, age, and gender, the crime rate would be uniform. Finally, studies on protest policing suggest that clashes between police and demonstrators occur because extreme fringe groups utilize "urban guerilla tactics."[127] As a whole, said studies suggest that communities with more criminal gangs and more youthful minorities may be more likely to practice disorderly political activism.

In sum, why do some protests in response to conflicts abroad become radical and violent, while others remain peaceful? In locales where minorities are well-connected with foreign, radical networks, extreme forms of political protest are likely to occur. In such communities, hundreds or more individuals may belong to violent-radical groups *and* regularly travel abroad for ideological guidance or paramilitary training. Furthermore, localities with active, provocative radical groups are likely to experience disorderly activism. In such communities, politically active groups with at least several dozen members and radical ideologies are likely to express their views confrontationally. Events organized by such radical fringe groups are likely to prompt counter-rallies from extreme right groups. These rallies increase the possibility for clashes among supporters of both groups. To conclude, the case studies will show how both the presence of radical groups in the community—and links to radical networks abroad—contribute significantly to political violence related to foreign policy events.

In summary, the rest of this book will show that triggers framed as important by community leaders frequently galvanize communities into action. In response to foreign policy events, migrant-background Muslim communities frequently tend to mobilize on the basis of their ethnic and sectarian divisions, whereas in regard to domestic policies, their Islamic identity commonly dominates. In such communities, interaction between the nature of immigration context and characteristics of minorities determine the nature of the mobilization. Communities residing in localities characterized by policies allowing immigration of violent radicals, presence of well-established radical groups, and existing linkages to radical networks abroad, can lead to political hostilities including violent protests and terrorist plots. Poor integration without extensive civil-society inter-group ties also can increase the appeal of radical activism. This is summarized in Table 2.2 below, which outlines the two types of reactive conflict spillover that are differentiated from each other by their level of overt violence, the importance of triggers, and the nature of causes.[128]

Finally, from a policy perspective, it is essential to distinguish between reactive conflict spillover associated with contemporary migration and spillover associated with diasporic activity.[129] Managing reactive conflict spillovers initiated by these two different "mechanisms" also requires different approaches. First, spillovers associated with contemporary migration can be notably reduced by placing restrictions on the immigration of violent radicals. Second, to lessen the threat of violent spillover to diasporic communities, it helps to build civil society inter-group ties involving minority community leaders, and local government and law enforcement representatives. More broadly, policies aimed at lessening socioeconomic disparities and discrimination are likely to greatly contribute to the creation of an environment where radical politics do not find fertile ground (for more on policy prescriptions, see Chapter 8).

Table 2.2 Two Types of Reactive Conflict Spillovers

Type	Trigger	Cause
Street Violence Spillovers (e.g., violent protest)	Important	Policies allowing immigration of violent radicals
		Poor economic integration without extensive civil society inter-group ties
		Local radical groups
Mobilized Violence Spillover (e.g., terrorist act)	Not important	Policies allowing immigration of violent radicals
		Poor economic integration without extensive civil society inter-group ties
		Connections with radical networks abroad

Notes

1 Hanagan 2002, 56.
2 Trask 2006.
3 See Zolberg 2006b, 95–100.
4 Hanagan 2002.
5 Cohen 1997.
6 Dhillon 2007.
7 Dhillon 2007.
8 "Sikh Extremism Spread Fast in Canada," *ExpressIndia.com*, 23 May 2007.
9 Roberts et al. 2005, 270.
10 Blaise and Mukherjee 1987.
11 Marcus 2007, 249.
12 Marcus 2007, 291.
13 Miller 2000.
14 Hurriyet, "Bir Dönemin Acı Bilançosu," July 16, 2008.
15 Marcus 2007, 65.
16 Marcus 2007, 65.
17 Lyon and Uçarer 2001; Marcus 2009.
18 Marcus 2007, 66.
19 Miller 2000.
20 Blaine Harden, "Turkish Kurds' revolt sparks wide violence," *The Washington Post*, March 25, 1992, A25.
21 Schmidbauer 1995, 8.
22 Miller 1981.
23 Kushner 2003, 153.
24 Huliq, "Turkish Grey Wolves Hold Violent Rallies in Europe," October 27, 2007.
25 Rosenberg 2006, 66.
26 Cross 1983, 106–108.
27 Rosenberg 2006, 67.
28 Rosenberg 2006, 67.
29 Hewitt 2005, X.
30 Hewitt 2005, 193.
31 Weiner 2007.
32 Stewart Bell, "8,000 Tamil Guerillas in Toronto: Police," *National Post*, June 17, 2000.
33 Stewart Bell, "Gangs Linked to Terrorism, Study Finds: Members, Tactics Overlap," *National Post*, March 5, 2002.
34 B'Tselem 2008.
35 Dreyfus and Laurence 2002.
36 Taspinar 2003.
37 Marc Perelman, "Antisemitic Incidents Rise in France as Worry Increases About Ethnic Divisions," *The Jewish Daily Forward*, January 21, 2009.
38 Klausen 2009.
39 Klausen 2009.
40 Miller 2000.
41 Miller 2000.
42 Miller 2000.
43 *New York Times*, "Indian and Pakistani Immigrants Live Together Peacefully in America (New York)," June 1, 2002.
44 Laitin 1998, 325.
45 For more, see Ripiloski 2011.
46 Finlan 2004, 64.

47 Brown 2004.
48 Hockenos 2003; Sullivan 2004.
49 For example, in 2000, intense violence occurred between Jewish and Muslim communities in France following the beginning of the Second Intifada. However, Jews and Muslims coexisted in relative peace in Britain during the same time.
50 Violence between Jews and Muslims in France has been common for the last several decades. However, following the Second Intifada, French police information indicates a notable increase in offenses committed by Muslims against Jews (e.g., see Taspinar 2003).
51 For a pioneering work on how migrants can represent a security threat, see Weiner 1993; for the possibility of the replication of homeland violence, see Wæver et al. 1993, and Pargeter 2008.
52 Byman and Pollack 2007; Salehyan and Gleditsch 2006; Zolberg et. al 1989.
53 Lucassen 2005, 22–3.
54 Lucassen 2005, 23.
55 Abiri 2000.
56 Chebel d'Appollonia 2008; Chebel d'Appollonia and Reich 2008.
57 Wittgenstein (1958) introduces the concept of "family resemblance" as an alternative to the commonly used term, "necessary and sufficient conditions." In contrast to necessary and sufficient conditions, family resemblance requires that the given phenomenon of interest only meet a certain number of conditions to be placed in a certain category. Collier and Mahon (1993) suggest that family- resemblance categories allow limitations placed on research by traditional concepts, such as necessary and sufficient conditions, to be supplemented and overcome.
58 Krebs and Levy 2001.
59 Alexseev 2005, 231; Kirshner 2006, 64.
60 Chebel d'Appollonia 2012, xi.
61 Chebel d'Appollonia 2015, 141–144.
62 Horowitz 1985.
63 Horowitz 1985, 295.
64 Dahlberg-Acton 1967, as quoted in Shain 2007, 9.
65 E.g., see Mearsheimer and Walt 2007.
66 Gurr 2000, 89.
67 Gurr 2000, 90.
68 Lake and Rothchild 1998, 25–29.
69 For Kosavar and Bosnian conflict spillover to trans-border kindred communities, see Grigorova-Mincheva 2000. For contagion of the 2005 riots in France's Muslim-migrant communities to migrant communities in Germany and Belgium, see d'Appollonia 2008, 223.
70 Hill and Rothchild 1986.
71 See Klausen 2009.
72 Doug McAdam 1982.
73 McAdam, Tarrow, and Tilly 2001.
74 See Zolberg 2006b, 95–100.
75 Wiktorowicz 2005, 200.
76 Lyon and Uçarer 2001, 932.
77 McAdam, Tarrow, and Tilly 2001, 9.
78 Migration-security scholarship includes Miller 2000, and Weiner 1993; ethnic-conflicts scholarship of migration includes Harff and Gurr 2004.
79 Horowitz 2001; Kaufman 2001, 2006.
80 Horowitz 2001.

81 However, the role of triggers is likely to be more subdued in such deliberate reactive conflict spillovers, like bombings and terrorist attacks. Such acts tend to result from meticulous planning, not spontaneous reactions to trigger events.

82 Community-leader support for a conflict may or may not be related to the overall magnitude of the conflict. For example, community leaders may advocate on behalf of a smaller conflict, while they overlook another conflict involving multiple deaths and a dire humanitarian situation.

83 Shain 2007; Smith 1999, 501.

84 For more, see Chapter 5.

85 For many layers of diasporic identity, see Berkovitch 2007, 19.

86 E.g., see Diehl and Schnell 2006; Lucassen 2005.

87 Laqueur 1999.

88 E.g., see Gest 2010, 57–58.

89 See Hizb Ut-Tahrir Britain 2007.

90 Nesser 2006.

91 d'Appollonia and Reich 2008; Salehyan and Gleditsch 2006; Zolberg et. al 1989.

92 Alexseev 2005 231; Lahav 2010; Kirshner 2006, 64.

93 Crul and Schneider 2010; Varshney 2002.

94 E.g., see Gurr 1970; Walker and Smith 2001.

95 Pettigrew et al. 2008.

96 Grant 2010.

97 Franz 2007.

98 Sageman 2004, 95.

99 Roy 2003; Kepel 2002; Vidino 2010.

100 Denemark 2008; Thompson 2007.

101 Abrams 2008.

102 Tablighis are quite religious, yet relatively apolitical, Muslims.

103 Naqshbandi 2008.

104 E.g., see Mueller and Stewart 2012.

105 Varshney 2002, 11, 47.

106 Varshney 2002, 11.

107 Brass 1997, 289.

108 Bass 1997, 285.

109 Bass 1997, 286.

110 Sageman 2008, 102.

111 Pargeter 2006.

112 E.g., see Pargeter 2008.

113 Miller 2000; Lyon and Uçarer, 2001; Marcus, 2007; Pupcenoks 2010, 26–28.

114 Shain 2007.

115 Baran 2004, Introductory Note.

116 Baran 2004, 1.

117 Cesari 2004.

118 Irvin 1999, 30.

119 Irvin 1999, 32.

120 Irvin 1999, 18.

121 E.g., see Benjamin and Simon 2003.

122 Neumann 2009a.

123 Mueller 2000, 42.

124 Horowitz 2001, 225–6.

125 Guiraudon and Joppke 2001.

126 However, the authors also imply that the crime rate among immigrant-background communities would resemble the national crime rate if one were to set age and offenses related to immigration-law violations as controls. Moreover, immigrant communities can also become the focus of political attacks by right-wing groups, as is the case in Eastern Germany, France, and Sweden. These political attacks increase the crime rate and cause mobilization.

127 Della Porta, Peterson and Reiter 2006, 4.

128 Even though there is some overlap, as the causes are not always mutually exclusive.

129 Diasporas without noteworthy contemporary immigration are possible, such as Jewish diasporas in numerous places all over the world.

3   Pakistanis in London, Arabs in Detroit

This chapter serves as a more thorough introduction to the Muslim communities in London and Detroit, before analyzing their political activism in the subsequent chapters. It starts with an overview of Muslim migration to Europe and the US, examines studies of Muslims in the UK and London and the US and Detroit, provides descriptive information on the said communities, and outlines their views and actions on political matters.

Migrant and Muslim Communities in Europe and the US

As a result of labor shortages in a booming post-war economy, Europe experienced a large influx of foreign workers and their families following World War II. France, Germany, and Switzerland admitted the majority of such guest workers between 1945 and 1973.[1] By the 1980s, the rapidly growing stock of immigrant-background individuals suggested two things. First, European states needed to come to terms with the fact that they *were* states of immigration. Second, in light of increasing migrant-background-individual political activism, migrants could no longer be viewed in purely economic terms.

In the 1980s and 1990s, three forces converged: the fall of the Soviet Union and the end of the Cold War, a re-conceptualization of "security," and increasing socio-political activism among Western European migrants and minorities. The post-Cold War re-conceptualization of security led officials to accept "new" security threats, which they previously overlooked because of more conventional security threats from interstate rivalry. Some of the "new" security threats were climate change and threats presented by migration.[2]

Lucassen (2005) points out that, contrary to popular belief, fears about the perceived differences between locals and immigrants are nothing new. In the early twentieth century, Italians migrating to France were considered intellectually inferior and socially troublesome. Eastern Europeans and Irish immigrants arriving to the US in the late twentieth century often encountered unwelcome environments. Irish immigrants arriving in the US in the first half of the 20th century faced harsh discrimination, for they were *not* perceived to be white.[3] Recently, there has been much scrutiny from both contemporary academic and journalistic sources of Muslim migration to Europe.

On both sides of the Atlantic, many have feared that Muslims are different from other waves of migrants of the past and less able to integrate.[4] Asad insists that, for centuries, hostility existed between Muslim states and European kingdoms; as a result, many Europeans perceive the Muslim as the "other." Many in the US hold similar views,[5] and there is a long history of negative stereotypes of Muslims in both Europe and the US.[6]

Prominent political scientist Samuel P. Huntington emphasized the perceived clash between Islam and the West in his 1993 *Foreign Affairs* article "The Clash of Civilizations?" Huntington claimed that conflicts along the fault line between Western and Islamic civilizations had been ongoing for 1,300 years and that the situation was unlikely to improve. Many have debated the credibility of the Huntington thesis ever since.[7] Various authors have stated that civilizations do not control states, but states control civilizations; that personal, not cultural, identities are the main cause of conflict; and that distinct cultural boundaries do not exist in the contemporary world.[8] Nevertheless, despite the common rhetoric of Muslim "otherness," Muslim historical presence in certain parts of Europe is frequently overlooked.

Muslims have long been present in Europe. After the conquest, Muslim Moors ruled parts of Iberia from 711 to 1492.[9] Indigenous Muslims have lived in Balkans for centuries, a legacy of the Ottoman rule.[10] In modern-day Bosnia and Herzegovina, and Macedonia, Muslims constitute close to half of the population; Albania and Kosovo are almost exclusively Muslim. In addition, the United Kingdom, France, Germany, and other Western-European nations are historically linked to Muslim lands.

The history of contemporary Muslim mass-migration to the West began after World War II. Estimates of European Muslims vary, but Pew (2015) estimates that there were 43 million (6 percent) Muslims in Europe in 2010, and this number is to increase to more than 71 million (10 percent) by 2050. Some of the largest Muslim communities are in Western Europe. Germany and France are each home to about five million Muslims, and the United Kingdom is home to about three million Muslims.[11] Meanwhile, in North America as a whole, the Muslim population will increase from about 3.5 million (1 percent) in 2010 to over 10 million (2.4 percent) in 2050.[12]More specifically, in the US Muslims represent only a small minority of all Americans, about three million (1 percent) in 2010, and Pew (2015) projects that there will be about 8 million (2.1 percent) Muslim Americans by 2050.

Roughly two-thirds of all Muslims in the US immigrated after the 1980s. The earliest known Muslims arrived in America during the slave trade of the 16th century.[13] Individuals from the Middle East and South

Asia have migrated to the US since the late 19th century. During the 20th century, increasing Muslim migration to the US was largely made possible because of changes in immigration laws, including the repeal of the quota system of 1924, the codification of the McCarran-Walter Act in 1952, and the Immigration Act of 1965.[14] Each of these actions aimed to ease restrictions on foreign nationals entering the US. Since the end of World War II, migrants from Muslim countries, including Syria, Lebanon, Egypt, Afghanistan, and Iraq, have continuously entered the US.[15] Many Arabs immigrated to the US following escalating violence in Palestine in 1948 and in Iraq in 1958.[16] In the 1980s, internal turmoil in Pakistan, a revolution in Iraq, and the Soviet invasion of Afghanistan triggered further outward migration.[17] In the 1990s, Muslim migrants escaping chaos in Somalia and conflicts in the former Yugoslavia and Iraq fled to the US.[18] More recently, Muslim migrants have come from the Asia-Pacific region, the Middle East, and North Africa, especially Iraq, Iran, Bangladesh, and Pakistan. Additionally, particularly since the 1960s, many highly educated Muslims from all over the world have entered the US.

Meanwhile, as former colonizers of numerous Muslim countries, European states have commonly remained in close contact with many of their former colonies, states with whom they were connected politically and economically. Critics have frequently castigated European meddling in the Muslim world, particularly European military involvement. Muslim and minority communities in Europe have notably opposed European military campaigns, from the 1991 Operation Desert Storm in Iraq to the more recent wars in Afghanistan and Iraq. Meanwhile, resurgent Islamists across the globe have cried that Muslims worldwide should unite and protest trespasses committed against the global *ummah*, regardless of where they occur. A tiny minority of Muslims have joined violent Islamist groups such as Al-Qaeda and ISIS.

Following the 9/11 attack, bombings in Madrid (2004) and London (2005), and other attempted terrorist acts in the transatlantic area, the public came to fear political violence from European Muslims even more. Amidst a moral panic[19]—largely induced by vivid portrayals of attempted terrorist attacks and excessive media attention given to Islamic radicals—it was easy to develop an exaggerate threat perception. Despite resurgent and violent Muslim radical terrorism occurring in Western Europe and America, the vast majority of Western Muslims did not sympathize with radical Islam or with political violence.[20]

Studies of British Muslims

Scholarship of British Muslims is a recent phenomenon, with Phillip Lewis' 1994 *Islamic Britain* widely considered to be the first major study of British Muslims. In this book, the author describes the history of the diverse Bradford's South Asian community. Daniele Joly's (1995) study of Muslim communities in Birmingham, *Britannia's Crescent: Making Place for Muslims in British Society*, closely followed Lewis' work. These works predate other studies of British Muslims. Such early studies tended to describe and celebrate British Muslim communities, which were previously neglected in academic studies.

More recently, studies concerning British Muslims tend to assess the security threat that these rapidly growing European Muslim communities may present for European countries. Controversial, yet widely read, works by predominately American journalists and some scholars such as Bat Ye'or's *Eurabia* or Christopher Caldwell's *Reflection on the Revolution in Europe*, delineate the perceived "dangers" of an "immanent" Islamization (societal acceptance of the superiority of religious and cultural values popularly associated with Islam) and the rise of Islamic radicalism in Europe.[21] Walter Laqueur (2007) claims that Muslim migrants are irreversibly changing Western European countries, and that Muslim communities create high economic and social costs for receiving states.

Numerous recent publications warn of growing Muslim radicalization within poorly integrated British Muslim communities.[22] In 2006, during a US Congressional hearing, Europe was labeled as "the Third Front in the War on Terrorism."[23] Nevertheless, the overwhelming majority of Muslims have integrated, and radicalism appeals only to tiny fringe groups of British and European Muslims.[24] Meanwhile, European and British Muslim scholars have become increasingly concerned about discrimination and attacks, predominantly by far-right groups.[25]

Additionally, more recent and comprehensive studies of European and British Muslims reveal complex dynamics of migrant-background population integration.[26] The seminal *When Islam and Democracy Meet: Muslims in Europe and the United States* goes beyond describing how Muslims adapt to their new environments and criticizing contemporary Islamophobia. Cesari (2004, 5) argues that Muslim immigration to Europe and North America has created a new, still unanalyzed "transcultural" space. Interestingly, a key finding in this book claims that while European and American Muslims consider Islam inseparable from ethno-national identity, Muslim diasporic, transatlantic communities increasingly attempt to develop "transethnic" Islam.[27] Overall, these writings reveal that results of Muslim integration in Europe are mixed and uneven across different countries and different ethnic Muslim communities in these countries.[28]

Another strand of studies focuses on the relationship between state policies and integration. Crul and Schneider (2010, 1257) suggest that Muslim participation and belonging among migrant-background populations in European cities is strongly dependent on the integration context or institutional arrangements in education, the labor market, housing, religion, and legislation. Joppke (2010) argues that what a government-driven integration policy can achieve is limited. Nevertheless, most of these more comprehensive studies tend to be optimistic and tend to suggest that, in many aspects, European Muslims are more integrated than they were in the 1970s, for example.[29]

Scholarship on British Muslim communities predominately analyzes the community experience or assesses the threat that such communities provide post-9/11. Many of these studies tend to emphasize the religious similarities that Muslims share. Commonly, scholars study one ethnically Muslim community (especially Pakistanis—the largest ethnic Muslim community in the UK, constituting more than one-third of the entire British Muslim population) and then apply the findings to the entire British Muslim community. Such studies are problematic, as they fail to emphasize the impact of ethnicity on the mobilization of diverse Muslim communities. Such accounts grossly overlook the importance of diversity. In addition, many scholarly and policy publications have exaggerated the perceived security threat that growing, radical Muslim populations present to European governments.[30]

Politics of Muslim and Pakistani Diasporas in London

According to the 2011 Census, there are one million Muslims in London, constituting 12 percent of the city's population of 8.2 million.[31] In 2011, the three boroughs with the highest proportion of Muslims were Tower Hamlets (35 percent, or 88,000), Newham (32 percent, or 98,500) and Redbridge (23 percent or 65,000).

Along with Turks and Bangladeshis, Pakistanis represent one of the largest ethnic communities in London. According to the UK's Office of National Statistics (2001, 2011), the population of London's Pakistanis has increased from 143,000 or 2 percent in 2001 to 224,000 or 2.7 percent in 2011. From the entire London Pakistani population, 60,000 live in the Inner London and 164,000 in the Outer London. The main concentrations of Pakistani settlements are located in the Northeast, West, and Southwest areas of the city. The three boroughs with the highest proportion of Pakistani Britons are Redbridge (11 percent), Newham (10 percent), and Waltham Forest (10 percent), yet Pakistanis are notably dispersed all over London (See Table 3.1). Major Pakistani communities are also located in the Midlands and Northern England.

Most British Pakistanis come from the Kashmir and Punjab regions of Pakistan, and they tend to practice the Barelvi denomination of Islam.[32] The Barelvi and Deobandi schools were established following the failed 1857 mutiny against British colonial rule on the Indian subcontinent.[33] In comparison to their main Deobandi rivals, Barelvis are comparatively more tolerant and apolitical. Newly arriving immigrants tend to share similar histories, cultures, and language. However, the Pakistani community in London has diversified through time, and it has lost many of its

Table 3.1 Pakistanis in London Boroughs, 2011

Region	Population	Pakistani Population	Pakistanis as a %	10 Boroughs with the Highest Pakistani Populations
Greater London	8,200,000	224,000	2.7%	Redbridge 31,051 (11%) Newham 30,307 (10%) Waltham Forest 26,347 (10%) Ealing 14,711 (4%) Brent 14,381 (5%) Hounslow 13,676 (5%) Croydon 10,865 (3%) Wandsworth 9,718 (3%) Hillingdon 9,200 (3%) Haringey 9,200 (4%)

Source: UK Office for National Statistics 2011

initial commonalities in the process. For example, some British Pakistanis have recently converted to the Wahabbi current of Islam.

Sizeable Pakistani immigration to the UK started in the 1950s and 1960s, and is still ongoing. Over 70 percent of Britain's Pakistani community can trace their ties to the impoverished, rural Mirpur region of Pakistani Azad Kashmir.[34] Many British Pakistanis also arrived from the Punjab province of Pakistan.[35] Overall, they tend to be less educated, belong to the working class, and endure more poverty than other socioeconomic groups in London. Nevertheless, Pakistanis constitute one of the oldest and well-established Muslim communities in London, and have participated in British politics for decades. About one half of British Pakistanis are second- or third-generation migrant-background individuals.[36]

Even though Islamic protest politics in the UK are a relatively new phenomenon, London's Muslims and Pakistanis have been particularly active in London and in the UK already prior to 9/11.[37] Unfortunately, scholars of British Muslims commonly overlook the scholarship on migrant political participation in the post-World War II period—even though several important connections emerge through the integration of studies on British migrants and Muslims. More importantly, the scholarship on migrant political activism prior to 9/11 reveals that minority political mobilization patterns based on ethnicity and race were established in the post-World War II era, and were not swept away by 9/11.

Migrants and minorities have played an important role in post-World War II politics.[38] In the UK, immigration became a subject of political debate as early as 1958, following race riots in Notting Hill in London and other areas.[39] The British Conservative Party won the 1970 election due to the popular appeal of its strong anti-immigration message.[40] Nevertheless, a pamphlet published by the Community Relations Commission in the 1970s also highlighted the growing electoral significance of immigrant-background ethnic minorities, and even the Conservative Party began to recruit minority members as a result.[41] The 1980s witnessed the emergence of shrewd Afro-Caribbean and Asian politicians.[42] Black and Asian Britons, many of whom were Muslims, actively participated in the 1983 and 1987 general and local elections.[43]

Historically, "colored" migrants had little voice in British parties and political institutions.[44] Even in the 1980s, nonwhite access to the British political agenda remained minimal and problematic: "While overt hostility towards nonwhites may have diminished over the years, indifference to their situation is still the norm, among both elites and masses, but especially the latter."[45] This is not to say that Conservatives and, particularly, Labour Parties have not provided small concessions to their nonwhite constituents. For decades, both Parties have adopted positions supporting British South Asians on issues including promotion of shared family values and conservative moral standards.[46]

Additionally, while the mainstream British political culture eschews political radicalism, British fringe radical groups have been promoting hostile activities against immigrant-background individuals. Some political anti-immigrant campaigns in Britain encouraged racial violence.[47] Contemporary British far-right groups have demonstrated similar occasional engagement in political violence;[48] while such activism is less prevalent in the US.

Moreover, while facing institutional discrimination and racist violence, Britain's minorities mobilized through non-electoral channels.[49] For example, British Afro-Caribbean and Asian youth organized self-protection groups against racist attacks in the 1980s. Faced with discrimination, British Black youth rioted in many inner-city areas in 1981 and 1985.[50] Riots occurred in Brixton's predominately immigrant Christian Afro-Caribbean community in 1981; smaller riots followed in Liverpool and the Midlands.[51] While British Muslims and Pakistanis did not play a major role in these riots, the upheaval of the 1980s created a foundation for later Muslim contentious politics and a distrustful relationship with the national government.

Largely influenced by disenchantment due to deeply entrenched class inequality and urban poverty, smaller outbreaks of unrest occurred in the early 1990s and in Bradford in 2001.[52] In response to the government's failure to tackle the roots of racism in the 1980s and 1990s, New Labour prioritized the issues of urban deprivation and social exclusion following its victory in the 1997 general election.[53] While most of the rioters were non-Muslims, these riots showed that a general pattern of minority political mobilization based on race and ethnicity was already established in the 1980s.

In recent elections, there has been a fierce competition for the Muslim vote. British Muslims and migrants in the United Kingdom, contrary to migrant-background communities in almost all other Western countries, tend to have high voting rates. South Asians, many of whom are Muslim, tend to be highly concentrated in certain localities. In some parliamentary constituencies they constitute 10 to 20 percent of the voters, while in a few local electoral districts they even constitute a majority.[54] Surveys conducted after the 2005 British general election indicated that more than 70 percent of Bangladeshi and Pakistani respondents voted. These percentages were significantly higher than the national average of 61 percent. By the early 2000s, minority and migrant voters were able to affect electoral outcomes in 30–60 of Britain's 650 constituencies,[55] and their voting preferences have influenced electoral results in recent elections.

There is some evidence that, in some of the competitive areas, Muslims played a key role in the Labour Party's losses in the 2005 general election. The Labour Party lost much of its traditional support from British Muslim communities after its decision to take part in the Iraq War of 2003.[56] Similarly, Muslims played a major role in determining electoral outcomes in certain constituencies in the 2010 national election.[57] Compared to past elections, more Muslims voted for Liberal Democrats in 2010; however, there was not a consistent pattern of Muslim defection from Labour overall.[58] Muslim voters played a major role in at least 32 constituencies in the 2015 national election.[59] By 2007, there were already 257 councilors and mayors of Pakistani descent.[60] Furthermore, two British Pakistanis (Bashir Khanbhai and Sajjad Haider Karim) have served in the European Parliament.

Additionally, recent decades have witnessed the creation of several major Islamic organizations as instruments of political representation and participation. The Muslim Council of Britain (MCB) is the largest and most influential Muslim umbrella group in the UK, and Pakistanis have the biggest presence in it of all ethnic groups.[61] It represents some 500 smaller organizations. Since its creation in 1998, MCB, for a majority of the time, enjoyed a close relationship with the New Labour-led government.[62] The Muslim Association of Britain (MAB) and the Islamic Society of Britain (ISB) are two other important British Muslim organizations.[63] Tellingly, the MCB is led by South Asian Muslims, while its main competitor, the MAB, is ideologically close to Egyptian Muslim Brotherhood.[64] Other key religious organizations for British Pakistanis include the UK Islamic Mission, the British Muslim Forum, the Union of Muslim Organizations, the Islamic Society of Britain, the Federation for Student Islamic Societies (FOSIS), and the Muslim Student Trust.[65]

In addition, there are also many smaller fringe groups with more hardline fringe ideologies, such as the Islamist Hizb ut-Tahrir and the now-defunct radical Islamist group Al-Muhajiroun.[66] Many additional Muslim organizations were established following 9/11. Unfortunately, despite the recent acute proliferation of Muslim organizations, these groups generally tend to be out of touch with everyday Muslims.[67] Leaders of such groups frequently fail to relate to mainstream Muslims and to adequately articulate their needs.[68]

British Muslim Views on Political Activism and Violence

Perceptions of what are appropriate political actions can partially explain controversial protests and political hostilities. Certain displays of public aggression by fringe groups, like the routine hostilities of British-football hooligans, violent anti-globalization protests, and other forms of activism, are accepted in the UK. As Mustafa (2015, 167) observes, "Britain has seen many violent protest, riots and bombings in the name of political causes." Meanwhile, although British Pakistanis have engaged in violent acts in London, a likelihood of a Pakistani engaging in a terrorist activity is about the same as their percentage of the population. Furthermore, in the decade following 9/11, the British Muslim community has largely discredited any kind of radical activism.

It is commonly believed that the 1988 British Muslim protests again Salam Rushdie's *The Satanic Verses* were a turning point in the development of a British Muslim consciousness and protest politics.[69] According to Rushdie, the novel:

> Celebrates hybridity, impurity, intermingling, the transformation that comes of new and unexpected combinations of human beings, cultures, ideas, politics, movies, songs. It rejoices in mongrelization and fears the absolution of the Pure . . . *The Satanic Verses* is for change-by-fusion, change-by-conjoining. It is a love-song to our mongrel selves.[70]

In reality, many Muslims in London and elsewhere found the novel to be insensitive and insulting. This was the first time that Muslims from all branches of Islam in Britain became united to advocate for a single cause. This activism transcended "differences between sects, generations and localities."[71] These protests also signified the British Muslims' "wider expression of unease at British societal values."[72] Muslim political activism against *The Satanic Verses* in the UK eventually became confrontational and violent. On February 14, 1989, the Iranian Ayatollah Khomeini issued a *fatwa*, or an Islamic ruling, sentencing Rushdie to death for apostasy.

Campaigning in Britain against *The Satanic Verses* took various forms, including demonstrations, the circulation of petitions, and lobbying of Members of Parliament (MPs) demanding that the book be withdrawn from circulation, destroyed, and not re-published.[73]Additionally, unsuccessful Muslim attempts at reforming the British blasphemy law further illustrated the weak influence that British Muslims had in the British political system in the late 20th century. This law provided for prosecution of those who criticized Christian beliefs central to the Church of England, but did not provide similar protections to other religions. Despite Muslim pressure that the law be extended to safeguard their beliefs from ridicule, the law was not amended—until it was formally abolished in 2008.

Protesters publically burned copies of the book in London streets. British bookstores received hundreds of threats requesting removal of the book, and several of them were bombed.[74] As a result, British bookstores across the nation did not sell the book openly. Many of the protesters, especially young people, appeared to be articulating a "self-conscious identity as Muslims for the first time."[75]

Olivier Roy claims that the Rushdie Affair exemplified "the shift from diasporic to universalist Islam."[76] More importantly, the Affair indicated the beginning of British Muslim religiously inspired politics. Today's British Muslim activists and radicals were children at the time when their parents' generation burned *The Satanic Verses* in the streets.[77] Today's young British Muslims largely see political violence (including rioting, burning cars, and vandalism) as unpopular because of the indirectly illegal status of such activities, and some also view them as un-Islamic.[78]

As of 2015, there were over 1,600 masjids in the UK, and more than 400 mosques in London alone.[79] With regards to the school of thought and ethnicity associated with British mosques, Lewis (2015: 237) observes that, "600 are Deobandi, 550 Barelvi 60 Islamists, 75 Salafi and 65 are Shi'ite," in addition to a number of mosques catering to specific ethnicities. Only a handful of these mosques had been associated with radical Imams and radical activism, and under their old leadership, radical mosques in Finsbury Park and in London's Brixton neighborhoods allegedly played a role in radicalizing convert Richard Reid, the shoe bomber, and Zacarias Moussaoui, the 20th 9/11 hijacker.[80] However, radical Imams like Omar Bakri Muhammad, Abu Hamza, or conservative-radical Imams portrayed in the popular UK documentary *Undercover Mosque*, are exceptions to the status quo in London. Only very few British mosques are associated with radical Islam.[81] Furthermore, many radical mosques were reformed under new leadership. For example, Yvonne Riddley, a Muslim convert with a loyal audience, controversial for her hardline views and close association with the Iranian funded Press TV, explained that, generally, mosques in the UK are not led by activist Imams and do not promote political action:

> If one goes into mosques today, for example, the Regent Park mosque, there isn't political speech in these mosques, there's no talk about Iraq.[82] There are even notes in Urdu there stating that there is not to be any political speech . . .. *khutbas* are first sent to the Egyptian embassy for approval. The mosque is supported by [the] Saudis and Egyptians.[83]

Indeed, many former radical leaders have been removed from London mosques and steps have been taken to promote good relations between different Islamic sects. For example, the Mosques and Imams National Advisory Board (MINAB), an organization representing most Islamic sects, was established in 2006. A major function of MINAB is to promote cooperation and goodwill amongst British Muslim mosques belonging to different schools of thought, improve the governance of mosques, and training of Imams.[84] Currently, more than 600 mosques are members.

More recently, some have expressed fears that Muslim political activism could lead to political violence and terrorism, as up to 15,000 of Britain's two million Muslims may sympathize with Al-Qaeda.[85] Meanwhile, although the vast majority of British Muslims do not consider political violence to be legitimate, a minority still does. Sobolewska (2010, 28) surveys the public opinion polls to conclude that between 2 and 5 percent of British Muslims, "support political violence and terrorism in general, the specific attacks of 7/7 or agree that terrorism is justified in the Koran." Between 7 and 13 percent of British Muslims hold extreme views.[86] O'Duffy (2008) believes that these percentages indicate that "the potential pool of recruits for violent jihad networks in Britain is between 112,000 to 208,000."[87] A 2006 Pew poll shows that 69 percent of British Muslims are concerned about Islamic violence globally, and 58 percent of British Muslims acknowledge that a struggle between moderates and Islamic fundamentalists exists.[88]

Furthermore, British government officials have frequently voiced widely varying estimates of the presence of radicalized British Muslims and Pakistanis, which suggests that precise information about domestic British potential terrorists is lacking. Even before the 7/7 bombings, a leaked 2004 government report insisted that: "Intelligence indicates that the number of British Muslims actively engaged in terrorist activity, whether at home or abroad, or supporting such activity is extremely small and estimated at less than 1%."[89] Post- 7/7 estimates claim that there are somewhere between 200 and 15,000 Muslim terrorists in the UK.[90] This great variance in estimates also suggests that, in absence of credible information, it is quite possible that the government and the media have exaggerated the threat presented by violent Islamic radicals due to the atmosphere of heightened fear following the 7/7 attack.

Studies of American Muslims

It has commonly been argued that American Muslims are better integrated in the US than in Europe, yet some recent studies document rising discontent and increasing tensions between Muslims and non-Muslims in the US.[91] Many significant differences exist between American and European Muslims. American Muslims tend to be better off financially and, despite the alleged recent tensions, are more integrated than their counterparts in Europe.[92] European Muslims are less educated and less upwardly mobile. In the United Kingdom, France, and several other

Western European countries, growing Muslim populations constitute 3 to 6 percent of the population. While in the US, most estimates place their numbers at just around 1 percent.[93] Moreover, during the next two decades, the Muslim population in the transatlantic area is expected to grow at a slower pace than it did in the previous two decades.[94]

The US is a melting pot where certain cultural values—namely the belief in the American Dream, individualism, and grassroots voluntarism—have made American Muslims less likely than their European counterparts to accept the narrative that there is a war against Islam.[95] European Muslims tend to live in enclaves, unlike the US Muslims.[96] Such segregated districts resulted from the unintentional consequences of the European guest worker programs during the 1950s-1970s. As Europe was undergoing a period of rapid growth after World War II, it assumed it could import people to fill its demand for workers; however, many of the foreign workers remained afterwards. Once reunited with their families, such immigrants often lived in *banlieues* in major cities across Western Europe. Nevertheless, on both sides of the Atlantic, Muslim communities are faced with challenges presented with Islamophobia. American Islamophobia tends to focus more on the religious aspects of Islam, in contrast to pre-9/11 European Islamophobia, which was mainly focused on cultural aspects associated with Islam.[97] The American approach is exemplified by the proliferation of various writings warning against threats presented by Islam and Muslims.[98]

Several post-9/11 studies and well-known polemical journalistic accounts argue that Islam and Muslim militants present a serious threat to the Western World and the US. Controversial, yet influential, Pipes (2002) and Spencer (2003), suggest that the government should closely monitor American Muslims. While supporters applaud their conservative views, critics have commonly noted that experts such as Pipes present biased analyses of Muslims in the West, in which they greatly overstate the extent to which Muslims sympathize with radical beliefs. Camarota (2002) provides evidence that foreign-born, Muslim extremists posed a dangerous security threat to the US even in the decade leading up to 9/11, and Leiken (2004) warns of the dangers presented by radicalized Muslims.

Another set of studies investigate alleged anti-Muslim discrimination in the US Scholars sympathetic to American Muslims argue that anti-Arab racism and anti-Islamic sentiment in the US has been prevalent and that, in essence, such prejudice is similar to anti-Semitism.[99] Abraham (1994, 162) argues that, following a rise of political violence in the Middle East, hate crimes against Middle Easterners in the US increased, especially in instances where US citizens are involved; such situations are "played up by the administration and the press." Several other studies show that negative Arab stereotypes prevalent after 9/11 existed prior to the 1980s.[100] A number of recent studies criticize the harsh measures taken by the US government against American Muslims.[101] Other more recent works provide accounts of the experiences of different American Muslim communities in the post-9/11 environment.[102] Meanwhile, a study by a well-known postcolonial scholar, Ali Behdad (2005), claims that, with regard to immigrants and foreigners, Americans have long fluctuated between hospitality and hostility.

Since the 1980s, a growing body of scholarship has addressed the presence of Arabs and Muslims in Detroit. Journalists and scholars have commonly portrayed the city as a hub of Muslim and Arab political activism. Every day, Muslims and Arabs from the community are likely to corroborate this image. Barbara Aswad writes that, because of constant immigration, "events in the Middle East are strongly reflected in the community and are often played out in the formal and informal institutions such as the mosques, coffee houses and clubs such as the Lebanese Athletic Club."[103] Studies of Arab Detroit from the 1980s on have emphasized how the community has remained active in local politics, US foreign policy, and the politics of their home countries.[104]

In sum, the scholarship on Muslims in the US and Detroit notes that even though American Muslims are better integrated than their counterparts in Europe, many have expressed concerns about Muslim radicalization in the post-9/11 environment. Tellingly, writings on Muslims in America tend to highlight the existing internal heterogeneity.

Politics of Muslim and Arab Diasporas in Detroit

Arabs and Muslims have been present in Detroit since the 1920s, when Henry Ford encouraged Arab migration to the area to help resolve labor shortages in his auto manufacturing factories. The auto industry was an important magnet for Arab migrants, especially Lebanese.[105] Rapid Muslim migration to the area has occurred since the 1980s. Currently, the majority of Detroit's Muslims are first-generation migrants.

Arabs constitute a notable proportion of more than 10 million Michigan inhabitants, four million of whom reside in metro Detroit. It is estimated that there may be as many as 490,000 Arabs in Michigan.[106] Somewhere between 200,000 and 350,000 Arabs live in the metro Detroit area.[107] Slightly less than half of Detroit's Arabs are Muslim, and non-Arab Muslims constitute a sizeable minority.

There are also varied estimates of the Muslim presence in the greater Detroit area. The University of Michigan's *Building Islam in Detroit* exhibit places the number of Muslims in the metro Detroit area at only 150,000, whereas the local Institute of Social Policy and Understanding (ISPU) sets the community between 125,000 and 200,000 strong, and as equally divided between Arabs, South Asians, and African Americans and Converts as of 2004.[108] Even though the ISPU study has been well-received, some have criticized it for using an unreasonably conservative formula for estimating the Muslim population.[109] Overall, estimates of Detroit Arabs and Muslims vary greatly, yet it is reasonable to estimate that there were certainly more than 200,000 Muslims in the Detroit metropolitan area as of 2010.

The Muslim population in the Greater Detroit area is roughly estimated to be equally divided between Arabs, South Asians, and African American Muslims.[110] There are certain segregations between, and even within, the three communities. This is caused in part by their geographical concentration in different parts of Detroit: Arab Muslims in Dearborn; South Asians in Canton, Hamtramack and other nearby suburbs; and African American Muslims in inner Detroit. Arab Muslim areas are further divided into predominately Lebanese, Yemeni, or Iraqi neighborhoods.

The Arab population in the US nearly doubled in the two decades leading up to the 2000 US Census, especially in the 1990s.[111] The community's rapid growth following 9/11 is especially surprising. The American Community Survey of 2005, conducted by the US Census Bureau, conservatively estimates that the Arab population of Michigan increased from 116,331 in 2000 to 153,843 in 2005, a 32 percent increase.[112] Furthermore, the 2010 US Census shows that Dearborn has the highest concentration of Arabs in the US, with 40 percent or 40,000 of the city's 100,000 inhabitants. This represents a significant increase from the 2000 Census, which showed that Arab Americans composed 30 percent of the total Dearborn population of about 100,000.[113] Because of that, some have called Detroit "The Arab Capital of North America,"[114] while others have advertised it as a great place for Muslims to live.[115] Far right-wing bloggers have lamented about perceived Muslim misconduct in "Detroitistan" and "Dearbornistan."

The majority of Michigan's Arabs are either Lebanese or Iraqi (both Muslim and Christian), and significant populations of Yemeni[116] and Palestinian populations are present as well. In addition to these populations, sizable African American Muslim, Convert, and South Asian Muslim communities also reside in the metro Detroit area. Overall, Arab Muslims in the Detroit metro area are more influential, organized, and active than other local Muslim groups.[117] Lebanese Arabs are the most influential of the different Arab communities.[118]

Research on Arab Detroit from the 1980s on has emphasized how the community has become increasingly involved with local politics, voicing its opinions on US foreign policy and the politics of its home countries.[119] Such narratives include reflections on activism in response to foreign policy events, ranging from celebrations of various events in Lebanon throughout the streets of Dearborn in the 1980s, to more recent street protests against American intervention in the Middle East. In the post-9/11 era, the community has been under particular scrutiny, yet efforts to find violent Muslim extremists in Detroit have yielded paltry results.

Meanwhile, with the exception of Arab American political activism studies in Detroit, very little has been written within academic literature about the level of American Muslim political participation. Additionally, American political and media attention on Islam has been almost entirely an after-effect of 9/11.[120] Both of these bodies of literature—one focusing on Arab Americans and the other addressing Muslim Americans—are used interchangeably by scholars of American Arabs and Muslims. Nevertheless, the relative dearth of scholarship on American Muslim political participation makes it harder to make claims about what key features (e.g., race, religion or ethnicity) influence their political mobilization. However, as in the UK, key Muslim organizations are led by representatives of certain ethnicities, which emphasizes the importance of ethnicity in American Muslim political mobilization.

Bagby (2004) criticizes the existing localized studies of American Muslims' political participation for being limited in scope or methodologically simple and unsophisticated.[121] Several recent studies have attempted to remedy these shortcomings.[122] Generally, they suggest that immigrant Muslims from diverse backgrounds are integrating into America. This scholarship also implies that discrimination against Arabs and Muslims in the US was present prior to 9/11, although it became more expressed in the post-9/11 period.[123]

In the 1990s, the American Muslim community's historic reluctance to participate in American political processes started to change. For example, in the 1994 elections, "Muslim groups backed 77 congressional and gubernatorial candidates."[124] By the turn of the century, the Muslim voter registration rate was close to the national average of 70 percent. Some Muslim candidates have been elected to municipal positions in Oakland, CA; Chattanooga, TN; and Detroit, MI. Several American-born Muslims are now working for the federal government, including two members of the House of Representatives, Keith Ellison and Andre Carson.

Nevertheless, as voters, Muslims are an "unreliable" constituency. While they tend to vote for the Democrats, they also tend to emphasize the Republican position on social issues and foreign policy. Recently, most Muslim organizations endorsed Republican George W. Bush in the 2000 presidential election, although they also supported Democrat Barack Obama in 2008. Therefore, the inconsistent voting pattern has not allowed Muslims to become an important constituency.[125] Furthermore, one recent study found that American Muslims who are highly religious do not affiliate primarily with either one of the two major parties (Democrats or Republicans); instead, "high religiosity, coupled with perceptions of discrimination against Muslims, may lead many to oppose both major political parties."[126]

Meanwhile, increasingly favorable treatment of Arab Americans by mainstream parties suggests that their political significance has increased through time. In the 1980s, Walter F. Mondale returned Arab American donations made to his 1984 presidential campaign, and Michael S. Dukakis told a group of Arab Americans during his presidential campaign that he was not interested in their vote.[127] In contrast, Bill Clinton's re-election campaign made an effort to woo new ethnic voters in 1996. In the following decade, Arab Americans were seen as key voters in the 2004 and 2008 elections. Furthermore, in addition to political participation through common electoral channels, American Muslims and Arabs have developed several capable organizations.

While some Muslim social and political organizations already existed, it was not until the 1980s that American Muslims started to build potent political institutions. Following World War II, the first national organization, the Federation of Islamic Associations of United States and Canada, was established in 1954. Arab and South Asian students founded the Muslim Student Association in 1963. The Islamic Society of North America (ISNA) was established in 1983, with the mission to take on a leadership position in the community. The ISNA's South Asian counterpart, Islamic Circle of North America (ICNA), was founded shortly thereafter. Although these two large umbrella groups tried to bring together diverse American Muslim ethnic communities, they remained relatively isolated and fragmented.[128]

Finally, several prominent Muslim political organizations were created in the 1980s and 1990s. The Council on American-Islamic Relations (CAIR) was established in 1994 and was entrusted with advocacy for Muslim human rights. The Muslim Public Affairs Committee (MPAC) was established in 1998, and the American Muslim Council (AMC) in 1988, for purposes of lobbying in Congress regarding issues of interest to American Muslims. Additionally, the American-Arab Anti-Discrimination Committee (ADC) was founded in 1980 by former US Senator James Abourezk, aiming to defend the rights of people of Arab descent. Muslim Arabs submit the vast majority of cases handled by the ADC. Regardless, the ethnic nature of American Muslim politics was evident even when these prominent organizations were established; the AMC was led by South Asians, and the MPAC and CAIR by Arabs.[129] More importantly, public opinion polls show that none of the American Muslim national organizations have much grassroots support.[130] Similar divisions, based on ethnicity, are evident in the city of Detroit as well.

American Muslim Views on Political Activism and Violence

Pew and Gallup public opinion polls have consistently shown that the support for extremism has been negligent among American Muslims.[131] From all American religious groups studied in the 2011 Gallup poll, Muslims were the most staunch opponents of military attacks on civilians (78 percent stated that such attach attacks are never justified, and 21 percent noted that they are sometimes justified). Compared to

Muslim populations that Pew has polled globally, American Muslims are among the most likely to reject suicide bombing (78 percent oppose suicide bombing and other forms of violence against civilians).[132] Very few American Muslims endorse al-Qaeda: 68 percent gave it an unfavorable rating, 27 percent refused to answer the question, and 5 percent gave al-Qaeda a favorable rating.[133] The majority of American Muslims also express worries about the possible rise of Islamic extremism in the US.[134]

On a local level, studies show that Detroit Arab lives are characterized by the constant juxtaposition of their ethnic, religious Arab identity and their American identity. Studies show that Muslims are being Americanized, embracing many American norms and mores, including democratic means for expression of disagreement.[135] A study by Bakalian and Bozorgmehr (2009, 2) finds that Middle Eastern and Muslim Americans have responded to the challenges of the post-9/11 environment in a "typically American fashion—through political activism and legal challenges." Unlike some European Muslim communities, Detroit Arab Muslims have internalized orderly ways of protesting.

In addition, as exhibited through the political activism of Reverend Martin Luther King Jr. during the Civil Rights movement and other clergy after him, political activism by religious leaders is perceived to be uncontroversial in the US. In recognition of this, American Muslim leaders have been active in politics, particularly following 9/11, when they felt a need to speak out in defense of American Muslims and their interests.

In Dearborn, community activists and leaders explained why provocative protest is neither legitimate nor effective in an American setting. South Asian Muslim student activist Muhiuddin Abdullateef revealed that:

> I feel like we go about things we try to do things as effective as possible. And we realize that if you go to that extreme, nobody is going to listen to you. If you're right in the middle. You're moderate, do things in orderly fashion—you'll get more attention, you'll get more support. So there's somewhat of a level of professionalism amongst these efforts.[136]

A male, second-generation Arab Muslim Palestinian student leader at UM-Dearborn expressed his opposition to hardline Islamist groups:

> Not to condemn the group like that, it's sometimes good not to have a group like that [Hizb ut-Tahrir] around here. Sometimes they do send the wrong message . . . it's wrong. They look at Palestine as Islamic issue. That's wrong, because that will only get Muslims out. You should get everybody out on this . . . it's all human rights.

A second-generation Palestinian Muslim student activist at UM-Dearborn strongly insisted that provocative protests reflect poorly on the protesters and their cause: "When you have a productive protest, people know that in order to let [the] message out, to let Congress and policy makers know, you need a well-organized protest." He warned that overly emotional protests can lead to civil disobedience, which in turn can make the protesters appear unreasonable and may hurt the prospects of their cause. Finally, an Iraqi Chaldean Christian leader, Joe Kassab, suggested that Arabs and Muslims in the Detroit Metropolitan Area eschew radicalism as they adopt norms of American democracy.[137] Radical politics have no appeal in Detroit, where violent actions are perceived as illegitimate.

In sum, vibrant and active Muslim communities exist in London and Detroit. They both have taken vocal stances on conflicts abroad, but their activism has unfolded following different trajectories. The next chapter examines foreign policy-inspired activism in both London and Detroit, and questions what role domestic and global triggers have in political mobilization.

Notes

1 Plewa 2007, 11.
2 Such threats include (but are not limited to) threats to the government, human and drug trafficking, and increasing crime.
3 Ignatiev 1996.
4 Caldwell 2009; Lucassen 2005.
5 Asad 2003.
6 Ernst 2013b, 3.
7 Council of Foreign Relations 2010, 1996; Huntington 1998, 1993.
8 Ajami 1993; Berman 2003; Sen 2006.
9 See Carr 2010; Fletcher 2006; Harvey 1990; Kennedy 1996.
10 Norris 1993.
11 Pew Forum 2009a, 2011.
12 Pew 2015.
13 Blassingame 1979; Diouf 1998; Gomez 1994.
14 Castles and Miller 1993; Coleman 1996; Mehdi 1978.
15 E.g., see Cohen 2008.
16 Suleiman 1999.
17 Ghayur 1984.
18 Duran and Pipes 2002.
19 A moral panic is an intensified, often exaggerated, feeling of concern about an issue that appears to threaten the social order.
20 E.g., see Mogahed and Nyiri 2007; Nyiri 2010.
21 Caldwell 2009; Ye'or 2005.
22 Abbas 2007; Alexiev 2005; Baxter 2007; Brachman 2009, 161–182; Glazer 2010; Leiken 2005; Phillips 2006; Roy 2003; Wiktorowicz 2005.
23 Frederick Kempe, "U.S. Sees Europe as Front against Radical Islam," *Wall Street Journal*, April 11, 2006.
24 Laurence 2012; Mogahed and Nyiri 2007; Nyiri 2010.
25 Ameli et al. 2004; Ansari 2006; Modood 2007.
26 Abbas 2001; Bowen 2009; Cesari 2013, 2010; Husain 2007; "Islam, America and Europe," *Economist*, Special Report, June 24, 2005; 2008; Lewis 1994; Miller 2006b, 2007; Ramadan 2004; Shibli 2010.

27 Cesari 2004, 178; However, such "transethnic" Islam still describes the beliefs of only a few Muslims in the transatlantic area (Ibid).
28 Crul and Vermeulen 2003.
29 Abbas and Reeves 2007; Bolognani 2009; Bowen 2007; Tomlinson 2007.
30 Vaisse 2010.
31 UK Office for National Statistics 2011.
32 Mahmood Neqshbandi, interview, August 31, 2009.
33 Ziya-ul-Hasan 1963, 21.
34 Pargeter 2008, 141.
35 Joly 1995, 46.
36 Ali 2008.
37 Jacobson 1998, 33.
38 Freeman 1979.
39 Castles and Miller 2003, 269; Freeman 1979.
40 Studlar 1978.
41 Castles and Miller 1993, 252; Layton-Henry 1981.
42 Layton-Henry 1992, 104–5; Layton-Henry and Rich 1986.
43 Castles and Miller 1998, 274.
44 Cohen and Layton-Henry 1997.
45 Studlar and Layton-Henry 1990.
46 Brown 2006, 126–7.
47 Layton-Henry 1992, 228.
48 Eatwell 2006; Goodwin 2008.
49 Castles and Miller 1998, 258; Layton-Henry 1992.
50 Sivanandan 1982; Benyon 1986.
51 BBC News, "Short History of Immigration," 2002.
52 Solomos 2003, 246. In addition to poverty and discrimination, unfair policing practices (e.g., Brixton riots of 1981) and far right group provocations (e.g., Bradford riots of 2001) served as causes which incited rioting (Economist 2011b).
53 Solomos 2003, 246–255.
54 Brown 2006, 125.
55 Castles and Miller 2003, 270.
56 Quinn 2006.
57 H.A. Hellyer, "For Some MPs the Muslim Vote Will Be Vital." *The Guardian,* 20 April 2010.
58 Heath et al. 2011, 265.
59 Simon Hooper, "Could the Muslim Vote Sway the UK's General Election?" *Al Jazeera,* 13 March 2015.
60 Samad 2013, 303.
61 Samad 2013, 301.
62 Birt 2005, 92–95.
63 Laqueur 2007, 73; Samad 2013, 301.
64 Economist 2006; The Change Institute 2009, 40.
65 The Change Institute 2009, 40.
66 Pupcenoks and McCabe 2013.
67 Madeleine Bunting, "Muslim Voices Have Been Lost in the Rush to Make Headlines," *The Guardian,* October 10, 2005; Ziauddin Sardar, "Young, Bright, Muslim, Ignored," *The Guardian,* October 11, 2005.
68 Mirza et al. 2007.
69 Hewitt 2005; Jacobson 1998; Malik 2009; Phillips 2006, 12; Werbner 1996.
70 As cited in Jacobson 1998, 38.
71 Joly 1995, 18.
72 Brighton 2007, 7.

73 Jacobson 1998, 38.
74 "The Rushdie Affair Lives," *The New York Times*, April 16, 1989; Hewitt 2005. In 1988, Collets and Dillons bookstores in London were bombed on April 9; several other bombings took place in the towns of High Wycombe and London in May; other bombings took place in the Penguin stores in London and York; and unexploded devices were found in the Penguin stores in the cities of Guildford, Nottingham, and Peterborough.
75 Jacobson 1998, 39.
76 Roy 2003, 66.
77 Pargeter 2008, 145.
78 Mustafa 2015, 167–8.
79 See Lewis 2015; MuslimsinBritain.org.
80 Archick et al. 2005.
81 E.g., see Swinford 2011.
82 However, before the mosque's "makeover," it was a hotbed for radicals.
83 Yvonne Riddley, interview, August 5, 2009.
84 Lewis 2015, 239.
85 Table 3.1: Terrorism Figures as Quoted in the Media, in Hewitt 2008, 81.
86 Home Office 2004. O'Duffy (2008, 41–42) explains that "these figures are based on responses to questions as to whether the September 11, 2001 attacks were justified, as conducted by Eastern Eye Mori in November 2001, BBC ICM in November 2001, and Telegraph YouGov in December 2002."
87 O'Duffy 2008, 41.
88 Pew 2006, 11–12.
89 UK Foreign and Commonwealth Office/Home Office 2004.
90 See Table 3.1: Terrorism Figures as Quoted in the Media, in Hewitt 2008, 81.
91 Better integrated: Cesari 2004; Mollenkopf and Hochschild 2010; recent tensions: Ahmed 2010.
92 Fisher 2009.
93 Pew Forum 2009a, 2011.
94 Pew Forum 2011.
95 Sageman 2008, 98.
96 Leiken 2004, 59.
97 Cesari 2004, 40.
98 Cesari 2004; Ernst 2013.
99 Salaita 2006; McCarus 1994.
100 Jamal and Naber 2008; Stockton 1994, 126.
101 Bakalian and Bozorgmehr 2009; Cainkar 2009; Peek 2011.
102 Ewing 2008; Khan 2002.
103 Aswad 1992, 177.
104 Abraham and Abraham 1983; Suleiman 1999; Abraham and Shryock 2000; Detroit Arab American Study Team 2009; Pupcenoks 2012.
105 However, there was a substantial Ottoman Arab migration to the US already in the 1880–1914 period (Balgamis and Karpat 2008).
106 Hassoun 2005.
107 Arab Detroit Website 2011; Baker and Shryock 2009, 4.
108 Building Islam in Detroit Exhibit 2009; Bagby 2004.
109 Muqtedar Khan, "The Remarkable Moderation of Detroit Muslims," *The Detroit News*, July 4, 2004.
110 Bagby 2004.
111 Michigan Daily, "U.S. Arab Population Doubles Over 20 Years," December 4, 2003.
112 Shryock and Lin 2009, 282.

113 US Census Bureau 2010.
114 Salloum 1998.
115 Heather Laird, "Southeastern Michigan is a Great Place for Muslims to Live," *SE Michigan Islamic Examiner*, October 11, 2009.
116 Yemenis are especially concentrated in jobs in the auto manufacturing sector.
117 For example, Detroit's Arab Muslims have played an essential role in the creation of many influential social, economic, and political organizations (e.g., the Arab Community Center for Economic and Social Service, and the Arab American News).
118 For example, Lebanese Arabs tend to hold many leadership position with Arab organizations and to be particularly active in local politics.
119 Abraham and Abraham 1983; Abraham and Shryock 2000; Detroit Arab Study Team 2009; Suleiman 1999.
120 Cesari 2004, 4.
121 Bagby 2004.
122 Bagby 2001; Pew 2007.
123 Jamal and Naber 2008.
124 Mazrui 2006, 501.
125 However, Muslim voters can play an important role in swing districts. Some Muslim leaders have argued that during the contested 2000 presidential election, the Muslim vote delivered the state of Florida—and the presidency—to George W. Bush.
126 Barreto and Bozonelos 2009, 200.
127 Holmes 1996.
128 Bassiri 1997.
129 Leonard 2003, 19.
130 Gallup 2011, 25.
131 Gallup 2011; Pew 2009b, 2011b.
132 Pew 2009b.
133 Pew 2009b.
134 Pew 2011b, 5.
135 Shryock, Abraham, and Howell 2011; Detroit Arab American Study Team 2009; Abraham and Shryock 2000.
136 Muhiuddin Abdullateef, interview, December 5, 2009.
137 Joe Kassab, interview, November 30, 2009.

Part I

Transnational Mobilization

4   The Role of Triggers

Khan and Esposito (2005) suggest that certain social and political triggers are important to Western Muslim political mobilization. However, it is less clear if triggers are a necessary first step before any transnational mobilization can happen and whether all triggers are equally important for mobilization. Thus, before seeking to understand the divergent responses to the wars in Afghanistan and Iraq in the following chapters, this chapter first considers patterns revealed by the recent history of foreign policy-related mobilization in both communities.

This introductory empirical chapter serves three main aims: (1) to question what conflicts abroad matter to Pakistani Muslims in London and Arab Muslims in Detroit, (2) to evaluate whether triggers play a major role in generating reactive political activism (or whether mobilization generally occurs regardless of triggering events), and (3) to show that triggers that are framed as important play a significant role in galvanizing the community into action related to conflicts abroad. It argues that triggers are frequently important in igniting reactive political violence. Primarily by drawing on data from public opinion polls, studies of Muslims in the West, and interviews with Muslim leaders and activists in London and Detroit, this chapter suggests that the disregard for upheavals in Africa, and idealization of the Arab World (the birthplace of Islam) will strongly influence the framing of community reactions. Nevertheless, the long-lasting Arab-Israeli conflict is commonly perceived as an Islamic conflict, and support for the Palestinian cause frequently transcends ethnic lines.

Foreign Policy-Inspired Activism in London

Since the 1990s, London's Muslims and Pakistanis have been particularly mobilized in reaction to conflicts in the Middle East (Lebanon, Iraq, Palestine); Europe (Chechnya, Bosnia); and Asia (Afghanistan, Kashmir, Pakistan), whereas conflicts in Africa have been overlooked. Although the community has debated the horrors of the recent conflicts in Muslim countries of Somalia and Darfur, these hostilities have not been framed as strategically important, and there has been a lack of community leadership in regard to generating reactive mobilization to these conflicts. British Islamist groups do not hesitate to side with Islamists in Pakistan and in the Middle East, yet they largely overlook African conflicts. As a result, a significant public response to calamities in Africa has not happened. Overall, London Muslims and Pakistanis are particularly likely to politically mobilize in response to conflicts that: involve Palestine, are supported by an already well-established migrant or minority community, and concern confrontation between a Muslim country and non-Muslim country or countries.

As an outcome of a growing politicization of their identities, British Muslims united behind the Palestinian issue after 9/11.[1] Said Ferjani, the Head of Policy and Public Relations for the Muslim Association of Britain (MAB), a Muslim Brotherhood-affiliated organization best known for actively participating in anti-Iraq war protests[2] and a former Chair of the Mosques and Imams Advisory Board, noted that Palestine matters for British Muslims because "[they] look at it from the window of rights and the failure of the international law . . . Pakistani origin people care more about Pakistan. But now Palestine has become the center for everybody, for all Muslims."[3] Indeed, participation in an alliance with the Stop the War Coalition in the organization of anti-Iraq war protests allowed the MAB to become the most visible British Muslim organization involved with the protests, and to be "elevated from a relatively obscure group to one with a national profile."[4] As an outcome of the anti-war protests, the MAB's membership increased from 400 to as many as 1,000.[5] Although a number of MAB's members left the UK for the Middle East following the Arab Spring, it is believed that the organization still has about 1,000 members.[6]

A youthful South Asian male and Muslim leader insisted that a major reason why the Israeli-Palestinian conflict draws so much attention in the community is due to a popular awareness of the problem: "Palestinian people aren't the most oppressed people in the world, but they get the most media attention. Also the lengths of the conflict matters and Palestinians have been oppressed for so long." A Bangladeshi male leader explained: "So much attention has been put on Palestinian cause because Zionists are the main adversaries. It's not some Sudanese guy who's demonizing Muslims, its Zionists. People like Melanie Phillips, Rod Liddle."[7] A senior, male South Asian Muslim leader noted how history of the conflict and unfairness could serve as triggers for activism. "Since all know about Palestine, there are more reactions to it. A perception of unfairness in a given location can create a spontaneous protest," he added.

Furthermore, Chris Doyle, the director of the Council for Arab-British Understanding (CABU), a non-profit, cross-party advocacy organization aiming to improve the relations between the Arab World and the UK since 1967, stated that the issue of Palestine has historically transcended other foreign policy matters. He further elaborated that the conflict represents such a tectonic issue for Muslims worldwide because it has been going on for over a century and because key Arab states and the British government have taken extremely active positions on the issue. These positions are consistent with CABU's key stances, as the organization has been known to advocate for Palestinian interests and, for example, the Palestinian Liberation Organization's representatives have spoken at CABU meetings in the past.[8] In addition, like many others leaders, Doyle expressed his incomprehension about the lack of activism in response to grave conflicts in Africa:

> It's strange there isn't more interest in Darfur. There is some but concerning the scale . . . but also lack of interest in Congo . . . my impression is . . . this notion that all Muslims somehow care about is not necessarily true. Just because there are Muslims involved in Sudan doesn't mean that all Muslims will be up in arms about it. National reasons predominate here. Arab Muslims will get more upset about Palestine. On the whole, they identify more with Palestinians than people from Sudan.[9]

Furthermore, shared opposition to the Iraq War unified the British Muslim community and allowed it to build bridges with non-Muslims. Overall, British Muslims overwhelmingly opposed wars in Iraq and Afghanistan and the broader War on Terror.[10] For example, a Guardian/ICM poll of British Muslims conducted one year after the beginning of the 2003 war reveals that 80 percent of British Muslims opposed the war, and were overwhelmingly skeptical of Western intentions in Iraq.[11] Similarly, in 2005, 83 percent of British Muslims disapproved the war in Iraq, and different surveys showed that between 72.8 percent and 83.5 percent of British Muslims similarly disapproved of the war in Afghanistan in 2010.[12] Muslim organizations such as the Muslim Council of Britain and Muslim Association of Britain—along with non-Muslim civil society groups—spearheaded and were highly visible in anti-war protests.[13] Chris Doyle claimed that anti-Iraq war protests were "the first time members of the community were opposing it side by side with huge segments of non-Muslims from the country with a broad spectrum of political viewpoints, backgrounds."[14] Abdul Rehman Malik, a Pakistani Muslim writer and a key leader of the Radical Middle Way, a largely British government-funded Muslim organization created right after the 7/7 London bombing and intending to promote a version of moderate Islam,[15] explained that "Iraq was a major national issue. Iraq did more for community cohesion than any government program would. Muslims from broader community now think that they're engaged with a broader society for a noble cause."[16] He sadly admitted that there is an unjustifiable, exaggerated amount of attention to Arab causes, especially a fascination with Saudi Arabia among South Asians at home and in diaspora:

> There is this sense that we raise Arab issues above all the other issues. There is a sense that Arab world was the cradle of Islam. Arabic language is the language of Koran. It's not necessarily right; the vast majority of world's Muslims aren't Arabs. Most of the exciting, progressive, noble things in Islam didn't come from the Arabs.[17]

Malik also expressed his regret about the lack of attention paid to Africa: "African Islam—a huge dark spot. Considering that Africa has one billion people, 60–65 percent Muslim . . . . massive Islamic culture, civilization."[18] Ed Husain (2009), a well-known British-Bangladeshi Muslim intellectual better known in the UK for his work with the Quilliam Foundation, a counter-extremism think tank, suggested that Muslims worldwide have largely ignored the conflict in Darfur. Consistent with these insights, Tehmina Kazi, a liberal British-Pakistani woman with the NGO British Muslims for Secular Democracy, elaborated that conflicts in Africa are often ignored:

> Somalia and Darfur don't get as much attention. Maybe it's a racial thing . . . the bulk of Muslims in this country are of Pakistani origin. If there is something going on in Pakistan or Kashmir . . . maybe they can relate to it more, there is a natural sympathy there. . . . Also, because there is less British and American involvement, Darfur is seen as more of an internal problem. Not like Gaza, where Israel is an invading superpower.[19]

Many of the respondents highlighted the importance of the duration of residency to reactive political activism. Shamiuiul Joarder, a British-Bangladeshi trustee for the Muslim Safety Forum—a Muslim umbrella group that between 2001 and 2011 organized regular meetings between the Metropolitan police and representatives of Muslim organizations—and the Head of Public Affairs for the pro-Palestinian organization Friends of Al-Aqsa, stated that a major cause of the dearth of activism regarding conflicts in Darfur is the lack of leaders willing to engage with the issue. In contrast, due to the presence of interested groups, there has been a great deal of activism in response to upheavals in the Middle East:

> Here are many Middle Eastern and Palestinian groups. As a result, there is much activism on affiliated causes as well. If there are organized groups, there will be more protests. Yet groups do seem to be picking and choosing their advocacy of issues abroad, it appears that based on what seems to be more convenient. Ideologically, injustice

is injustice in Somalia or Palestine, and, theoretically, Muslim groups in London should support both causes. Yet it's not the case with regards to Somalia . . . There are 100,000 Palestinians living here, a half million individuals from Kashmiri/Pakistan area. With such numbers, these become issues in themselves.[20]

Furthermore, 77 percent of British Muslims opposed the UK's military actions in Afghanistan and Pakistan and were strongly opposed to any intervention in these countries.[21]

Some interviewees suggested that it is more difficult to mount responses to foreign conflicts when both sides are Muslim (such as the ongoing Somali Civil War). The Somali community in London is a relatively new community, and it has not yet developed a cohesive community identity or gained political influence.[22] The majority of the current British Somali community constitutes of individuals who left Somalia while the civil war was raging in the 1980s and 90s.[23] According to the 2011 UK Census, more than 100,000 Somali-born individuals live in England and Wales, about 65,000 of them in London. The first Somali councilor, Mohamed Ali, was only elected in 2004. More than a dozen Somali candidates ran in the 2010 local elections; and seven of them were elected, and nine Somali candidates were elected in the 2014 local elections.[24] Nevertheless, the political activism of Somalis is a fairly new phenomenon, and it is likely that the relatively new Somali community in London will have to go through a maturation process similar to what the better-established Bangladeshi and Pakistani communities went through in the 1960s and 1970s.

Islamist leaders and activists offered slightly different perspectives. Political Islam, or the belief that Islam—besides guiding the believers on the personal level—should also influence public and political life, is supported by a notable minority of the British Muslims. For example, a 2006 poll revealed that 28 percent of British Muslims would prefer to live under the *Sharia* law and 9 percent were "hardcore Islamists."[25] Perhaps the most popular Islamist group in the UK is Hizb ut-Tahrir, or an organization that sees itself being dedicated to the restoration of the Islamic Caliphate. At its peak in the 1990s, it had about 10,000 members. The group has been known to hold regular conferences calling for the creation of caliphate, advocating for the protection of Islam in the UK through nonviolent means, and expressing support for Islamist groups in conflicts in the Muslim world. For example, during the 2009 "Struggle for Islam and the Call for Khilafah" conference in Birmingham, Hizb's leader, Taji Mustafa, expressed his sympathy for Pakistan's Taliban and advocated for an end to the Pakistani government's action against the Taliban.

Many Islamists also tend to embrace the Palestinian cause. During an interview in London, arguably the most well-known and controversial British Islamist, Anjem Choudary, offered his perspective on why political violence surrounding Palestine is of importance to British

Muslims: "The reason why Palestine is still in the hearts of Muslims, is because it has a central part in our beliefs. It's the [place of the] third holiest site—Jerusalem."[26] Choudary has long been associated with the al-Muhajiroun movement and its successor groups, and known for controversial statements such as claims that the UK will become part of an Islamic Caliphate. Similarly, Moazzam Begg, a notable Pakistani Islamist leader and former Guantanamo Bay detainee, the author of *Enemy Combatant* (2006) and a spokesperson for prisoner and human rights group CagePrisoners, insisted that support for Palestine and pro-Palestinian protests unite all Muslims. He was disappointed that the conflict in Somalia did not generate much attention:

> Very sad to say this . . . when it comes to Africa, people don't care. Value of African life is so low . . . People in London—when they talk about Somalia they do say how there is a proxy war fought there by the US by sending in Ethiopians. Spoken about it, not much protest.[27]

Overall, Islamists suggested that any conflict abroad where Muslims are countered by non-Muslims, or where secular Muslim governments are assaulting Islamist forces, matter to Muslims and Pakistanis in London and to all Muslims who are part of the global Muslim community, the *ummah*. Nevertheless, the empirical evidence shows that even Islamist support for conflicts abroad is selective. Conflicts in Arab lands appear most germane for Islamist political activism. Issues in South Asia are also included, because they appeal to a predominately South Asian British Muslim community. Finally, how to explain that the Palestinian cause has been one issue that has drawn support all across the Muslim communities in the West?

In a major study of Muslim interest groups in the US, the UK, and Canada, Liam Radcliffe Ross finds that not all conflicts where Muslims are suffering were prioritized.[28] Western Muslim interest groups have adopted the Palestinian cause, as well as other global causes where Muslims are victimized, as non-controversial issues that could unify heterogeneous Western Muslim communities. However, even the events surrounding the Palestinian cause were covered selectively, and "developments generally considered positive or progressive in conflicts between Muslims and non-Muslims, such as the Israeli disengagement from the Gaza Strip, were not commonly discussed [by Muslim interest groups in the West]."[29] Thus, the Palestinian cause has been embraced by various Western Muslim communities largely for pragmatic reasons (the need to embrace a non-controversial cause) and the coverage of this cause has been purposefully selective.

Furthermore, triggers serve as intervening variables in galvanizing individuals to take reactive action to conflicts abroad, but the level of mobilization that a certain conflict and trigger will generate in a community depends on strategic framing. The Muslim and Pakistani community in the UK is engaged with advocacy in response to various conflicts abroad, especially conflicts dealing with relatively nearby countries (Bosnia), former home countries of well-established communities (Pakistan), conflicts in the Middle East (Arab-Israeli conflict), or well-publicized conflicts involving the British or Israelis (Iraq, Arab-Israeli conflict). Despite a growing Somali community in London, Somali conflicts—as well as other major African conflicts—have received relatively little political attention. Most likely, more will be seen as the relatively new Somali community in London matures.

Meanwhile, interviews with community leaders and activists revealed that domestic and global triggers often initiate episodes of peaceful and hostile political mobilization. Particularly in instances with prolific media coverage of the given conflict, significant triggers can galvanize the community into action. The following table lists key such triggers.

Domestic triggers generally centered on domestic counter-terrorism policies and perceived unfair policing practices.[30] Early British counter-terrorism efforts rose in reaction to threats represented by Irish terrorist groups. In response to an escalation of the IRA violence in 1974, the British government enacted the Prevention of Terrorism Act, which conferred emergency powers upon police forces in instances where they suspected terrorist activity. The Act delegated Home Secretary the power to ban alleged terrorist organizations, enabled police to detain suspects for up to seven days, and allowed the authorities to exclude certain people from entering the UK. Although initially perceived as a temporary measure, the Act was renewed and modified in 1976, 1984, and 1989. Most of the provisions were eventually incorporated into a permanent legislature, the Terrorism Act of 2000.

The Terrorism Act of 2000 extended police stop-and-frisk powers and banned 14 Irish paramilitary organizations. Twenty-five international

Table 4.1 Key Triggers for London's Muslim Community

Triggers	
Global	*Domestic*
Iraq War, 2003–2011	Domestic counter-terrorism policies
Israeli-Palestinian conflict	Perceived unfair policing practices
Publication of Prophet Muhammad cartoons, 2005	
Alleged desecration of Koran in the Guantanamo Bay detention facility, 2005	

groups, 18 of them Islamic, were added to the list by September 2001. British counterterrorism measures in place by 2000 were among the most repressive in Europe. More than 1,000 people were arrested in the UK between September 2001 and December 2006 under the Terrorism Act of 2000. The subsequent Anti-Terrorism, Crime and Security Act of 2001 gave the government the right to detent and remove non-citizens suspected of involvement with terrorism. The 2001 Act gave the government power to detain foreign residents suspected of terrorism without trial, and in cases where deportation was not possible, they could be held indefinitely. Eventually, to counter criticism of the challenges raised due to the Act's treatment of foreigners, it was replaced with the Prevention of Terrorism Act of 2005. This legislation replaced indefinite detention with "control orders." Such orders allow the Home Secretary to place foreign individuals and citizens suspected of involvement in terrorism under house arrest. In 2008, 15 control orders were in force, almost all of them on foreign citizens.

The Prevention of Terrorism Act of 2006 was enacted after the 7/7 attacks. It created new offenses for terrorism, amended existing ones, and increased the power of the Home Secretary and the police. It outlawed incitement of terrorism, distribution of terrorist literature, and reception or provision of terrorist training. It enabled the government to ban groups that glorify terrorism. Additionally, the 2006 Immigration, Asylum and Nationality Act now allowed the government to remove British citizenship or right of residence from individuals if their presence was determined to not be conductive to the public good. Finally, the Counter-Terrorism Act of 2008 created additional new powers to gather and share information. The law allowed post-charge questioning and established longer prison sentences for convicted terrorists.

Many aspects of British counter-terrorism laws and policing practices have been seen as problematic by many British Muslims. Said Ferjani, the spokesperson with the Muslim Association of Britain, identified a number of triggers for political activism: existence of oppressive laws, codification of new British anti-terrorism acts, unjust American and British foreign policies, and unfairly favorable Western policy towards Israel.[31] A Bangladeshi leader added: "Anti-terror legislation, approaching general elections, potential war with Iran—all serve as triggers that influence action and spur people to work together." A Muslim youth leader explained that "MI5 allegations of spying on students, [perceived to be unfair] anti-terror legislations, all of this over the time builds up and spurs action." However, political mobilization can also occur without triggers, in reaction to domestic policies perceived to be unfair. For example, a senior Bangladeshi Muslim leader insisted that: "It's a combination of trigger and things adding up to the point where action seems to be required you join in because something is being organized, because you hear somebody else doing something, you decide to get active as well."

Overall, views expressed suggested that both domestic policies perceived to be objectionable and allegedly unfair policing practices can lead to political mobilization, a view that has been well documented in studies about British Muslims.[32]

Meanwhile, key global triggers included the 2003 Iraq War, the Israeli-Palestinian conflict, the publication of the Prophet Muhammad cartoons in 2005, and the alleged flushing of a Koran in Guantanamo Bay. Also, trigger events frequently covered in the media were the most effective. Shamiul Joarder, a representative from the NGO Friends of Al Aqsa, explained the importance of Muslim media sources, whose coverage of conflict abroad has been imperative to political activism in London: "On Press TV[33] one could see quite graphic images of the Israeli incursion, that triggered to start political activism. These pictures weren't seen on BBC."[34] A female Pakistani leader insisted that some issues, like the conflict in Gaza, quickly mobilize people, and that "media plays a large role in community political activism. When they see images on the TV and they feel similar to that, it's almost as it's happening to them; for them it's a real emotional response."

A Bangladeshi Muslim human rights leader further illustrated how trigger events have increased the power of certain groups in the community. He shared a story in which he attended a mosque on the eve of the Iraq war, yet the Imam spoke of an allegory about the hand of Allah. There were no references to the looming Iraq war. At another time, he was in a mosque while Israel bombed Lebanon in 2006, yet the *khutba* did not address it. Instead, the Imam spoke of a need to marry daughters young so that fathers could keep control over them. Then, as the masses left the mosque following the prayers, they were greeted by Hizb Ut-Tahrir activists shouting their opposition to Israel's actions, calling for the establishment of a *khilafah* as a solution to various social and political ills. Eventually: "People start listening to groups like that. They like the foreign-policy focus, they join in even if they don't necessarily care about the *khilafah* part." The leader displayed regret that mosques tend to stay clear of important contemporary foreign policy issues. Additionally, political protests were also evident in London following the publication of Prophet Muhammad cartoons in 2005 and in the aftermath of the flushing of a Koran in the Guantanamo, also in 2005.[35]

Meanwhile, British Islamists tend to solely blame the British foreign policy as the key trigger for terrorist attacks against the UK. Islamist Moazzam Begg insisted that prior terrorist acts in London were triggered by British foreign policy. He advocated a common Islamist position, which blamed the actions of the West for the terrorist attacks:

> [the] bombings that happen on 7/7 didn't happen after invasion of Afghanistan, they happened after the invasion of Iraq. It's very important . . . and that's because the massive opposition to war in

Iraq . . . look at the testimony of the bombers themselves and what did they have to say why they did it—I am a soldier of Islam and I'm doing this because I hate the West.[36]

Similarly, Anjem Choudary insisted that the historic British military involvement in the Middle East is a key trigger for would-be terrorists.[37]Such statements are consistent with extensive literature produced by Hizb Ut-Tahrir—predominately blaming the Western foreign policy for radicalization and political violence among Muslims.[38]

Although a trigger event is not always a pre-requisite for political mobilization, domestic and global triggers frequently spur communities and individuals into action. Certain triggers elicit spontaneous nonviolent action (e.g., an escalation of the Israel-Palestinian conflict), whereas others may serve as a cause for later terrorist acts (e.g., the invasion of Iraq). Conflicts and triggers popularized in the media tend to be particularly potent, especially if the community is united on the issue. Finally, many of those Muslim and Pakistani individuals who have attempted terrorist acts in London have claimed to be influenced by British and American involvement in the 2003 Iraq War, and to a lesser degree, anger regarding conflicts in Palestine, Kashmir, and the Western governments' foreign policy towards the Muslim world.

Foreign Policy-Inspired Activism in Detroit

Since the 1990s, Muslim and Arab communities in Detroit have been vocal about conflicts in the Middle East, although political activism has been more subdued in the post-9/11 era. The main conflicts during this time have been Palestine, Iraq, and Lebanon. Similar to London, there has been little activism on Afghanistan and Africa. In contrast to London, virtually none of the interviewees (including their politically active religious leaders) see conflicts in Afghanistan, Iraq, and Pakistan as Islamic conflicts. Arab Muslims tend to be predominately concerned about conflicts that involve Middle Eastern countries or former homelands. The Israeli-Palestinian conflict, however, is commonly viewed through Islamic lens.

Overall, the most important and recent foreign policy issues for the Arab Muslim community concern situations in Palestine and Lebanon. Compared to ethnic Muslim communities in Europe, the Arab Muslim community in Detroit engaged in relatively little anti-war activism and expressed a partial support for the Iraq War of 2003-2011. Additionally, the relative lack of anti-Iraq War activism was unusual, compared to the community's high level of overall activism and its traditional opposition to American involvement in the affairs of the Middle East.[39]

Thus, as in London, the Palestinian issue and other Middle Eastern conflicts are central to local political mobilization in Detroit. For example,

Imad Hamad, the Regional Director and the Senior National Advisor for Public Affairs of the American-Arab Anti-Discrimination Committee (ADC), noted that the key issues for the community related to foreign policy are the Arab-Israeli conflict, Iraq, and Afghanistan; the US role in the Middle East and even Iran; and "if it rains in the Middle East, we carry umbrellas here."[40] The ADC was founded in 1980 by the first Arab American US Senator, James Abourezk, and has since become the largest Arab American civil rights organization in the US. Prior to retiring in 2013 in the face of growing allegations of sexual harassment, Hamad was well-known for working closely with the federal law enforcement agencies.[41] National public opinion polls corroborate such views. For example, American Muslims opposed wars in Afghanistan and Iraq to a larger extent than average Americans. As succinctly and effectively summarized by Clements (2015, 227):

> In the US, the Pew Research Center's (2007: 49) Muslim Americans survey, found that 75.0 percent of Muslims thought that invading Iraq was the wrong decision (compared to 47.0 percent of American in general). In both 2007 and 2011, 48.0 percent of Muslims thought the use of military force in Afghanistan was "wrong decision" compared to 29.0 percent (2007) and 35.0 percent (2011) of the general United States population.
>
> (Pew Research Center 2011: 73)

Furthermore, American Muslims in general tend to rally behind the Palestinian cause, which is commonly viewed through Islamic lenses. For example, a female Arab Muslim youth and human rights activist in her 20s suggested that Palestine is different from other foreign conflicts abroad, as it transcends ethnic lines:

> In certain situations and circumstances you'll see the entire community to come up and support. So when, for example, the Gaza massacre was happening. Everyone knew about it, everybody supported Gaza . . . There were Lebanese and Yemenis, there were everybody there. Even non-Arabs. . . . when it's just Palestine in general, you'll see mostly just Palestinians. It really depends on what the issue is and how it's being presented to everyone.

Similarly to other religious groups in the US, the majority of American Muslims (81 percent) support a two-state solution in Palestine.[42] With the exception of the opposition to the Iraq War (a notable segment of Detroit's Arabs supported it), the pattern of political mobilization in Detroit largely resembles that of American Muslims overall.

However, there has been little to none activity regarding to other conflicts. A secular, middle-aged male and lifetime Palestinian cause activist confirmed that, with the exception of the Muslim Student Associations, there has been marginal community engagement with conflicts in Afghanistan, Darfur, and Somalia. He explained how particular ethnic groups take leadership positions in organizing community political protests on different issues. Thus, the Lebanese led the 1996 protests following the Qana Massacre/Shelling of Qana (where the Israeli army shelled a Lebanese village, killing more than 100), while the Arab community participated heavily. In support of the Palestinian Second Intifada, Palestinians and Islamic leaders led the 2002 protests. Osama Siblani, the publisher of Arab American News, played a major role in organizing public protests in 2000, 2006, and 2008. The Congress of Arab American Organizations (CAAO) was a major player in the organization of protests against Israel's incursion in Lebanon in 2006 and political protests since then. This narrative underlines the importance of a certain ethnic group taking the leadership position following a trigger abroad—if reactive political activism is to occur.

As in London, biases against and popular disregard for Africa are key reasons for the absence of attention to humanitarian crises on the continent. Khadigah Alasry, a Yemeni Arab youth leader with the conservative, Muslim Brotherhood-affiliated Muslim American Society, suggested that community prejudices are largely to blame for the lack of attention concerning Africa: "I think there's a lot of racism and it's all over. It's in Arab community as well. Africa: irrelevant. They're black, and I'm not. No connection. Once again, it's not an ideological thing."[43] As a result, the community attention is focused on upheavals in the Middle East at the expense of major African conflicts.[44]

However, some attention was paid to the conflicts outside of the greater Middle East on college campuses. South Asian community youth activist Abdullateef Muhiuddin suggested that he was actively involved in activism on African causes with a local Amnesty International chapter while still in college. Another Arab youth activist at UM-Dearborn, a Palestinian Muslim second-generation male student, insisted that campus student groups stay active on issues in Africa, even though it is rare to see events on African conflicts outside the campus.

As in London, certain triggers have been persuasive in generating political activism when strategic framing ascribes them importance. Community activism has been solely focused on Middle Eastern conflicts, while largely overlooking the existence of humanitarian catastrophes in Muslim countries in Africa. As in London, domestic triggers have played a major role in prompting political activism in Detroit. Some important events that elicited an immediate response are listed in the following table.

Key domestic triggers involved domestic counterterrorism policies and perceived unfair policing practices. Due to a preoccupation with the Cold War and nuclear threat, only miniscule attention was paid to domestic terrorism in the US in the 1960s and 70s.[45] During the 1980s,

Table 4.2 Key Triggers for Detroit's Muslim Community

Triggers	
Global	*Domestic*
Israeli-Palestinian conflict	Domestic counter-terrorism policies
Iraq War, 2003–2011	Perceived unfair policing practices
Execution of Saddam Hussein, 2006	
Israeli invasion of Lebanon, 2006	

counterterrorism was linked to increasing Puerto Rican militia activity, while in the late 1980s and early 1990s, the focus on counterterrorism was on environmentalist groups such as Greenpeace.[46]

In the 1990s, the focus of counterterrorism efforts turned to violent Islamic radicalism. Following the first Gulf War, there were fears concerning Saddam Hussein's retaliation.[47] On February 26, 1993, Islamic terrorists were arrested and later convicted for the bombing of the World Trade Center in New York City. Prior to 9/11, the deadliest attack on American soil was perpetrated by American white supremacist Timothy McVeigh. On April 19, 1995 McVeigh bombed a federal building in Oklahoma City, killing 168 people. Following the attack, the Clinton (1992–2000) administration passed the Antiterrorism and Effective Death Penalty Act of 1996 (AEDPA), and the Illegal Immigration Reform and Immigrant Responsibility Act of 1996 (IIRAIRA). These laws largely targeted individuals from an immigrant-background. They made it easier to criminalize and deport aliens. After the Oklahoma City bombing, alien deportations increased rapidly.[48]

The USA Uniting and Strengthening America by Providing Appropriate Tools Required to Intercept and Obstruct Terrorism Act (PATRIOT) was codified in response to 9/11. The act dramatically reduced restrictions on law enforcement agencies' ability to search telephone, electronic, and other records. It eased restrictions on foreign intelligence gathering in the US and broadened powers of law enforcement and immigration authorities to detain and deport immigrants suspected of terrorism-related activities. The US government arrested more than 1,200 individuals with Arab and Muslim backgrounds in the two months after 9/11.[49] The Homeland Security Act of 2002, establishing the Department of Homeland Security, was codified soon thereafter. Most of the PATRIOT Act's provisions were subsequently renewed.

The introduction of the PATRIOT Act has had significant impact upon the policing policies, and actions taken by both local police, and federal policing agencies. In particular, the creation of an entirely new department of the government, the Department of Homeland Security, had an impact upon policing. In direct reaction to the challenges facing

the changes in policing enacted by the PATRIOT Act, the FBI specifically created a position for Law Enforcement Coordination, as a way of
smoothing communication between all levels of local, state, and federal
policing.[50] Community policing also became a major focus of the US Justice Department.[51]

Many have argued that the PATRIOT Act deprives citizens of rights to
due process.[52] Critics of US counterterrorism measures oppose indefinite
detentions of immigrants and extensive law enforcement powers to conduct searches and surveillance. In a manner strikingly similar to the UK,
only a handful of some 4,000 individuals arrested on terrorism charges
following 9/11 were charged; lesser charges such as immigration violations were much more common.[53]

Some additional discriminatory policies include the use of informants
in mosques and investigations and harassment faced by Islamic charities.[54] Many Detroit Muslims were outraged by the realization of the FBI
infiltration of local mosques, and mistrust between Muslims and the FBI
was furthered by other controversial policies, such as the creation of the
list with mosques for further investigation, and secret investigation of
radiation levels in mosques.[55] Nevertheless, Detroit Muslims have developed a remarkably close relationship between community leaders and
law enforcement officials, which helped to ease many of the tensions.[56]

Globally, key triggers surrounded the Israel-Palestinian conflict, the
Iraq war, the execution of Saddam Hussein, and the 2006 Israeli invasion
of Lebanon. Interviewees frequently complained that community activism on foreign policy causes is reactive in nature and that there is a lack
of sustained activism. A female Arab Muslim youth human rights activist
in her 20s went as far as to insist, that if not for human rights violations
in Palestine, which generate many responses in the community, Detroit
"would have been a sleepy town." A Sunni Imam of a Lebanese background, Steve Mustapha Elturk, with the Islamic Organization of North
America, claimed that community activism resulting from events abroad
is almost exclusively in response to triggers abroad:

> Usually, unfortunately, it's how it has become. It's all reactionary
> response to these big events . . . I don't want to say we're passive, but
> you have to go with what's happening on the ground. . . . Only when
> it explodes, when there is a need to react to something that is about
> to happen, you find everybody coming together . . . but afterwards it
> kind of dies out . . ."[57]

Ron Amen, a middle-aged community leader of a Lebanese background,
a Shia Muslim and a Vietnam War veteran, mentioned that media plays
a major role in popularizing certain triggers, ". . . in Iraq or Afghanistan,
the media gives great attention that this was Shia mosque that was blown

up and suspected Sunni insurgents were the perpetrators."[58] Such coverage stirs emotions and propels individuals into action. Following the execution of Saddam Hussein, Detroit experienced some sectarian tensions between local Sunnis and Shias. The 2006 Israeli invasion of Lebanon led to almost daily protests in Detroit. In sum, the most important foreign policy activism among Detroit Arab Muslims occurs in response to trigger events from the Middle East.

Some Conflicts and Triggers are More Important than Others

Muslims in London and Detroit have a rich history of activism concerning conflicts abroad and triggers play a particular role in this activism. Triggers have been almost omnipresent in instances of political activism. Nothing stirs emotions and generates response like the dawn of the American and British invasion in Iraq, or Israel's incursion into the Palestinian Territories or Lebanon.

This chapter showed that those triggers that are framed as important generate reactive political activism. Consistent with the majority of studies of Muslims in the West, leaders in both communities emphasized the importance of conflicts in the Middle East. The Palestinian cause in particular is widely supported among Muslims regardless of their ethnicity or sect. Media coverage often served an important factor in generating awareness and activism. Interestingly, Detroit Muslims were significantly more likely than London Muslims to invoke the importance of homeland conflicts. Furthermore, properly framed triggers tend to lead to nonviolent spontaneous activism, such as street protests. For example, in certain environments, the Iraq War of 2003 led to immediate, spontaneous street protests, as well as to the more distant terrorist acts undertaken in London.[59]

Nevertheless, besides religion, sect and nationality strongly influenced perceptions of what conflicts and triggers matter. Certainly, more religious Muslims tended to see foreign policy events through Islamic lenses, and were more likely to support advocacy for more conflicts in Muslim lands. More commonly, however, members of the two communities studied perceived the importance of conflicts through ethnic lenses. London interviewees emphasized the preeminence of conflicts in home states and upheavals in the Middle East. Meanwhile, a number of Detroit interviewees mentioned that there is a sizeable segment of local Shias from Lebanon and Iraq that are not at all concerned with Palestine, which is perceived by some to be a Sunni issue. The following chapter further develops this assertion and provides evidence that—in addition to a common Islamic identity—ethnic divisions are important in explaining the nature of London's Pakistani and Detroit's Arab Muslim political mobilization in response to foreign policy events.

Notes

1 Greene 2013, 152. Prior to 9/11, British Muslims were significantly less active regarding the Palestinian cause, and conflict in Kashmir commonly was of a greater interest (Ibid).
2 E.g., See Abbas 2005, 103–103; Hamid 2014; Phillips 2008; Phillips and Iqbal 2008.
3 Said Ferjani, interview, August 11, 2009.
4 Phillips 2008, 105.
5 Phillips 2008, 105.
6 Robert Mendick and Robert Verkaik. "Downing Street Set to Crack Down on the Muslim Brotherhood," *Telegraph*, 19 October 2014.
7 Phillips and Riddle are British journalists well known for their articles portraying European Muslims as threats to European social order and state security.
8 Edmunds 2000, 33; Vaughan 2015.
9 Chris Doyle, interview, August 18, 2009.
10 Field 2012.
11 Alan Travis, "Muslims Abandon Labour over Iraq War," *Guardian*, 14 March 2004.
12 Clements 2015, 223.
13 Birt 2005.
14 Interview, August 18, 2009.
15 However, some have asserted that a few people associated with the Radical Middle Way sympathize with the Muslim Brotherhood.
16 interview, September 4, 2009.
17 Abdul Rehman Malik, interview, September 4, 2009.
18 Abdul Rehman Malik, interview, September 4, 2009.
19 Tehmina Kazi, interview, August 12, 2009.
20 South Asian Muslim Religious Leader.
21 Clements 2015, 227.
22 E.g., see McGown 1999.
23 Harris 2004, 23.
24 Tarbush 2010; "A Record 9 British-Somali Councilllors Elected in UK Local Elections," *Warya Post*, June 6, 2014
25 Basham, Patrick, "Many British Muslims Put Islam First." *CBS News*. August 14, 2006.
26 Anjem Choudary, interview, August 10, 2009.
27 Interview, August 24, 2009.
28 Ross 2013, 296.
29 Ross 2013, 297.
30 Ansari 2006; Majeed 2010; Rankin and Cowen 2012.
31 Interview, August 11, 2009.
32 E.g., Ansari 2006; Majeed 2010; Rankin and Cowen 2012.
33 Press TV, a channel controversial due to its affiliation with the Iranian state, lost its license to operate in the UK in 2012 due to numerous violations of the UK's broadcasting code (e.g., broadcasting an interview with journalist Maziar Bahari. This interview was obtained while Bahari was held under duress in a jail in Tehran).
34 Interview, August 19, 2009.
35 E.g., see Klausen 2009.
36 Interview, August 24, 2009.
37 Interview, August 10, 2009.
38 E.g., see Hizb Ut-Tahrir Britain 2007.

39 Detroit's lack of the anti-war activism is consistent with a surprising lack of protests nationwide, despite widespread opposition to the US invasion of Iraq (see Mueller 2008). However, some anti-war protests amounting to several thousands of participants did take place in activist strongholds such as Madison, WI (Castles and Miller 2009, 284).

40 Interview, November 11, 2009.

41 Warikoo, Niraj. "Civil Rights Leader Imad Hamad Retired in the Face of Sex Harassment, Assault Allegations," *Detroit Free Press,* November 22, 2013.

42 Gallup 2011, 29.

43 Interview, December 13, 2009.

44 For more, see chapter 7.

45 Constanza, Kilburn and Helms 2009, 96.

46 Borgeson and Valeri 2009.

47 Costanza, Kilburn and Helms 2009, 96.

48 Miller T. A. 2005.

49 Welch 2002.

50 Morreale 2004.

51 Docobo 2005.

52 Costanza, Kilburn and Helms 2009, 105.

53 Welch 2002; Cole 2003.

54 Howell 2011, 152.

55 Youmans 2011, 275; Isikoff 2003; Kaplan 2005.

56 Howell 2011, 153–4.

57 Interview, December 19, 2009.

58 Interview, November 24, 2009.

59 A number of testimonies by alleged terrorists state that they were conducting their hideous acts largely as a response to the war and occupation of Iraq.

5 The Importance of Ethnic Fragmentation

Although many insist that religious identity is a key building block for minority identities, especially for Muslims, this perspective is challenged by studies that emphasize the role of ethnicity and other variables in identity construction. The scholarship on internally diverse Muslim communities in the West tends above all to focus on their common Islamic identity.[1] Meanwhile, some scholars of diasporic studies warn against perceiving groups as united by world religions (such as Islam), borderland cultures (Mexicans in the US), and stranded minorities (East European Russians) as diasporas, because such communities tend to lack cohesive identities.[2] Publications by many Muslim scholars highlight the existing heterogeneity among Muslims in the West.[3]

The scholarship on diasporic activism commonly identifies cohesiveness and group identity as necessary prerequisites for any actions taken by diasporic communities.[4] Several criteria can be used in describing and defining diasporas: most importantly, certain ethnic, national, linguistic, cultural, or religious attributes and commonalities. Shain (2007) generally suggests that migrant-background individuals can be contentious regardless of their length of presence in a country (e.g. first or second generation). Therefore, it can be expected that diasporic communities that retain strong, well-developed identities are likely to react to conflicts abroad.

Literature on diasporas in conflict elaborates on the role of migrants in regard to homeland conflicts. Some of these studies investigate the extent of diasporic community influence on host or home state domestic policies.[5] Others assess the impact of expatriate monetary contributions on parties involved in conflicts, or analyze the influence that diasporas may have during the post-war period.

Hazel and Stares (2007) and Shain (2007) show that diasporic communities can serve as agents in their own right—especially in international relations, where they are able to influence foreign policies of their homelands and receiving states, and have a limited agency in regard to their ability to impact the resolution of homeland conflicts. Subsequently, diaspora activism studies suggest that a cohesive community identity is a pre-requisite for migrant-background community mobilization. Commonly, such claims remain at a high level of abstraction, without identifying the particulars of what such an "identity" encompasses.

Meanwhile, recent rapidly growing scholarship on internally diverse Muslim communities in the West tends to emphasize the importance of their common Islamic identity, above all.[6] A number of studies make the case that Muslims worldwide belong to a global Muslim community, or *ummah*.[7] The authoritative study of Modood et al. (1997, 301) claims that Muslims place their religion before nationality. Islamist groups, as well as many mainstream Muslim organizations in the West, also propagate such views.[8] A notable radical British Islamist, Anjem Choudary, proclaims his perceived unity of Muslims worldwide:

> We see ourselves as a Muslim community worldwide, even though we may differ on sectarian matters, issues on how to interpret divine texts. Yet they are still our brothers and sisters and we have a duty and obligation to all of them. I must raise my voice for brothers and sisters in Palestine, Kashmir, Azerbaijan, Chechnya, Iraq, Afghanistan.[9]

Despite their marginal status within Western Muslim migrant-background communities, Islamist voices, such as this, have received disproportional attention and media coverage, largely due to their controversial messages, including: the desire to create an Islamic caliphate, typically heated anti-Western rhetoric, and strident critique of Western democracies.

Additionally, studies by Connor (2010), and Givens, Freeman, and Leal (2008), provide evidence that Muslim communities in the West tend to be more religious than receiving populations. Overall, this literature implies that Muslim communities in the West are likely to mobilize predominately on the basis of their religious identity.

In the post-9/11 period, Western governments and foundations have been frequently encouraged to study Islam as a monolith. The UK government started to offer public funds to British Muslim organizations claiming to be working on counter-radicalization policies following the 7/7 attack through its PREVENT program.[10] The British government has strived to find organizations that could represent British Muslims as a whole. Since the mid-1990s, with varied success, the government has engaged with several organizations, such as the Muslim Council of Britain, the Sufi Muslim Council, and the Quilliam Foundation. In the US, the Russell Sage Foundation funded research on Muslims and Arabs. In Detroit, well-established Arab organizations succeeded in obtaining government grants, which further increased the perception of the existence of a unified Arab community in Detroit.[11]

At the same time, publications by many Muslim scholars highlight the existing heterogeneity among Muslims in the West.[12] Additionally, functionalist and constructivist theories of ethnicity, nationalism, and national identity argue that ethnic identities often can be based on many different markers, of which religion is just one such component.[13] To what extent, then, are actions by Muslim communities in the West influenced by their common religious identity, as opposed to other divisive identity-makers?

Indeed, Western Muslim communities are decisively heterogeneous and divided along national, religious-sectarian, and racial lines. Such divisions are frequently important in Muslim socioeconomic life, and Muslims commonly interact with their co-ethnics based on divisions such as nationality, sectarian cleavages, or racial/sectarian differences. The following analysis shows that, although an Islamic identity influences Muslim activism on local and national matters, ethnic differences frequently influence mobilization in response to foreign policy events more than religious commonalities do.

Identity in London's Pakistani Mobilization

Despite the attempts by a number of studies and mainstream Muslim community organizations to refer to a "Muslim community" in London, for most purposes, such a community does not exist.[14] A 2009 in-depth report, commissioned by the British Government, warns against the tendency to homogenize British Muslims and highlights the importance of the existing diversity of characteristics in different ethnic Muslim communities in the United Kingdom.[15] Such ethnic differences are frequently more helpful in understanding characteristics and actions of different ethnic Muslim populations than more abstract commonalities shared through the faith as "Muslims." Many Muslims in the West practice what Cesari calls "Ethical and Cultural Islam;" they live largely secular lives, but observe the major Islamic rites of passage, including circumcision, marriage, and burial; or are non-practicing believers who largely identify with what they perceive to be the key cultural elements associated with Islam.[16]

Both on the national level and in London, public opinion polls and surveys show that Muslims in London have a strong globalized identity as Muslims and strong ethnic identities, yet a weak national identity.[17] In an authoritative Pew study, 77 percent of British Muslims felt that Islamic self-identification is increasing, and 86 percent of British Muslims thought that such intensifying of the Islamic identity is a good thing.[18] Eighty-one percent of Muslims polled saw themselves as being first Muslim, then British.[19] Critics have spoken out against polls and surveys asking Muslims to identify with being either British or a member of their faith first, and have pointed out that such framing implies that there is a friction between being British and Muslim. As studies on diasporic identity show, members of diasporas tend to have multi-layered identities, where more than one identity plays a major role in shaping one's actions.[20] Indeed, a study of 24 prominent British Muslims reveals many diverse ways of being Muslim and finds that British Muslims have diverse, plural identities.[21] Meanwhile, British Muslims have been under major pressure by the media and government to publicly articulate that they view themselves as British first and Muslims second.

In London, South Asians constitute the largest ethnic segment of Muslims. They hold a significant number of leadership roles in Muslim organizations, and they appear to be better established than other ethnic groups. For example, one qualitative study suggests that British Pakistani youth in general are actively plugged into political activism.[22] Through their active engagement in British socio-political life, South Asians and Pakistanis dominate the national debate about what it means to be a Muslim in London and the UK. Furthermore, interviews help to further illustrate observations captured by public opinion polls and surveys—that British Muslims have strong global-religious and ethnic identities. They also show that Islam can be seen as a major force in mobilization for domestic issues, whereas ethnic differences dominate many social decisions and much of foreign policy-influenced activism.

Religious Identity in Activism in London

Muslim men and women tend to be more religious than members of other religions in the West.[23] Common Islamic identity clearly serves as a powerful mobilizer on a number of local and domestic issues (such as opposition to perceived Islamophobia or opposition to anti-terrorism laws seen as unfair). However, ethnic identities and divisions play a more dominant role in influencing activism in response to foreign policy events.

Some interviewees stated that Muslims are united through their faith and common problems that they face as British Muslims (such as Islamophobia and discrimination), and pointed to the unifying influence of increasing Muslim religiosity in the post-9/11 period. For example, Peter Neumann, the director at the International Centre for the Study of Radicalisation and Political Violence (ICSR) at King's College in London, noted that after 9/11 and 7/7, Muslim religious self-identification has been strong, meanwhile:

> Racism against Muslims because they're Muslims has quite increased in Britain. It used to be the case that they were insulted as "Pakis," the former national identity was perceived as the most common insult. In making such an insult, different diaspora groups are being thrown together—Hindus, Muslims, and others.[24]

Eventually, the term "Islamophobia" was coined by the Runnymede Trust in the late 1990s. Afterwards, [some] "Muslims started to believe from early on that they cannot succeed because they're Muslim, and it largely became a self-fulfilling prophecy."[25] For example, South Asian Muslim activist Shamiul Joarder claimed: "There is a common Muslim identity: *Ummah*, the global community."[26] Ghayasuddin Sidiqui, a senior Muslim and Pakistan leader, echoed a similar view: "Muslim identity in London is very diverse, but for London's Muslims their religious identity comes before their ethnicity."[27]

Another male South Asian leader stated that, for Pakistanis in London, religious identity was stronger than ethnic identity, but it was the other way around in the parts of the UK, where Pakistanis live in isolated settlements. For example, in Bradford, a city where 20 percent of the population is Muslim: "You can go in the city all day without speaking English or running into a white person. The community is largely composed of Pakistanis, the community in Bradford seems like a Mini Pakistan."

Some of the most articulate claims about the unity of the British Muslim community via religion are advocated by the conservative and angry Islamist groups such as Hizb ut-Tahrir and Islam4UK. Although these are fringe groups, they have historically had a disproportionately large influence on political discourse in the UK.[28] It is largely overlooked that, despite their strident rhetoric, Islamists' selective reactive activism to conflicts abroad does not match their claims about the unity of the Islamic *ummah*.

When asked about the features of British Muslim and Pakistani identity, an Islamist activist insisted that: "Yes, there is identity for Muslims, it's Islam. It's usually associated with practice. Mosques transcend ethnic lines. Being practicing Muslims is what unites Muslims. . . . Muslim youth is recognizing now the importance of Islam." The leader further emphasized the importance of identification with the *ummah*, while simultaneously contradictorily claiming that ethnicity still matters greatly in generating political protest:

> When Palestine and Gaza was being bombed earlier in the year [2009], it mattered to the Muslim community as a whole, not just Bengalis or some other ethnic group. Yet there are some issues that are specifically important to certain ethnic groups like Bengalis. In the West, nationalism is strong. In Islam it's duty-bounded.

Islamist Anjem Choudary similarly claimed that Muslims are united through the commonality of faith, and that the nationalism that exists among some Muslims is a disease that needs to be overcome.[29] Islamist and *CagePrisoners* activist Moazzam Begg echoed a similar opinion, as he insisted that Islam does serve as the identifying factor for the community in London, even though the community is extremely diverse.[30] Nevertheless, even Choudary felt forced to admit that the majority of Muslims in the UK are not practicing, thus putting into question to what extent can Islam serve as a unifying force for Muslims and Pakistanis:

> There are many people that want to affiliate themselves with Islam, but when it comes down to it, we find that the majority of people

aren't practicing and they are affiliating themselves based on the country, on the basis of background. But among practicing, we find that they're divided along the sides of sects.[31]

Despite their statements emphasizing the worldwide unity of Muslims, empirical evidence shows that even Islamists support foreign conflicts in Muslim lands selectively, as ethnic considerations frequently trump assessments about the severity of conflicts. Conflicts in Africa tend to be ignored. In contrast to mainstream groups, Hizb ut-Tahrir is active in supporting Islamists in Pakistan; however, British Pakistanis also constitute the key ethnic group among the Hizb's supporters. To some extent, such divisions are recognized by Islamists themselves. Such leaders frequently publicly proclaim the unity of the *ummah*, while also admitting that ethnicity and nationality still matter a great deal.

Views that British Muslims are united by their membership in the global Muslim *ummah*, and through shared problems (such as dangers presented by Islamophobia), are considered to be common knowledge. As exemplified in this section, a number of studies and Muslim leaders have been supportive of this view. Meanwhile, it is frequently overlooked that, despite popular assertions suggesting that a global Muslim community exists, British Muslim and Pakistani reactive political activism regarding issues concerning Muslims worldwide has been selective. Numerous rallies were held in opposition of the Iraq War of 2003, while virtually no political actions have been taken on more extensive bloodshed in Africa. Although the majority of British Muslims share concerns about the perceived rise of Islamophobia in the UK, ethnicity usually serves as a key lens through which Muslims process foreign policy events and conflicts.

The Importance of Ethnicity in Diasporic Muslim Socio-Political Life

Although common religious identity certainly plays an important role in galvanizing British Muslims into action against perceived Islamophobia and unfair policies, the role of ethnic identities in the daily lives of Muslims is often overlooked or underplayed. The 2001 British Census showed that, paradoxically, Muslims in London in relation to Sikhs, Jews, or Hindus are less segregated; however, there is "a high level of intra-Muslim ethnic segregation . . . [and] . . . Intra South-Asian mixing irrespective of religion is greater than intra-Muslim mixing, irrespective of ethnicity."[32] Peach (2006, 264), explains how different Muslim ethnic and racial groups tend to occupy separate areas of London, and she concludes that

Bangladeshi Muslims, who [in 2001 Census] form London's largest Muslim group, are highly encapsulated, showing little residential mixing with any other groups. White Muslims and Black Caribbean Muslims are separated from both Indian and Pakistani Muslims. The *Ummah* exists spiritually, but is not manifested in residential terms.

Representatives of certain ethnicities tend to hold the key leadership positions in different major Muslim organization. For example, Chris Doyle, the director for the Council for Arab-British Understanding (CABU), noted that with "Pakistani[s] being the largest [group], and they tend to dominate, for example, the MCB [Muslim Council of Britain]. Muslims of other ethnic backgrounds don't necessarily view that organization the same way."[33] Similarly, the Muslim Association of Britain is led by Muslims of Arab ethnicity, and there are numerous ethnicity-specific Muslim organizations.

In London, ethnicity frequently serves as an important dichotomy, which determines what mosque or social group individual Muslims will join, and in what circles they will they spend their time. In comparison to other British minorities, South Asians tend to "show greater co-ethnic choice with respect to partners, friends, church and associational involvement than do the black groups."[34] A Change Institute (2009, 40) study of British Pakistanis finds that, within British Muslim communities, "There are splits along sectarian, denominational and geographical lines, and particularly in relation to the countries of origins. Mosques are generally associated with specific communities such as Pakistanis, Indian Muslims and Bangladeshis." Indeed, much distinction still exists as far as mosque attendance is concerned, as Bangladeshi academic Shahab E. Khan explained: "Pakistanis don't go to Bangladeshi mosques, both groups follow different Eid dates and so on."[35] For British Muslims, country of origin often dominates as a point of reference, and, as CABU's Chris Doyle explained, "the different Muslims in London live in different places not because they are Muslim, but because they're from Bangladesh . . . you see the same with Lebanese, Egyptians, Somalis and others."[36]

In addition, some of London's Muslims have developed localized identities, whereas others have an ambivalent relationship with Islam. Abdul Rehman Malik, a Radical Middle Way representative, explained that although there are commonalities among Muslims in London based on the faith of Islam, London Muslims also display strong, localized identities:

> Muslim experience in Tower Hamlets is very different than that from Western London. Different culture, different vibes that young people have. They have their own language, "Banglish."[37]

Additionally, the vast majority of Muslims have an "ambivalent relationship with Islam," and the vast majority of them do not go to mosque:

> Even the East London mosque on Ramadan . . . every floor of the building is full, there are a lot of young people there. But there are also

a lot of young people that aren't there. If the East London mosque fits 5,000 people, we have 60,000 people in Tower Hamlets.[38]

Furthermore, ethnic differences are quite important in social interactions. Tehmina Kazi, with the British Muslims for Secular Democracy, stated that the Muslim community is very fractured and diverse, and insisted that different factions (Arabs, Somalis, Eritreans, etc.) "don't keep in touch with each other's activities as they perhaps should."[39] "People often put ethnicity first," she added. "They may not say it, but their actions show otherwise. . . . For example, when looking for brides, immigrants tend to look for similar ethnic/racial background people to marry."[40] Indeed, a British government's survey for years 1997–2002 showed that 94 percent of Pakistani women married their co-ethnics, and "0.7 per cent of Pakistani women had an Indian partner and 0.5 per cent a Bangladeshi partner."[41] In fact, at least 55 percent of British Pakistani couples marry their first cousins.[42]

In sum, in addition to an Islamic identity, ethnic identities play an important role in British Muslim and Pakistani socio-political life. The Islamic identity is particularly important in galvanizing British Muslims to organize to counter the perceived Islamophobia and unfair counterterrorism laws and practices. It is also important in mobilizing the community in responding to the Arab-Israeli conflict or conflicts involving a Muslim state and the UK (e.g., the Iraq War of 2003). However, it is important not to overlook the importance of ethnic identities in political mobilization. Most of London's Muslims and Pakistanis interact with other co-ethnics, and most mosques and Muslim organizations are led by representatives of certain ethnicities. London's Pakistanis are concerned with conflicts in Pakistan and Kashmir, and major conflicts in Muslim countries in Africa have received little attention. Moreover, as will be further explained in the following chapters, connections with groups in Pakistan will serve as a key cause explaining many instances of reactive conflict spillover in London.

Identity in Detroit's Arab Muslim Mobilization

Surveys and public opinion polls of American Muslims on the national level reveal that they identify less with religion than most other Muslim populations in the West, and a growing number identify with being American. Forty-seven percent in 2007 and 49 percent in 2011 of American Muslims see themselves as Muslims first, while 28 percent in 2007 and 26 percent in 2011 identify with being Americans first.[43] In the 2011 survey, 18 percent stated that they see themselves as both Muslims and Americans first.[44] Thus, American Muslims are less likely to identify with religion than British Muslims. Interestingly, American Muslim primary self-identification with religion is similar to that of American Christians (42 percent of the latter see themselves as Christians first); but notably lower with regards to primary self-identification as Americans (48 percent of Christians identify as Americans first).[45] 93 percent of Muslims surveyed by Gallup perceived that Muslims living in the US are loyal to the country.[46] Ninety-two percent of American Muslims are either integrated or tolerant of other religions, and only 8 percent are isolated or believe in the superiority of their own religion and explicitly reject other belief systems.[47] American Muslims identify equally with their family and the US.[48] Overall, this data shows that whereas American Muslim self-identification with religion is similar to that of Christians, their national identification is still somewhat lower to that of other religious groups.

Additionally, Arab Americans also have a strong Arab identity. It is widely accepted that the 1967 Arab-Israeli war served as a major cause for the development of Arab American identity.[49] During this time, Arab American politicization in support of Palestinians led to the emergence of organizations supporting the Palestinian cause.[50]

Much research on Muslims in Detroit focuses on Arabs.[51] Meanwhile, a slight majority of Arabs in Michigan are Christian, and the Arab Muslim community in the greater Detroit metropolitan area is roughly divided equally between Sunnis and Shias.[52] Sizeable African American and South Asian Muslim communities reside in the greater Detroit metro area as well. Detroit is known to be one of the most segregated cities in the US, and cleavages among class, race, and ethnicity are prevalent among Detroit Muslims.

Arab Muslims, in particular, dominate the community organizations and activism; thus, in order to properly understand Muslim activism in Detroit, one should place a particular emphasis on Arabs. A vibrant and politically active Arab Muslim community, with powerful local organizations, press, events, and growing community electoral influence, resides in the city. Incentives to promote violence are virtually nonexistent, and community leaders and activists do not endorse contentious mobilization. Additionally, in interactions with the government, Arab and Muslim politics are predominately based on domestic issues.[53]

However, with regards to foreign policy events, ethnic divisions dominate. Interviews similarly highlight the ongoing process of Detroit Arab Muslim integration, and provide evidence of how their Islamic identity guides many political activities on local and national levels, while ethnic Arab identity usually guides transnational activism.

Religious Identity in Activism in Detroit

To outsiders, Islam appears to be a formidable force in local Detroit politics.[54] As in London, common identity as "Muslims" galvanizes mobilization in reaction to Islamophobia and anti-terrorism laws perceived as unjust. In fact, American Christian Arabs worked together with Muslims on some of these problems (e.g., discriminatory laws) seen as affecting all individuals of Middle Eastern background. Whereas the Arab-Israeli conflict is an exceptional struggle that is seen through the religious lenses, ethnic identities commonly filter Detroit Arab Muslim views on foreign policy events.

For example, Sofia Latif, a Muslim woman and South Asian youth and community activist, believed that, despite all their differences, Muslims in the Detroit area are united by their common belief in Islam: "There are commonalities whether they're religion or culture or social tendencies, but I do see all Muslims as one entity, even within America. There are definitely commonalities across the board, but I definitely think it's very, very diverse."[55] Nevertheless, like many of the interviewees, she explained that an additional localized identity based on Arab culture is emerging in Dearborn. At the same time, she pointed out incoherent aspects of this emerging Arab-centric identity:

> I'm sure you've seen that within the range of people you've spoken to, some are very comfortable with Arabic language. Others . . . are educated here, their parents are educated here. They have a very different view. They've assimilated. Their names are no longer festive Arab names. Some of them don't practice religion anymore. Others, who have come in the past five years, are still very unaware of what they are faced with in this culture, they're still beginning to form their identity, [and] their parents are very sensitive how their children are adapting to the culture.[56]

Furthermore, Abdullateef Muhiuddin, a South Asian, Muslim student activist, highlighted that Muslims in Detroit tend to have multilayered identities; they can both simultaneously identify with either their nationality or ethnicity and a common Muslim identity: "You do see some nationalism . . . people that are Lebanese, Yemeni, Egyptian. . . . but I think that everybody identifies [as] being Arab American or South Asian American."[57] "In the same sense you can talk about all Muslim Americans as a one community," he continued. "Especially in American politics. . . . because in America we're seen as a minority. In any minority you have similarities and the same, we're in it together."[58]

One such issue that Detroit Arab Muslims view through Islamic lenses is the Palestinian cause. For example, a second-generation, male, Muslim Arab Palestinian student activist at UM-Dearborn explained that all Muslims show their support for the Palestinians, regardless of their ethnicity. Thus, as shown in these excerpts from interviews, for some Detroit Muslims, their faith is the most important variable in identity construction and political activism on the local issues—and on the Palestine cause.

Whereas the London members of conservative and angry Islamist groups presented some of the most assertive claims about the strength of Islamic identity, the Detroit sample does not include any Islamists, as none of these groups were present in the city as of 2009. Interestingly, the staunchly Islamist group Hizb ut-Tahrir, which was fairly well-known in the area prior to 9/11, has since vanished.[59]

In sum, it is evident that for many of Detroit's Arab Muslims, religious identity serves as a mobilizer for domestic issues. It can also not be denied that religion serves as a powerful force that influences the way the community perceives the Arab-Israeli conflict. Nevertheless, the following section will illustrate in what way ethnic identities are important in political activism.

The Importance of Ethic Arab Muslim Divisions

Contrary to popular belief in high Muslim religiosity, academic studies show that only 10 to 20 percent of Muslim Americans attend mosques regularly.[60] A 2004 local Muslim Institute for Social Policy and Understanding study found 33 mosques in the area. A couple of years later, the Building Islam in Detroit project, by accounting for more recently established mosques and using a more inclusive methodology, almost doubled the mosque count, to 55.[61] Another authoritative study finds that Muslims who attend mosques are willing to integrate and to move from the "margin to mainstream,"[62] and that as many as two-thirds do not have an affiliation with a mosque.[63] Evidence from Detroit corroborates these figures, even though there is some evidence claiming the opposite. A 2007 Pew Research study shows that 40 percent of American Muslims attend mosques at least once a week, while 72 percent pray daily.[64]

It cannot be denied that Islam is a formidable force in proactive Detroit Muslim politics on numerous domestic issues. Many Arab and Muslim organizations and civil society groups operate in Detroit. An increasing number of Arab and Muslim politicians compete in local elections.[65] Several studies show that Muslims in Detroit often find more common ground on which to organize in relation to the domestic front of the War on Terror than they do in relation to overseas concerns.[66]

However, with the exception of the support for Palestinians, ethnic divisions are more important with respect to mobilization in response to conflicts abroad.[67] This view was substantiated through interviews with Detroit's Arab Muslims. Some respondents stated that ethnic Arab identity matters more than religious commonalities, and others emphasized the importance of national and sectarian dividers in their daily lives. This observation is consistent with Jocelyne Cesari's (2004, 178) findings that, in their daily lives, Muslim Americans predominately associate with co-ethnics.

Interviews in Detroit illustrated the importance of ethnic identity. For example, Aoun Jaber, a male Lebanese community leader, perceived that "Arabness" has been more important than "Islamness" for the community, and that even secular, non-practicing Muslims could adopt Islamic practices such as the wearing of a *hijab*.[68] A female Arab Muslim youth and human rights activist in her 20s suggested that there are divisions in the community based on ethnic and cultural lines, but they are not that deep, and "there's a common Arab identity that people will always recognize." Sally Howell, a senior area scholar of Arab Detroit, describes the development of such localized identity:

> There is an emergence of an Arab-American identity in Detroit. It's being created by the ACCESS [Arab Community Center for Economic and Social Services], the ACC [Arab and Chaldean Council], Arab-American National Museum, Arab TV shows, ME comedy shows, activity on Warren Avenue—it's a place where we see a production and reproduction of the Middle Eastern consumer culture. . . . There is a growing number of local Arab novels, Arab identity is promoted in mosques, and in some churches. . . . Almost every Arab can identify with parts of it, but no one can identify with all of it.[69]

Meanwhile, Shia Imam Husham Al-Husainy, from the Karbalaa Islamic Education Center in Dearborn (the mosque serves mainly individuals of Iraqi and Lebanese descent) explained that Arab Muslim diasporic identity in Dearborn remains quite layered:

> There is . . . an overlapping of different elements of the belonging and the character of the Arab-Muslims in the US, and especially here. I think it's hard to draw a line because this is an individual situation . . . Some people who're practicing Islam more than others, they'll think of their identity as Muslim. Some others, they don't practice Islam much. They think they're Arab more than they're Muslim. Some people are too close to their nationalities, so they think they're more Lebanese or Iraqis than Muslim and so on.[70]

During a meeting with a focus group of five religious South Asian and Arab community leaders in the greater Detroit area, the group repeatedly voiced that it is of the utmost importance that Muslims in Detroit are not perceived as monolithic. They explained how community identity in each locality chiefly depends on the demographic dominance of a certain ethnic group. Thus, Dearborn is dominated by Lebanese and Iraqi Arabs, inner Detroit by African American Muslims, Canton/Oakland by South Asians, and Hamtramack by Bangladeshis. A number of Arab and non-Arab interviewees from outside Dearborn stressed that Dearborn has a particular Arab character due to a high Arab concentration. For example, an Egyptian community activist and young Muslim male professional, insisted that:

> There's the Dearborn community which has so many similarities . . . especially the second generation Arabs. They have a particular way, a particular culture . . . how they get dressed. You can . . . find out that this is a Dearborn Arab if you see them anywhere else in Michigan.

Furthermore, many of the interviewees illustrated the importance of national and sectarian differences in community organizations. Khadigah Alasry, a Yemeni Arab Muslim youth leader and the Assistant Director of the Muslim American Society Detroit Chapter, admitted that existing divisions among Detroit's Arab Muslims based on ethnicity or Sunni-Shia affiliation, emerge as a result of practical considerations.[71] Individuals from certain ethno-religious backgrounds tend to live and work together, and share a similar culture. Thus, ethno-religious divisions are more practical than ideological.

South Asian activist Saeed Ahmed Khan insisted that ethnic and national lines are the most important for political activism.[72] Therefore, because there is only a small Somali community in Detroit, there has been miniscule activism concerning Somalia.[73] Ron Amen, a middle-aged community leader of Lebanese background, a Shia Muslim and a Vietnam War veteran, regretfully admitted that ethnicity plays a major role in political activism on conflicts abroad:

> We stood by . . . and you heard very little when the slaughter was going on in Rwanda. Many Muslims died there. . . . and we were standing by when we saw what was going on in Somalia (ethnic Arabs killing their Muslim brothers because they're not Arabs). It's a sickening situation but it doesn't have the reaction.[74]

Aoun Jaber similarly stated that there have not been notable protests concerning Afghanistan, as there were not many Afghani migrants or organizations.[75] Meanwhile, the Palestinian cause is transnational, and when an issue involving Israel or Gaza arises, everyone takes action. An Arab Muslim religious leader explained that: "The situation in Pakistan is not as clear as Palestine. There are many different loyalties in the community locally."

Thus, an overwhelming majority of respondents highlighted the importance of ethnic identity markers in their self-identification and reactive political activism on foreign policy. Such an identity may encompass elements of a global "Arabness" (e.g., Arabic language and culture), a localized Arab identity (e.g., emerging Dearborn culture), or other national or sectarian divides. Therefore, in many instances, social and political activism beyond the Arab-Israeli conflict for Detroit's Arab Muslims is largely guided by ethnic cleavages, especially nationality and sectarian affiliations.

The Importance of Ethnic Identities in Foreign Policy Activism

This chapter shows that—in addition to a common Islamic identity that mobilizes Muslims regards certain domestic issues—national and sectarian cleavages are important for Muslim socio-political life and frequently influence how ethnic Muslim communities react to global conflict issues. However, religious Muslim identity indeed plays a major role in in domestic politics, especially instances where Muslim communities mobilize to oppose Islamophobia, oppose discrimination, and support the Palestinian cause.

These findings suggest that for these two communities, for purposes of foreign policy activism, identification as "Muslims" is just one of the layers of diasporic identity, and not necessarily the most important one. Although these findings are largely restricted to explaining mobilization in these two communities, they nevertheless question the contemporary wisdom of studying various ethnic Muslim communities as individuals motivated by their common Muslim identity, as opposed to being representatives of different national, sectarian, and racial groups. Ethnic and nationalistic divisions play an even larger role within Muslim religious organization in the West.[76] These findings further caution against placing an overly large emphasis on religious identity in regards to explaining foreign policy-influenced activism.

Indeed, ethnic divisions are important for the socio-political life of Muslim communities. For example, Pakistanis mainly interact with other Pakistanis, and Arab Muslims live often segregated lives in Detroit. Mosques and mainstream Muslim organizations are commonly managed by representatives of certain ethnicities. Finally, ethnicity-based considerations frequently determine what conflicts abroad generate political activism in Western Muslim communities, which will be further explored in the next two chapters. More specifically, the next chapter will inquire why, in addition to peaceful mobilization, London Muslim and Pakistani communities have also experienced reactive conflict spillover.

Notes

1 Baxter 2007; Bleich 2010; Ewing 2008; Joly 1995.
2 Cohen 1997.
3 Abbas 2005.
4 Sheffer 1986; Cohen 1997; Lyon and Uçarer 2001; Shain 1999.
5 The available research about how diasporas influence host state decision-making focuses almost exclusively on diasporas in the US.
6 E.g., see Baxter 2007; Bleich 2010; Ewing 2008; Joly 1995.
7 Ramadan 2004; Roy 2004.
8 In this book, "Islamist" refers to Muslim individuals adhering to the belief that Islam is both a religion and a comprehensive political system; see Hizb Ut-Tahrir Britain 2007.
9 Interview, August 10, 2009.
10 Between 2007 and 2011, 77 million British pounds were spent in the framework of the program. The money was spent on projects aiming at countering radicalization, and more general social welfare projects addressing the needs of Muslim communities (Pazoles 2009, 30).

11 The Arab Muslim community in Detroit is very diverse. About half of it consists of Christian Arabs, and the Muslims are roughly equally divided between Sunnis and Shias.
12 Abbas 2005.
13 Guibernau and Hutchinson 2004; Hastings 1997; Smith 1991; Smith 2009.
14 Bleich 2010.
15 Communities and Local Government 2009
16 Cesari 2004, 47–50.
17 Abdul Rehman Malik, interview, September 4, 2009; Pew Global Attitudes Project 2006.
18 Pew 2006.
19 Pew 2006.
20 Berkovitch 2007, 19.
21 Ahmad and Evergeti 2010, 1714.
22 British Muslims for Secular Democracy 2010.
23 Westoff and Frejka 2007.
24 Personal communication, Peter Neumann, August 5, 2009.
25 Ibid.
26 Interview, August 19, 2009.
27 Interview, August 26, 2009.
28 Pupcenoks and McCabe 2013.
29 Interview, August 10, 2009.
30 Interview, August 24, 2009.
31 Interview, Anjem Choudary, August 10, 2009.
32 Peach 2006, 353.
33 Chris Doyle, interview, August 18, 2009.
34 Heath and Demireva 2014, 169.
35 Shahab E. Khan, interview, February 26, 2010.
36 Chris Doyle, interview, August 18, 2009
37 Abdul Rehman Malik, interview, September 4, 2009.
38 Abdul Rehman Malik, interview, September 4, 2009.
39 Tehmina Kazi, interview, August 12, 2009.
40 Kazi interview, August 12, 2009.
41 Peach 2006, 354.
42 Peach 2006, 354.
43 Pew 2007, 2011b.
44 Pew 2011b, 7.
45 Pew 2011b.
46 Gallup 2011, 32.
47 Gallup 2011, 41–2.
48 Gallup 2011, 49–50.
49 McCarus 1994, 78–80.
50 McCarus 1994, 78–80.
51 E.g., see Abraham and Shryock 2000; Detroit Arab American Study 2009.
52 This pattern is quite different from the Muslim World, in which Sunnis constitute about 80 percent and Shias 10–15 percent of the total Muslim community.
53 Shryock 2008.
54 "Hockey and *Hijab*," *The Economist*, December 4, 2008.
55 Interview, December 9, 2009.
56 Sofia Latif, interview, November 20, 2009.
57 Interview, December 5, 2009.
58 Abdullateef Muhiuddin, interview, December 5, 2009.
59 Abdo 2006.

60 Haddad and Lummis 1987, 8; Leonard 2003, 17.
61 Bagby 2004; Shryock 2009.
62 Bagby 2010.
63 Saeed Ahmed Khan, personal communication, November 18, 2009.
64 Pew 2007.
65 Sinno and Tatari 2011.
66 Detroit Arab American Study Team 2009; Howell and Shryock 2003.
67 Economist 2008.
68 Aoun Jaber, interview, Detroit, November 20, 2009.
69 Sally Howell, personal communication, November 19, 2009.
70 Imam Husham Al-Husainy, interview, Detroit, December 1, 2009.
71 Khadigah Alasry, interview, Detroit, December 3, 2009.
72 Saeed Ahmed Khan, personal communication.
73 However, although people did not go out on streets over the humanitarian catastrophe in Somalia, some did raise money for the victims of this conflict, and brought concerns over this matter to their congressional representatives.
74 Ron Amen, interview.
75 Aoun Jaber, interview.
76 Vidino 2010, 9.

Part II

Reactive Conflict Spillover

6   Violence and Peaceful Mobilization
Pakistanis in London

London is at the forefront of Muslim political activism in the United Kingdom. The city has a sizeable, politicized Muslim population. It has experienced both peaceful and violent political reactions to the wars in Afghanistan and Iraq, as well as other conflicts abroad. In the decade following 9/11, London's Muslim activism ranged from peaceful to violent, including voting and lobbying, participation in protests, and involvement in terror plots. There have also been a number of protests, marches, and rallies critiquing British foreign policy and the country's actions while fighting terrorism on the global level.

Only a minute minority of the UK's Muslims have embraced extremist views, which has resulted in reactive conflict spillover.[1] Violent extremists involved in terror plots in London have come from various ethnic, economic, and cultural backgrounds. Would-be terrorists have included immigrants, British-born perpetrators, and converts. They have been rich and poor, cultured and uneducated. Some have come from Northern Africa, others from Jamaica, and yet others from South Asia: Turks, Pakistanis, and Bangladeshis make up some of the largest ethnic communities in London.

British Pakistanis have been involved in some of the most notorious terror plots, such as the 7/7 attack on London's public transportation system. On the morning of July 7, 2005, four men—three of whom were Pakistani and from outside of London—detonated four bombs, killing 56 people, including themselves. A year later, a number of London's Pakistanis were implicated for their involvement in a plot to detonate liquid explosives onboard several airplanes leaving Heathrow airport for the US and Canada. Individuals involved in such criminal acts commonly blame British foreign policy for their actions, especially the British involvement in the 2003 Iraq War. In light of such evidence, some have concluded that British Pakistanis have been somehow involved in almost every major Muslim extremist terrorist plot following 9/11.[2]

However, one should not leap to negative conclusions about British Pakistanis. The evidence presented in this chapter speaks for itself: British Pakistani engagement with terrorist activity in London mirrors their percentage of the British Muslim community.[3] Thus, British Pakistanis (the largest Muslim ethnic community in the UK) are generally not more likely to be involved with terrorism than other British Muslims. Instead, it is largely the structural situation in London that has left them with few significant ties to conventional society and—therefore—greater vulnerability to the triggers that can lead to conflict spillover incidents. Additionally, extremism and political violence is not a logical extension of peaceful political mobilization. Terrorist violence has been perpetrated only by a handful of misguided individuals.

This chapter provides an assessment of peaceful and violent reactions toward the War on Terror, specifically within the Muslim and Pakistani communities residing in London. It gives an overview of peaceful and radical protests to wars in Afghanistan and Iraq, and outlines instances of reactive conflict spillover. This chapter argues that reactive conflict spillover has occurred in London predominately due to the following causes: policies allowing migration of violent radicals, the presence of radical Muslim groups, and ties with radical networks abroad. The lack of economic integration—and inadequate political representation—also contributed to the radicalization of some Muslims.

London Pakistani Reactions to Afghanistan and Iraq, 2001–2010

British Muslims and Pakistanis have expressed concerns about Western involvement in the wars in Afghanistan and Iraq. They oppose the wars and denounce British and American participation in the conflicts. There has been a plethora of awareness-raising events and protest marches, and even some attempted bombings, in reaction to British and American actions in the War on Terror. In fact, most young British Muslims who participate in demonstrations and protests tend to focus on events focused on international war issues.[4] Awareness-raising campaigns tended to be organized by Pakistani groups, catering to individuals from Pakistani or South Asian ethnic backgrounds. However, larger public protests involved individuals across ethnic and religious lines. Commonly, trigger events galvanize the community into mobilization.

Trigger events are episodes where conflicts escalate, including the British decision to join the US in the 2003 Iraq War, and the following intensification of fighting among different Iraqi groups from 2003 to 2006. Triggers can be generated by intensified media coverage of a conflict or by significant events, such as the meeting of certain world leaders or attacks on significant religious or political landmarks. Reactions to conflicts abroad and reactive conflict spillover can also occur from a build-up of certain events.

The most visible street protests against the wars in Afghanistan and Iraq appeared shortly after an intensification of the situation abroad. The largest anti-war protest on the streets of London occurred on the eve of the British invasion of Iraq in 2003. In reaction to built-up frustration with anti-terrorism legislation, Muslims engaged in some other peaceful protests. A perception that the Coalition could lose the Iraq War between the years 2003 and 2006 allegedly inspired several attempted acts of reactive conflict spillover. However, reactive conflict spillovers (including the foiled 2006 Heathrow bombing plot) were the result of careful planning, not spontaneous reactions to an escalation of conflicts abroad. As the following sections will illustrate, London's Pakistanis (and existing connections with radical networks abroad) have been particularly important in leading to hostile mobilization and terrorism.

The beginning of British military actions in Afghanistan generated only a few major protests and did not lead to a spillover of violence in the time period from 2001 to 2003. However, the Iraq War and Occupation of 2003 has served as a major cause for British Muslim activism and radicalization. By the time the UK withdrew its combat troops from Iraq in 2009, the conflict had taken the lives of 179 British soldiers and hundreds of thousands of Iraqis, according to mainstream sources. As this chapter will explain, only a few protests took place in opposition to the British involvement in Afghanistan, whereas anti-Iraq War and Occupation activism (organized by Muslim groups alone and in alliances with major British organizations) has been spirited and ubiquitous (see Table 6.1 below).

Table 6.1 Protests in Reaction to the Afghanistan and Iraq Wars, 2001–2010[1]

Total Protest Count	Organizers of Protests	Themes of Protests	Key Demands of Protests
• three major protests against Afghanistan War	• Muslim Groups (MCB, Muslim Parliament of Great Britain British Muslim Initiative.) • Stop the War Coalition	• Opposition to air strikes • Opposition to UK involvement	• Stop air strikes in Afghanistan • No British involvement in Afghanistan
• 10+ major protests against Iraq War • Dozens of minor protests against Iraq War[2]	• Muslim groups (MCB, MAB, BMI, Hizb ut-Tahrir, Al-Muhajiroun, Islam4UK) • Mainstream British groups	• Anti-war • Against the involvement of British troops in the wars	• Do not invade Iraq • Withdraw from Iraq • Calls for violence against the British

Sources:
1 Compiled by the author (December 2010) and updated by Josh Heath (July 2013) using the Lexis-Nexis Academic database and internet research.
2 Anti-war protests have been routinely underreported by the mainstream British media (Bristol Evening Post, "Anti-War Protesters Criticize BBC," April 5, 2006).

In response to the beginning of American airstrikes against targets in Afghanistan, British Muslim leaders called for peaceful protests and vigils in 2001.[5] Nevertheless, in addition to several smaller Muslim protests and vigils, there were only three major street protests—on October 13, 2001, when 20,000 people marched in streets of London to demand a halt to ongoing US strikes in Afghanistan; and a general protest on November 18, 2001, when 15,000 protesters marched against the war[6] and the third protest, attracting thousands of anti-war protesters, took place on November 20, 2001. It is unknown how many of the protesters were Muslim. Overall, the conflict in Afghanistan never received significant attention among British Muslims. This lack of activism regarding Afghanistan was largely due to the fact that this war was perceived to be largely justified, and because there were very few British Muslim leaders who framed this conflict as important. It was not until the fall of 2002 that perceptions of the imminence of the upcoming war in Iraq galvanized British Muslims into reactive political mobilization.

Anti-Iraq War protests had already commenced in the fall of 2002, as British and American governments contemplated removing Saddam Hussein's regime. They continued until the British military withdrawal from Iraq in 2009. For example, some 350,000 demonstrators (including 100,000 Muslims) attended a protest organized by the Stop the War Coalition on September 28, 2002. The participants took a stance against the publically discussed plan to militarily intervene in Iraq with the goal of removing Saddam Hussein.[7] British Muslim organizations planned protests of their own and built remarkable coalitions with major British groups, most notably the powerful Stop the War Coalition. Protests organized by major British Muslim organizations generally remained nonviolent, whereas protests organized by Islamist organizations occasionally transformed into civil disobedience.

Major anti-war protests reached their peak from February to March 2003, after which regular protests continued to follow, although their attendance decreased over time. On February 16, 2003, the Muslim Association of Britain, along with the Stop the War Coalition and the Campaign for Nuclear Disarmament (CND), co-organized the largest public demonstration in British history. British police estimated that there were some 750,000 attendees, while the organizers put the number between 1.5 and 2 million.[8] The three-and-a-half-mile protest march unfolded peacefully and only a handful of activists were arrested, for minor offenses.[9] Additional anti-war gatherings took place in Glasgow and Belfast.

After the invasion of Iraq on March 20, 2003, both the Muslim Association of Britain and the British Muslim Initiative—in coalition with mainstream British groups—organized regular, nonviolent, anti-war activities. These protests most notably took place on annual anniversaries of the war and during the 2006–2007 escalation of the conflict. Unlike the "million march" against the war in 2003, only somewhere between 10,000 and

60,000 Muslims and non-Muslims marched in opposition to the war during the fourth anniversary of the conflict in 2007.[10] Meanwhile, parallel to mainstream activism, conservative and angry Muslim groups organized smaller, more provocative protests, which were widely covered in the media.

Representatives of radical Islamist group al-Muhajiroun (including its more recent reincarnations, such as Islam4UK) organized some of the most notoriously radical protests. For example, members of al-Muhajiroun used protests against the publication of Prophet Muhammad cartoons in 2006 to express their opposition to the War in Iraq, and to call for violence against the UK. A senior former al-Muhajiroun member, Umran Javed, who called for terrorist attacks during a protest against the Prophet Muhammad cartoons, was later convicted of soliciting murder.[11] Other radical Muslims, without identifiable ties to specific organizations, were tried and convicted on charges of instigating aggression during the cartoon protests. For example, Mizanur Rahman called for non-Muslims to be "annihilated" and "beheaded." Rahman also called for the destruction of British and American forces in Iraq, and for the return of British soldiers in "body bags."[12] Similar statements were voiced in later radical anti-war protests, including a notorious 2009 protest that triggered the emergence of the controversial English Defence League.[13]

On March 10, 2009, the London-based Islam4UK held a protest against the British presence in Iraq. The protest took place in the nearby town of Luton, concurrent with a parade in honor of British soldiers returning from Afghanistan. Despite extensive prior advertising and outreach efforts by the group's leaders, the protest only consisted of some 18 protesters holding provocative signs comparing British soldiers to terrorists; the protesters shouted slogans describing the soldiers as "murderers," "rapists," and "baby killers."[14] Actions by Islam4UK provoked a much larger counter-protest, police presence, and disproportionately widespread media coverage. The group was officially outlawed under British counterterrorism laws after it announced controversial plans to organize an anti-British soldiers' march through a military cemetery in the town of Wootton Bassett in January of 2010.[15]

Overall, the Iraq War galvanized significant support among mainstream and fringe Muslim groups. Mainstream Muslim groups organized massive street protests in association with British anti-war groups, while more radical organizations orchestrated poorly attended, controversial protests with widespread media attention. Yet activism in London is not solely limited to the use of democratic means.

Reactive Conflict Spillover in London

The following list provides a brief summary of the seven most important instances of reactive conflict spillover in London in the decade following 9/11.[16] This broad overview will show that Muslims (migrants,

British-born and converts) have occasionally engaged in political violence in London. In particular, British Pakistanis have been associated with a large number of these plots. This connection will be further examined in the following section.

- December 2001. The Shoe Bomber incident. Richard Reid, a Muslim convert, attempted to detonate an improvised explosive device in his shoe. He stated that the reason for his action was his belief that the US is at war with Islam, and that the US has caused much harm to predominantly Muslim states, such as Iraq.
- November 2002. Chemical attack on the London Underground. A group consisting of Britons with North African backgrounds was responsible for a failed chemical attack on the London Underground.
- 2004. The fertilizer bomb plot. The attackers intended to target locations in the UK, including London. The plot was barely averted thanks to the efforts of the British police. The plan's mastermind was Omar Khyam and, among the conspirators there were several other men of Pakistani background. Khyam was radicalized through his anger over the treatment of Muslims in Kashmir, and his opposition of British and American foreign policies toward Islamic countries.
- July 7, 2005. The London Underground attack. Suicide bombers detonated four bombs in various places within the London transportation system. The culprits were from Birmingham and other cities, yet some arrests were made in East London.
- July 21, 2005. London Bombings. Four bombs failed to detonate in London. The Abu Hafs al-Masri Brigade (a group loosely linked to Al-Qaeda) claimed responsibility and stated that it will continue terrorism as long as European soldiers are in Iraq. Two years later, several immigrant-background individuals from Somalia and Eritrea were convicted of participation in the conspiracy.
- 2006. The Heathrow Airport transatlantic airplane plot. London police thwarted a conspiracy to detonate explosives on several airplanes leaving the Heathrow Airport for the US. Twenty-four arrests were made in London, its suburbs, and Birmingham. The convicted men were of Pakistani background with extensive ties to radical networks in Pakistan.
- 2007. London car bomb plot. Several Muslim men were found guilty of a failed conspiracy to detonate four car bombs in London.[17] The alleged would-be terrorists claimed that their motive for the terrorist act was anger due to the occupation of Iraq, and the oppression of Palestinians in the Occupied Territories. Most of the perpetrators were medical doctors.[18]

As the handful of examples above indicate, there have been a number of violent protests and acts of violence initiated by individuals from the

Muslim community as a whole, and by individuals from the Pakistani community in particular. The following section will describe the key instances of reactive conflict spillover and will show that, regardless of the source of motivation, at least three-quarters of all groups surveyed by British domestic security have ties to Pakistan, and an overwhelming majority of implicated would-be violent extremists have had some connection with violent extremists in Pakistan.[19] It is interesting to note, however, that such would-be terrorists tend to lack institutionalized training and recruitment.[20] Although Al-Qaeda's safe haven in Afghanistan has been eliminated, elements of Al-Qaeda remain in Afghanistan, Pakistan's Northwest Frontier, and Iraq.[21] Furthermore, the Al-Qaeda associated social networks in the UK, connecting violent Afghani and Pakistani radicals with Britain's Pakistani community, with 40,000 visits per year in Pakistan, now constitutes "the base" of its activism in the UK.[22] Furthermore:

> Of the 48 persons charged, convicted, or suicided in the UK since 2001, 18 (39 percent) were of Pakistani descent. This proportion roughly corresponds to the proportion of British Muslims of Pakistani origin (43 percent according to the 2001 Census).[23]

This threat is not contained within the UK alone. In 2009, Bruce Riedel, a former CIA officer who advised President Barack Obama, claimed that: "The British Pakistani community is recognized as probably al-Qaeda's best mechanism for launching an attack against North America."[24] Dozens of Muslim militants with European citizenship are operating in lawless tribal areas of northwestern Pakistan.[25] At least 70 Germans have undergone paramilitary training in Pakistan and Afghanistan, and about a third of them have returned back home.[26] Western intelligence and counterterrorism officials have received information that terror plots in Britain, France, and Germany had been planned by Pakistan.[27] Furthermore, since 9/11, individuals associated with loose networks connected to Pakistan or British Pakistanis, some of them radicalized "lone wolves," have been implicated in several terror plots across Europe.

On December 11, 2010, one such lone wolf, Taimour al-Abdaly, an Iraqi-born, naturalized Swedish citizen, detonated two bombs in central Stockholm, killing himself and injuring two people. This was the first act of suicide terrorism in the Nordic countries. Al-Abdaly became particularly radicalized during the time he spent in Luton, UK, home to some 20,000 Pakistani Britons and 25,000 Muslims.[28]

Meanwhile, many British Muslims involved in key terrorist plots were either Pakistanis or individuals with links to radical groups in Pakistan. This is not to claim that terrorist acts could not be committed without links to Pakistan, or that terrorist motivation does not matter. British convert Richard Reid—a lone wolf without ties to radical networks—attempted to detonate an explosive hidden in his shoe. Numerous British Muslims of diverse backgrounds have planned terrorist attacks against the UK, inspired by a transnational motivation to avenge perceived injustices committed against the global Muslim *ummah*.[29] However, such plots by lone wolves tend to be amateurish and poorly organized and realized, whereas plots where individuals have received paramilitary training and guidance from violent extremists in Pakistan or another volatile area are more carefully prepared; therefore, they present a greater threat to national security.

Attempted Terrorist Acts with Links to Pakistanis

A sizeable proportion of terrorist acts committed by British Muslims in the UK and South Asia have Pakistani and Kashmiri connections.[30] The most infamous British domestic Islamist terrorist attack is the 7/7 bombing in the London Underground. Some have argued that the 7/7 attack constituted the advent of "compounded terrorism," "an amalgamation of the attackers' (foreign) ethnicity, culture, and extreme religious beliefs with their (domestic) citizenship."[31] Compounded terrorism is domestic in regards to the actors involved, but its motivation is transnational. Many of the individuals who engaged in political violence were influenced by the ongoing war in Iraq. Reports from the Chatham House and the Joint Terrorism Analysis Center, two think-tanks with close ties to the British government, have found that the US-led occupation of Iraq has been explicitly linked to terrorist activity and its subsequent increase in the UK.[32] Other studies suggest that violent extremists extended their European operations after the roundups following 9/11 and the invasion of Iraq in 2003.[33] However, the following analysis shows that reactive conflict spillover predominantly occurs in situations where actors, regardless of their motivations, have connections with radical networks abroad, which enable them to receive paramilitary training, frequently in Pakistan.

The 7/7 terrorist act consisted of four coordinated suicide bombers in London's public transportation system during rush hour. Three of the bombings were carried out in London's Underground and the fourth bombing came an hour later in a double-decker bus in Tavistock Square. All three blasts occurred within 50 seconds of each other.[34] The explosions appear to have been caused by homemade, organic, peroxide-based devices packed into backpacks and detonated by the four suicide bombers. The blasts resulted in 56 deaths, including the bombers themselves; about 700 people were wounded. The incident served as a wake-up call for British security services, which had previously paid very little attention to threats posed by domestic Muslim extremist terrorism. The terrorists claimed that their attacks were motivated by the British involvement in the 2003 Iraq War.

The 7/7 terrorist attacks were carried out by three British Pakistanis and a Jamaican. All four of the men resided outside of London. Sidique Khan and Shehzad Tanweer were second-generation British Pakistanis. Hasib Hussain was also a Pakistani. Garmaine Lindsay, also known as Abdullah Shaheed Jamal, was a Jamaican-born convert. Although for the general public this attack signified the emergence of a "new" terrorist threat emanating from British Muslims with South Asian backgrounds, several individuals with Pakistani background had already been arrested in 2004 during Operation Crevice. In fact, "almost every significant terrorist plot uncovered in the U.K. in recent years has some link to a Kashmiri militant group, which is significant because most British Pakistanis are of Kashmiri origin."[35] Although British Pakistanis continue to play a notable role in Muslim political violence in London as a reaction to conflicts abroad, the overwhelming majority of residents with Pakistani background in London remain law-abiding citizens who are overwhelmingly upset and disgusted by the actions of a few misguided individuals.

Both nationally and in London, individuals of Pakistani background have been implicated in several additional terrorist plots. Terrorists failed to carry out a similar attack just two weeks after the 7/7 bombings. On July 21, 2005, four attempted attacks disrupted London's public transport system. Three of the bombings occurred in the London Underground, another on a bus, and the fourth bomber abandoned his device without attempting to detonate it. Luckily, only the detonators of the bombs exploded and the attacks resulted in no casualties.

It was suspected that either the same group was culpable for 7/7 and 7/21 bombings, or that the second bombing was inspired by the first. The Abu Hafs al-Masri Brigade, an Al-Qaeda affiliate, claimed responsibility for the bombings. The group stated that terrorism will continue as long as European soldiers are in Iraq. On July 9, 2007, three defendants—Eritrean Briton Muktar Said Ibrahim from London; and Yassin Omar and Ramzi Mohammed, both of Somali background, from outside London—were found guilty of conspiracy to murder. Each was sentenced to a minimum of 40 years in prison for the attempted 7/21 bombing.

Some events that occurred in previous years can be viewed as warning signs for the 2005 attacks. In August 2004, as a part of Operation Rhyme, British police arrested eight British citizens on charges of planning terrorist attacks on financial institutions in the UK and the US. The arrests were made after receiving a tip from Pakistani police. In another massive attempt to control terrorists, on the morning of March 30, 2004 (during Operation Crevice), British police seized 1,300 pounds of ammonium nitrate fertilizer and arrested several British Pakistanis.[36]

In two dozen round-ups involving seven hundred officers, eight British-born Pakistanis and a naturalized Briton born in Algeria were arrested.[37] Six of the fertilizer bomb plot organizers had family ties in

Pakistan, and several of them had received training in Pakistan. One of the arrested individuals resided in London, yet the operation mainly exposed the presence of terrorist groups in the Thames Valley, Sussex, Surrey, and Brefordshire. In April 2007, five of these men were convicted of conspiracy to cause explosions that were likely to endanger lives.

One of the most catastrophic, but thwarted, Pakistani extremist terrorist attacks occurred in 2006. The Transatlantic Aircraft Plot consisted of an attempt to detonate liquid explosives on 10 airplanes leaving London Heathrow airport for the US and Canada. The plot was discovered and thwarted by the British police, and was followed by an unprecedented increase in security measures at airports. The restrictions were gradually lifted, yet the ability of passengers to carry liquids on an aircraft remained limited. A number of British Pakistanis were involved in the plot, many of them from London. Approximately 24 suspects were arrested. Eight men, including Ahmed Abdullah Ali, Assad Sarwar, Tanvir Hussain, Oliver Savant, Arafat Khan, Waheed Zaman, Umar Islam, and Mohammed Gulzar, were charged in connection with the plot in 2008. Three of them were found guilty of conspiracy to commit murder.[38]

In sum, the scale of London's Muslim political mobilization inspired by wars in Afghanistan and Iraq ranges from awareness raising events and street protests to violent radicalization and terrorist acts. Political violence in response to foreign policy events was largely enabled due to certain openings provided by the migration context and certain features of London's Muslim and Pakistani communities.

Context: Presence of Radicals, and the Lack of Economic Integration

The two main contextual variables that led to conflict spillover to London are migration and security policies allowing inflow of violent radicals, and lack of economic integration. First, until 9/11 the British authorities were generally willing to tolerate radical Islamists migrating to the UK, and they were not perceived to represent a national security threat. More recently, such policies have been revised to prevent migration of radicals, yet certain controversial policing practices and counterterrorism policies have caused tensions between Muslims and the state. Second, the lack of economic integration—accompanied by inadequate Muslim representation in British politics, and discrimination—also encourages the radicalization of some London's Muslims and Pakistanis.

British Policies Allowing Migration of Violent Radicals

The UK's government has pursued an increasingly restrictive asylum policy in the post-World War II period.[39] However, although exact numbers are unknown, it is generally accepted among policy-makers and scholars that the UK also simultaneously accepted—and consciously tolerated—a large number of extremists and foreign radicals in the few decades leading up to 9/11.[40] Such extremists played important roles both in participating in political violence themselves, and radicalizing others.

Predominantly due to concerns about race riots, the UK started to restrict its asylum policy already in the late 1950s.[41] In the 1980s and 1990s, the successive governments led by the Conservatives and Labour further restricted immigration and curtailed social citizenship rights afforded to asylum seekers in the UK.[42] For example, the 1999 Immigration and Asylum Act established the National Asylum Support System, which tightened border security, provided additional powers of search and arrest to immigration officials, and strengthened penalties for those transporting undocumented migrants.[43] By the mid-2000s, British immigration policy and screening of potential immigrants was significantly more thorough and restrictive.

During the 1990s and early 2000s, 314,000 of 499,000 asylum petitions were rejected.[44] From 2002 to 2006, over a third of asylum seekers were either removed or departed voluntarily, which represents a significant increase from less than 20 percent during the 1997–2001 period.[45] Two-thirds of 29,840 asylum claims filed in 2009 were rejected.[46] Meanwhile, during the New Labour-led government (1997–2010), the UK increasingly promoted selective migration while the attitudes towards asylum seekers hardened.[47] The 2002 Nationality, Immigration, and Asylum Act established that "appeals no longer suspended deportation" and suspended permission to work after six months.[48] Due to such restrictions, in November 2006 asylum applications for that year were at the lowest level since 1993.[49]

Paradoxically, despite the restrictions, the UK accepted more foreign political radicals than most other Western countries in the post-World War II period. Although the UK did indeed make its asylum policy more restrictive in the decades prior to 9/11 and 7/7, these restrictions were mostly influenced by economic concerns. The security dimension was missing from these considerations, and the screening aimed at identifying and preventing an inflow of violent radicals was not effectively implemented.[50]

In the 1980s and 1990s, British authorities were willing to "grant a significant degree of tolerance" to radical preachers such as the former Finsbury Mosque's Imam Omar Bakri Mohammed.[51] Furthermore, during this time period the British government did not believe that violent Muslim extremists posed as a security threat to the UK. On the contrary, the British government saw it to be beneficial that a number of radicalized British Muslims joined Islamic *mujahideen* fighting Soviet forces in Afghanistan in the 1980s. Additionally, mainstream British Muslim groups failed to denounce radicals among them until after 9/11.[52]

Additionally, the UK's physical proximity to the volatile Middle East appears to be a factor in the arrival of numerous foreign recidivists from that region; especially from the 1970s to the 1990s, when radical Islam was ascendant globally.[53] The relatively high acceptance of radicals is partially a result of the extensive British Courts' interventions to protect refugee rights and to promote more expansive conceptions of the refugee in the 1980s and 1990s.[54] Largely, this was due to the government's initial perception that Islamic radicals did not constitute a national security threat, a conception which has been since revised following 9/11 and 7/7.[55] Prior to 9/11, the British government pursued an explicit policy of non-repression of members of radical Muslim groups, as long as they did not directly attack British institutions.[56]

Thus, whereas the UK attempted to restrict the number of asylum seekers accepted, it did not attempt to prevent acceptance of Islamic radicals until 9/11. Thus, the growing number of radicalized Muslim individuals in London is largely an outcome of relaxed British policies, and as one prominent scholar and analyst states: "The rise of London as the main center of the *jihad* in Europe was probably due to its tolerant laws allowing for sanctuary and its large pool of potential *mujahedin*."[57]

By the 1990s, many Islamic dissident organizations operated in London and the city was known as a major center for Islamic radicalism in Europe. Such organizations included: Palestinian Hamas, Algerian GIA, Afghani Taliban, and Egyptian Jamaat al-Islamiyya. British immigration policies were further restricted after 9/11, and by 2003, there was an understanding among senior British governmental officials that the UK had become "a net exporter of terrorism."[58] Nevertheless, following 9/11 and the 7/7 bombings, British officials increasingly started to detain and deport radicals using the powers given by counterterrorism laws.

Additionally, the relationship between the British police and Muslim communities is frequently tense.[59] Policing programs within these communities are often tied to counterterrorism efforts.[60] On the surface, this appears to be a positive decision, but it could potentially be problematic if too much focus is spent on countering terrorist behavior, and not on day-to-day policing needs. This focus on counterterrorism has led to an increase in the deportation of key radicals, arrests, and increasing the scrutiny of Muslim communities, potentially with a loss of respect between police and Muslim citizens. [61] Moreover, Muslim groups that are working with the government may lose credibility among fellow Muslims.[62] Meanwhile, the British PREVENT program—initiated in 2007 and developed out of the Operation Contest program of 2006—aims to take measures to prevent violent radicalization in British Muslim communities.[63] The Operation Contest and PREVENT programs helped to instigate a drastic increase in the size of the MET, which is tasked with UK counterterrorism actions. Between 2006 and 2007, 6,000 officers were added to a staff of 30,000, and budgets tripled from

9/11 to 2009.[64] However, these numbers appear to have reduced since that time, decreasing to 31,000, and with the introduction of the new CONTEST strategy of 2011, some changes to procedure and personnel occured.[65] Along with increasing budgets, an increase in CCTV use can be seen, with more than 200 such devices used in two Birmingham Asian neighborhoods.[66]

Part of the PREVENT program, including providing funding for British Muslim organizations that work on de-radicalization projects, has brought forth mixed results. For example, government-funded anti-radicalization programs have helped to further a "civil war" among British Muslim communities, where certain Barelvis and Sufis have received support for their investigations of alleged extremism among their perceived rivals, the Deobandis and Salafis.[67] On the opposing side, a small number of Salafi and Islamist groups were actually empowered by the MET and the Muslim Contact Unit (MCU) to perform counterterrorism work and to assist in preventing the building of connections between Al-Qaeda and local youths.[68]

Indeed, critics have pointed out a number of deficiencies with PREVENT. In particular, community involvement decisions were made behind doors without Muslim consultation; for example, the manager of a Muslim community organization spoke about PREVENT-related programs: "The chief executives of the local authority drove it through, which means that the usual processes of consultation and accountability were bypassed. It was presented as a fait accompli."[69] A key premise of PREVENT is the idea that community involvement and consultation is essential; however, the search of the new CONTEST program contained no mention of the word consult or consulting.

Money flowing from this program into the coffers of British Muslim organizations also reduces the legitimacy of programs designed to interact with Muslim communities and their leadership.[70] PREVENT has alienated Muslims "by defining the government's relationship with them entirely in terms of reining in the worst elements," and by frequently creating conflicting positions.[71] This seems to be a systemic issue that leads to other policing issues and actions that lead to violence, particularly when policing political protest.

The British Home Office has funded a number of projects, "designed to 'counter the ideological and theological underpinnings of the terrorist narrative.'"[72] For example, the British government, especially the Home Office, has financed the Radical Middle Way, an organization with a key purpose to empower and promote mainstream (moderate) Islam. In 2009, this organization received £350,000.00 from the British government.[73] Another Muslim think-tank, the Quilliam, received some £2.7 million from 2009–2011, but the group's financial support from the government was largely decreased in the latter years.[74] The Quilliam is the world's first counter-extremism think tank, established in London in 2008. It argues, controversially, that political Islam is the key cause for Muslim terrorism. The Quilliam foundation was formed by two former Hizb ut-Tahrir leaders, Ed Hussain and Maajid Nawaz, with the stated goal of preventing extremism, specifically Islamism, which is allegedly the source of Muslim terrorism.

Another concern tied into these types of community-based policing and counterterrorism actions is racial or ethnic profiling. A report released in 2004 by the Home Office showed an increase in Asians stopped for search by 302 percent after the 9/11 attacks.[75] Such incidences bring to mind injustice and unfair targeting by those being searched and can lead to a view of discrimination and Islamophobia.[76] Profiling in the UK is a continuous problem that is a negative result of deeper problems, and one that targets Muslims and other individuals of South Asian background.[77] Publications by London's Muslim organization chastise the police's differing treatment of Muslim protests and non-Muslim demonstrations, and, at times, the police's failure to properly protect Muslim protestors from physical assaults from their opponents, usually fringe far-right groups.[78]

London is a microcosm of the way the United Kingdom treats, integrates, and polices their Muslim population. Certain policing tactics seem to have a negative effect, and often lead to violence, instead of being performed in a manner that reduces the possibility of violence. Unfair policing practices were a major cause for the Brixton riots of 1981.[79] More recent studies conducted by British Muslim scholars argue that hostilities during protests result from the London police's use of controversial policing techniques such as kettling.[80] "Kettling" consists of holding protesters for extended periods of time, which can last up to several hours behind a police cordon. Critics have noted that the technique violates human rights, and it may encourage the stranded protesters to turn to violence out of frustration

Such a situation does not occur overnight, and the trends in London and the UK in general contrast with the different approach taken by police in Detroit, which will be covered in a later chapter. In the UK, community involvement and interaction with police forces was minimal until the aftereffects of the 7/7 attacks, and even after, the focus of police forces was not on policing these communities harmoniously, but in preventing terrorism.[81] Particular policies include the stop and search procedures, which escalated after the 9/11 attacks, the distribution of materials outlining counterterrorism practices a focus on increasing feelings of integration, and imam training in counter-arguments to terrorist ideology.[82]

Overall, by the 1990s, a residual effect of the prior acceptance of numerous foreign extremists and radicals was the creation of an environment conductive for the reactive spillover of violence to the UK and, especially, London. Nevertheless, in the years following 9/11, immigration screening for extremism was conducted more effectively, and counterterrorism laws were used to detain and deport radicals. The long-term effects of these policies are likely to lead to a decreased risk of conflict spillovers in the UK.

The Lack of Economic Integration and Inadequate Representation

It is a common complaint that London's Muslims and Pakistanis are poorly economically integrated, frequently unemployed, and commonly under-educated. Relative to other faith groups, Muslims in the UK generally live in economically depressed areas, in overcrowded buildings, have high unemployment rates, and earn low incomes.[83] Furthermore, according to the 2001 Census, Muslims have the highest rates of ill-health.[84] The numerous Muslim organizations tend to lack notable grassroots support. Although the situation is improving, British Muslims (and their interests) are still underrepresented in national politics, and Muslims remain frequently distrustful of the government.

High unemployment rates in British Muslim and Pakistani areas can be seen as structural, and such rates have persisted from at least the 1970s.[85] Cesari (2004, 23) observes that:

> In 1991, the rate of unemployment among people of Pakistani origin between 16 and 24 years was almost 36 percent, whereas for "whites" it was below 15 percent. And while in 1998 the unemployment rate fell to only 21 percent among Pakistanis, this number still remained considerably higher that the "white" unemployment rate of the same year (estimated at 5 percent).

Nevertheless, in many aspects, Britain's Muslims and Pakistanis show high levels of social integration as measured in terms of bridging residential segregation and feeling of belonging to British culture and society. Although Pakistanis in particular show high rates of in-group marriage and frequent interactions with other members of their ethnicity, data also shows that Pakistani workplace segregation is low, that they commonly adopt a British identity and view positively British culture and society.[86] As it is frequently case with diasporic communities, which tend to have multi-layered identities, British Muslims and other minorities want to both keep their own traditions and integrate into broader British society.[87] Meanwhile, there is extensive evidence outlining the economic deprivation of British Muslims.

A recent, authoritative Open Society Institute study found that Muslims are the most disadvantaged faith group in the UK.[88] British Muslims have the lowest rate of employment out of any group, at 38 percent, and the highest level of economic inactivity, at 52 percent.[89] According to the UK Office for National Statistics, the Muslim unemployment rate stood at 13 percent in 2004. The Joseph Rowntree Foundation study of different ethnic minority groups in the UK found that 55 percent of Pakistanis live in poverty.[90] Muslims in the UK are also quite concerned about high levels of crime in areas where many of them live.[91] This data shows that British Muslims are poorly integrated and frequently disenfranchised.

Similarly, in London, Bangladeshis, and Pakistanis are among the very poorest ethnic groups.[92] Members of these two ethnic groups in London face chronic unemployment, and have the lowest average earning rate of any minority group.[93] 30 to 40 percent of Pakistani and Bangladeshi children in London live in workless households.[94] A study by Taylor et al. (2005) finds that East London's Bangladeshi, Indian, and Pakistani boys are at risk of being underweight.

According to the 2001 Census, only 41 percent of Muslims over the age of 15 held a high school diploma. Young Muslims in inner-city London fared even worse. Thirty-seven percent of Muslims between ages of 16 and 24 failed to complete high school, as opposed to 25 percent of the general population.[95] Many Pakistanis, most of whom came from the Mirpur region, were uneducated and employed in unskilled jobs to a greater extent than other migrants from the Indian subcontinent.[96] This evidence suggests that—similarly to other Muslims in the UK—London's Pakistanis are socioeconomically marginalized. In addition to the challenges presented by the marginalization of British Muslims due to poverty, such as the lack of education and unemployment, British Muslims must also face the challenges that are presented by rampant discrimination and Islamophobia.

Paradoxically, whereas there are plenty of Muslim organizations—such as the Muslim Council of Britain, and other organizations catering to Muslims and Pakistanis (e.g., Muslim Association of Britain, UK Islamic Mission, and so on), they tend to lack grassroots support. These results are consistent with the findings of Lorenzo Vidino, where only 10–12 percent of Western Muslims are engaged or belong to a Muslim organization.[97] Most likely, no single group will ever represent the British Muslim community, "for no such thing exists."[98]

Additionally, minorities, especially Muslims in Europe, face rampant discrimination, and the UK is no an exception.[99] The existing discrimination against Muslims in Britain further increases tensions and increases the likelihood of violent action. Numerous studies show that Muslims in the UK are routinely discriminated against by employers as well as public institutions.[100] British Muslims are 23.6 percent more likely than non-Muslims to report religious discrimination, and 12 percent more likely to report racial discrimination.[101] Additionally, numerous hate crimes are routinely committed against British Muslims and their institutions. It is estimated that between 40 to 60 percent of mosques, Islamic centers, and Muslim organizations have been attacked at least once since 9/11; at least 762 "Islamophobic offenses" were committed in London between April 2009 and June 2011. However, many suspect that such offenses are greatly underreported.[102] One study finds that Muslims in the UK are 12 percent more likely than non-Muslims to "indicate racial discrimination against their group."[103] A 2006 Pew study shows that 40 percent of the general public and 42 percent of British Muslims "see many of their fellow countrymen as hostile to Muslims."[104] Sixty-four percent of Britons doubt that Muslims want to adapt to local customs and way of life, and the opinion of British Muslims themselves is divided: 41 percent reported that they want to adopt national customs, whereas 35 percent desired to remain distinct from British society.[105] Finally, by analyzing public opinion polls from 1988 to 2008, Bleich (2009) finds that negative attitudes towards Muslims have risen in the UK over the last 20 years, and Muslims are generally viewed with tremendous suspicions by average Britons.

Furthermore, a 10-year study from the University of Exeter's European Muslim Research Centre shows that British Muslims undergo physical violence and discrimination on a daily basis—and many of these incidents are underreported.[106] Such violence against Muslims has been committed by far right groups such as the English Defence League, as well as by "individuals who have become convinced and angry by negative portrayals of Muslims in the media."[107] The claims of British Muslim marginalization are further supported by studies showing that a deep-rooted Islamophobia exists in parts of the British society.[108] Finally, British Muslims face ongoing media scrutiny and hounding. Asylum seekers, regardless of religion, tend to be covered in negative light in the British press.[109] Especially since the 1979 Islamic revolution, South Asian Muslims and Islam have been portrayed in the British Press in a particularly negative light[110] as well as commonly racialized.[111]

Public opinion data shows that significant portions of the British Muslim population perceive that they are not well-integrated and display insecurities about the future. According to a Pew survey, 80 percent of British Muslims are either somewhat (31 percent) or very (49 percent) concerned about the future of Muslims in the UK; 44 percent are very worried about unemployment, and 42 percent about Islamic Extremism in the UK.[112] From all Western Muslim populations surveyed, British Muslims are also the most worried about all other issues, including the influence of secular culture on their youth (44 percent very concerned), and adoption of modern roles in society by Muslim women (22 percent very concerned).[113] Such Muslim self-perceptions further illustrate the existing problems with economic integration and the notable insecurity that these communities experience.

Furthermore, many British Muslim grievances are addressed through their points of access in the Labour Party and the powerful Trades Unions Congress (TUC). Migrant and Muslim involvement with the TUC and the Labour Party has allowed them to draw attention to some of their problems. Historically, Muslim interests have been better represented by the Labour Party than fledgling Islamic organizations. The TUC is a national umbrella group representing the majority of British trade unions. Fifty-eight unions representing 6.5 million members are affiliated with the TUC, and this umbrella group has historically served as an important source of support for the Labour Party.[114] Although scholarship on Muslim participation in the TUC remains scarce, many British Muslims are members of the organization.[115]

In general, Muslim electoral loyalty to Labour is high.[116] In the late 1990s, there were 160 local British Muslim councilors, and British minorities and Muslims voted overwhelmingly for the Labour Party. The Party breakdown was as follows: 153 Labour, 6 Liberal, and 1 Conservative.[117] Muslims are represented at various levels in the Labour Party leadership, especially in districts with significant Muslim concentrations.[118] In Birmingham, the Labour Party's local managing committee included 13 Muslims, and significant numbers of Muslims were reflected in the Labour rank and file in the late 1980s.[119] Muslim voters and candidates played a part in securing the Labour majority on the Birmingham city council as early as the 1980s.[120] Following Labour's endorsement of the Iraq War of 2003, many Muslim voters transferred their patronage to the Liberal Democrats. Wars in Afghanistan and Iraq, along with immigration matters, were important issues in the 2005 election, particularly for Muslim voters.[121]

Despite some gains, British Muslim interests are not well-represented in the British political system.[122] For example, Labour's British councilors have expressed strong concerns that the Labour Party has failed to represent the issues that concern many Muslims, such as the problem of Muslim exclusion and discrimination in the UK.[123] As a result, British Muslims remain generally distrustful of the government. Additionally, Muslims remain quite underrepresented among elected officials. Following the 2010 national election, the number of Muslim MPs doubled to eight (out of 650), including several Muslim women. Despite the gains, this amounted to only to 1.2 percent of all MPs, whereas Muslims made up about 5 percent of the UK's population.[124]

Thus, despite some encouraging signs with regards to social integration, London's Muslims and Pakistanis are poor, marginalized, and discriminated against, which is likely to make them more vulnerable to radicalization. While it is now well-proven that a low socioeconomic status is not a primary driver for violent radicalization,[125] socioeconomic deprivation has been a reason for some Muslims to turn to fringe leaders and groups. Largely due to the perception that Muslim needs are not appropriately addressed, there exists a mutual distrust between London's Muslims and Pakistanis and the British government. Participation in the TUC and Labour has enabled British Muslims and Pakistanis to shed light on some of their grievances.

However, many British Muslims feel that the political officials have not paid adequate attention to their needs. Muslims are similarly underrepresented among the elected officials, although the number of Muslims politicians has recently increased, which offers reasons for cautious optimism. Furthermore, Muslims are generally similarly disappointed with local Islamic organizations, many of whom lack capable leadership and grassroots support. Additionally, in contrast to Arab Muslims in Detroit (for more, see the following chapter), civil society inter-group ties—capable of mitigating the negative effects of economic deprivation—are weak in London. For example, the Muslim Safety Forum, which from 2001–2011 organized regular meetings in London involving police officers and representatives from Muslim organizations (and which was later succeeded by the London Muslim Communities Forum) failed to build adequate trust.[126]

Migrant Communities: Moderate and Radical Leaders, Ties to Radicals Abroad

While there has been proliferation of both moderate and radical Muslim and Pakistani leaders, there is still a lack of well-established leaders who could command a following of significant segments of the British Muslim community. Although leaders commonly denounce the wars, they legitimize a wide variety of responses to it (including both peaceful and violent means). Finally, the two most important community variables explaining spillover are the presence of radical leaders and groups, and transnational connections with radical networks abroad. The presence of radical groups at home can lead to violent protests, and radical networks abroad can provide both leadership and paramilitary training to those British individuals willing to engage in political violence.

Moderate and Radical Leaders, and their Views on Wars in Afghanistan, Iraq

Key London Muslim and Pakistani leaders consist of a combination of Muslim organizations, mosques, and influential leaders. A number of Muslims perceive that there is a lack of well-established leaders trusted and endorsed by notable segments of London's Muslims. There may be leaders on certain issues—such as Imams on religious issues or certain members of parliament on political issues like Kashmir and Palestine—yet there is a shortage of well-rounded community leaders. Furthermore, although the vast majority of leaders denounce wars in Afghanistan and Iraq as unjust, they provide diverse suggestions of what community reactions should be to the conflicts. As a result, the lack of capable mainstream leadership has created an opening for radical fringe leaders to spread their messages and gain followings.

A 2009 UK government-sanctioned study found that there are few community leaders, and that there is a tendency for public institutions to deal with individuals who self-proclaim community leadership, regardless of their grassroots support base.[127] For example, Iqbal Sacrani, the former chair of the MCB, is highly regarded in the community. So are his successors, Dr. Abdul Bari and Farooq Murad. Some perceive East London's MP, George Galloway (a Christian), as a Muslim community leader in London due to his perceived support for Kashmir and other issues his Muslim constituents care about. Drs. Tariq Ramadan and Abdel Wahab al-Effendi, and other scholars, offer points of reference in debates regarding issues that are important in Muslim and Pakistani communities. Nevertheless, while many groups and individuals claim to represent British Muslims and Pakistanis, representative community leaders with a great deal of grassroots support are few and far between. In fact, public opinion polls of Western Muslims commonly show that there is not a Muslim organization that would represent majority interests.[128] For example, Shamiul Joarder, with the Muslim Safety Forum, lamented that the British government works closely with and assumes that organizations like the Quilliam represent British Muslims, while in reality, "some people I know spit when they hear Quilliam name."[129] His criticism is shared by some of the others, who are suspicious of Muslim organizations which—like Quilliam—have cultivated close ties with the government. Some believe that British Muslim organizations may compromise their integrity by working closely with—and accepting money from—the government.

Meanwhile, virtually all Muslim organizations in the UK are organized around either a unifying theme of common religion or an advocacy of homeland issues; therefore, such groups fail to represent a sizeable part of British Muslims, those who are only slightly religious, and those members who are no longer interested in the affairs of their former homelands.[130] As a result, much of the available research excludes those Muslims who have only slight associations with religious organizations.[131] Furthermore, some interviewees criticized community leadership for its incompetence and unaccountability, as well as sectarian divides in mosques, and undemocratic decision-making. Several female interviewees claimed to be underrepresented, as the community leaders tend to be men who either: (1) tend to focus on bigger political issues, instead of local community bread-and-butter issues, which are more important; or (2) discriminate against women.

In the absence of strong mainstream leadership, fringe groups have managed to receive some support. Hizb ut-Tahrir is known to recruit disaffected Muslims outside of mosques and on college campuses. Al-Muhajiroun and Islam4UK have recruited followers by using claims that the mainstream groups do not take enough action to protect the interests of British Muslims. Radical leaders from abroad have conveyed their messages over the Internet. Speeches by radical Omar Bakri Muhammad, the ousted former head of Al-Muhajiroun, are available online, where they remain popular in certain circles. Sageman (2008) observes that Internet sources and extremist "online leaders" play an important role in radicalizing Muslims in the West.

The rising availability of new kinds of electronic communication and social networking tools are empowering new kinds of leaders. One such leader is the controversial broadcaster Yvonne Riddley, who organized spontaneous protests against Israel's 2008–9 incursion into Gaza using social networking sites such as Facebook and Twitter, and text messaging. Activities took place in front of the US embassy in London. Riddley complained that she felt obligated to make this move due to a lack of activism by Muslim leaders in London, whom she perceived as overly law-abiding citizens. When the Israeli invasion in Gaza was ongoing in 2008–9, she went to Muslim leaders to ask for their help and support. She further added that when "Anti-Gaza protests were started by people, the leaders followed."[132]

Instead of extending their support, leaders spoke of a need to get protest permits from the police and take other preparatory and potentially lengthy actions before protests could be carried out. Riddley decided to call the police and inform them that she would advertise a protest via Facebook to her friends. When asked how many people would show up for the protest, she told the police that she only invited her friends. She was expecting a several dozen people, yet 4,000 showed up.[133] The journalist has used "new-media" tools (Facebook and Twitter) to promote protests many times since then. Additionally, text messages and electronic means of communication have enabled more effective action by Islamic fringe groups. For example, Islamist Anjem Choudary has used text messaging to advertise potentially controversial events with only a little prior notice.[134]

Furthermore, some studies have recorded a rapid proliferation of radical Islamic websites in recent years, have expressed concerns that the presence of such websites could lead to self-radicalization by disaffected Muslims.[135] However, studies and public statements by British officials overwhelmingly indicate that radical issues appeal only to a small minority of British Muslims.[136] In sum, despite numerous organizations and self-proclaimed Muslim and Pakistani leaders, many of London's Muslims feel underrepresented. To some extent, the weakness of mainstream leadership has created an environment in which fringe leaders and radical groups can gain some support.

Furthermore, community leaders almost unequivocally denounce wars in Afghanistan and Iraq as unjust—yet beyond that, no clear message emerges. Mainstream groups tend to criticize the wars and question if the War on Terror can be equated to a War on Islam. Angry Islamist groups (including HT, Islam4UK, and CagePrisoners) equate the War on

Terror with a War on Islam. Muslim mainstream as well as fringe groups articulate democratic means of expression, including lobbying and marching. Fringe Islamist groups, however, tend to engage in provocative and violent protests in order to gain media attention. Interestingly, although all mainstream leaders denounce terrorism on UK soil, some of them imply that political violence is permissible under certain instances; for example, to counter Israel in the Occupied Palestinian Territories. Mustafa's (2015, 172–175) study of young British Muslims found very similar results: Most of her respondents noted that Palestinians' political violence is justified due to the extensive grievances they face, whereas terrorist attacks in the West are not justified, because the key purpose of terrorists is to attack—not to defend.

Similarly, while known to be on the more "hawkish" side of British Muslims, influential broadcaster Yvonne Riddley denounces violence and asks for restraint in demonstrations in London, while legitimizing violence in some other places. She made a distinction about under what conditions violence is acceptable, as she denounced terrorism in the UK but endorsed it in certain other parts of the Muslim world: "In short, [the 7/7 attack] is a criminal act of terrorism. Not to be confused with a legitimate *jihad* in Palestine [or] Afghanistan where people protect lands that are occupied."[137] Meanwhile, violent Muslim extremist leaders call for terrorist acts against the UK in response to British foreign policy towards Afghanistan and Iraq. Such demands are stated in certain radical protests, on violent Muslim extremist websites, and during clandestine meetings with followers.

Mainstream leaders and activist tend to encourage democratic means of protest. For example, Tehmina Kazi, a liberal Muslim youth leader with the British Muslims for Secular Democracy, insisted that the best way for political activism is through large letter-writing campaigns, and she noted that there would be less political violence if the government would be more responsive to peaceful, democratic activism.[138] She explained that political violence occurs in some instances when protesters' passions spill over, and in instances when Muslim activists are confronted by far-right activists. Some Muslim and Pakistani leaders adopt provocative protest methods to gain popularity, as in the case of Anjem Choudary: "With the amount of attention he gets one would think he has ten times the following that he really does . . . The more moderate voices . . . we get some coverage . . . but it's not the same league."[139] She further insisted that radical Muslim leaders play a major role in radicalization and further alienation of the youth. Some other Muslim groups, including the Radical Middle Way and the Active Change Foundation, are actively involved in struggles to de-radicalize British Muslims.

Islamist groups also promote nonviolent expressions of protest. A Hizb activist noted that "Hizb demonstrations are against interference of the Western Governments in the Muslim world, to call for *Khilafah*, speak against colonial foreign policy and aid brothers in whatever way you can . . . Muslims have a message. Make clear to audience we're well behaved and followers know this. It's un-Islamic to have violence." Hizb is known to organize regular debates, demonstrations, pickets, and protests. The HT activist further explained that the purpose of such actions is to provide Muslims with outlets for their emotions, and to lead by example: "People in Egypt see protests in London for Gaza via media, [and] feel inspired."

The HT activist's position on Iraq is clear: the war is unjust. "There was a confusion among the British Muslims about how to react to Gulf War I. Iraq was much more clear—especially after the initial 'shock and awe.' The war was unfair." A Hizb leader during the organization's conference in Birmingham on August 2, 2009, similarly stated that: "The conflict now in Pakistan matters because it's on the forefront of war against Islam. What's the appropriate action? Education, knowing how to support Islam." In short, Islamist groups like Hizb often see conflicts with Western involvement through Islamic lenses. As such, the conflicts necessarily involve the Western intruder on one hand, and the Muslim world on the other.

For Islamist Anjem Choudary: "The main purpose of anything you do . . . a demonstration, a procession . . . is to please Allah."[140] He uses propagates Islam through the Internet, processions, demonstrations, conferences, leafleting, distribution of booklets, talks, and chat-rooms. Nevertheless, Choudary would endorse more aggressive expressions of protest, if he could ensure that they would take place without violence:

> None of our protests have really been that violent. But if . . . we would have a demonstration outside the Chinese embassy and we could occupy the embassy and draw more attention to it and pass the message without killing anyone or harming anyone, then that would be great.[141]

Meanwhile, Choudary's endorsement of nonviolence remained ambivalent, as he refused to condemn individuals committing terrorist acts in the name of Islam, while insisting that such individuals were convinced of the legitimacy of their acts:

> I may believe that for me it's not allowed because I have a covenant of security. But they will assess their own situation. And if they don't believe that they have one . . . they do something under that pretext.[142]

Overall, a desire to gain attention was commonly a leading cause behind provocative and violent protests. For example, Peter Neumann, with the International Centre for the Study of Radicalisation and Political Violence

(ICSR), asserted: "Choudary probably has 200 to 300 supporters in the UK, yet based on the media coverage received, he could be perceived as being one of the most visible Muslims in the UK. Media exaggerates his importance."[143] Yvonne Riddley explained that the "media continues to interview hard-lining Islamists and radicals," while she keeps on asking herself, "Why do we interview these people?"[144]

Chris Doyle elaborated on how the media gives undue attention to radical Islamists:

> John Reed, home secretary, went to announce a new policy change towards relations with Muslim communities and was heckled by Trevor Brooks [A.K.A. notorious British Islamist Abu Izzadeen] . . . Trevor came and heckled, and the next day was interviewed for 10–15 min on "Today's" program which is the leading flagship program on BBC. He basically stole the story by just simply heckling the home secretary. My problem is the profile that's given to those Muslims. Abu Hamza is probably the most famous Muslim in the country. He's sort of a made for cartoon figure. His face . . . you couldn't conjure up a better person to inspire fear . . .. Many Muslims in this country got quite upset that he got such a disproportionately high coverage. And he's not a little bit representative of the majority Muslims here. In a media driven age, if you shout and scream the loudest and come out with the most extreme comments, you get heard. Newspapers have to sell. Sensation sells.[145]

Shamiul Joarder expressed a similar view:

> Certain people would get a lot of media attention . . . [the] likes of Anjem Choudary . . . media, government whoever is giving them this airspace to talk. But, once again, there are many, many, many people who disagree with him, but they don't get exposure. We don't have these slots on Sky and BBC anymore. There is a number of young Muslims who don't know what to do, it's important for them to know different ways to get engaged, Choudary is not the only political active person, Muslim, out there.[146]

A senior general Muslim leader in London, Kashmiri by national origin, argued that the "media provokes fringe groups. For example, [the March 2009 provocative Islam4UK protest in] Luton was covered extensively, Choudary thrives on this attention. He does it for such attention." The Kashmiri leader further asserted: "Radical leaders, like Choudary, would die a sudden death if media would stop paying attention to them." He retold a story of a recent event where an Islamist group organized a pro-*Sharia* event. Some 40 people showed up, yet there were no media representatives. The organizers became quite angry because the media was not present. The interviewee noted that in May 2008, there was a Muslim event during which some women questioned an Imam about sexism. There was no coverage of this event, whereas Choudary's provocative events tend to be widely covered by the media.

Peaceful protests can become violent if angry and conservative fringe Islamist groups participate in them. Such groups can promote a more confrontational approach to demonstrating, which, in turn, can lead to political violence. Fringe groups can "hijack" peaceful protests and encourage the protesters' disobedience, or these groups can organize their own provocative protests. For example, activist Shamiul Joarder remembered past instances where some individuals in the back rows of a demonstration attempted to provoke violence with aggressive actions or rhetoric. He stated that mainstream Muslim groups have been struggling hard to ensure that such voices are properly silenced.

Furthermore, as witnessed during the Bradford riots of 2001, the presence of hardline groups from the other side can also change a peaceful protest into a violent one. Additionally, frequently violent anti-Muslim demonstrators from British far-right groups, like the English Defence League, can indirectly drive Muslims to radicalize.[147] In a number of instances, anti-war protests organized by Muslim groups have turned violent when the protesters were either verbally or physically attacked by radical groups far-right groups. At other times, counter-protests of far-right groups, including the English Defence League and Stop the Islamification of Europe, have clashed with Muslim-organized protests. In 2008, the annual Islamic Human Rights Commission's pro-Palestinian march in London experienced an outbreak of violence as the protesters were attacked by baton-wielding individuals from a far-right group. Chris Doyle similarly claimed that: "It's highly annoying for peaceful protesters if a small group comes to cause trouble. Occasionally, there will be some hardline pro-Israeli groups as well . . . that stir things up and vice versa. Pro-Israeli march will be countered by pro-Palestinians."[148]

Shamiul Joarder explained that there are usually very few individuals responsible for violence in protests.[149] For example, during the prophet Muhammad cartoon controversy there were demonstrations that ended in violence. He claimed that the violence occurred because mainstream Muslim organizations did not react as quickly as they should have:

> People need to vent their anger as well, feel that they need to do something. We were slow to react. Other people and individuals with misguided views decided to take streets . . . even if their numbers were in tens, that's all on front page. Week later when we went to Trafalgar square, that hardly got any public, that was completely peaceful . . . Important to organize events quickly . . . otherwise others will instigate what's not correct."[150]

British Muslims and Pakistanis denounce wars in Afghanistan and Iraq, but they are divided on legitimate means of response. The vast majority of British Muslim leaders denounce political violence in the UK, but some of them endorse violence under certain circumstances. Finally, a few violent extremists, drawing on only miniscule support from London's Muslims and Pakistanis, advocate more hostile tactics.

Ties with Radical Groups, Networks Abroad

Many Islamic activists and radicals sought refuge in Europe in the 1980s and 1990s.[151] The 1979 Islamic Shia revolution in Iran and the combined efforts of the Gulf States to promote Sunni Islam helped to craft the belief that Islam can bring about change and the establishment of more equitable societies.[152] Some British Muslims and Pakistanis are involved with non-violent radical groups, and a very small number of them have taken part in terrorist plots.

The 1989 Soviet withdrawal from Afghanistan and subsequent Afghani immigration to the UK paved the way for the infusion of violent extremism into England.[153] The Afghan War veteran home states in the Middle East and North Africa commonly prevented the return of their natives because they were aware that they had become the target of these *mujahideen.*[154] Many of these "Afghanis" fled to the UK, France, and Germany, among other European countries.

Fleeing dissidents from oppressive Muslim regimes frequently found their home in the UK during the years leading up to 9/11. Hizb ut-Tahrir[155] reached its peak of popularity in the late 1990s, a time when it was the most overtly militant group in the UK.[156] Mainstream Muslim organizations did not criticize radicals, such as Al-Muhajiroun, until after 9/11.[157] In the post 9/11 era, radicals have received disproportional amounts of public and media attention, which is not justified when considering their limited following.

Nevertheless, while it is still being debated whether or not groups like Hizb ut-Tahrir and Al-Muhajiroun serve as "conveyer belts to terrorism," the highest number of radicalized young British men is among Pakistanis, even though only small minorities of British Pakistanis sympathize with violent, extremist ideology or have been involved with terrorism.[158] Although apparently no former British members of Hizb have been involved with terrorism, the group's former non-British members include the 9/11 mastermind, Khalid Sheikh Mohammed, and Al-Qaeda in Iraq's former leader, Abu Musab al-Zarqawi.[159] Thus, the empirical evidence points to a paradox: Membership in Hizb ut-Tahrir-Britain does not encourage violent extremism, whereas membership in the group's non-European branches does.[160] At the same time, in some instances, British Muslims have self-radicalized.

Islamist Moazzam Begg believes that individuals who engage in provocative protest activism truly believe that they are protecting the rights of their Muslim brothers and sisters.[161] Consistent with findings of Olivier Roy (1998), he insisted that many of those who have engaged in Islamic terrorism have self-radicalized through the internet, on sites such as YouTube:

> In the past, you sit with a group of people, they show you videos and you may speak to somebody who radicalize you perhaps they go to Pakistan or Afghanistan . . . but it's not the case anymore. Because of Youtube. You can just sit there all day long without referring to any scholar, any group of people, and self-radicalize. You can carry the bombing out yourself, make your weapons yourself, you can do whatever you want.[162]

It is very important that virtually every recent post-9/11 terrorist plot has had connections with Pakistani militias operating in Kashmir.[163] Terrorist motivation may be transnational (e.g., opposition to the Iraq War), religious (e.g., a desire to avenge perceived injustices committed against the *ummah*), or inspired by invocation of symbolic appeals.[164] However, mere attachment to a certain ideology or to certain beliefs cannot alone explain why some individuals become violent radicals.[165] Instead, individuals who are capable of carrying out such acts have been linked to—and have received training from—radical networks abroad, in this case in Pakistan. Nesser (2006) finds that a significant number of terrorist cells in Europe are built around former *mujahideen* fighters in wars in Afghanistan and Iraq. One study estimates that one out of nine European fighters in wars in the Middle East has attempted to engage in terrorism after return.[166] Thousands for Western Muslim fighters are currently fighting with extremist groups in the Middle East. Those of them that will return will likely pose similar security challenges.

In summary, British migrants and Muslims are inadequately represented in British political institutions. In addition, the British Islamic community is undergoing an internal crisis of leadership, and the weaknesses of mainstream leaders and organizations empower radicals. Radical groups receive a fairly limited following among London's Muslims and Pakistanis, but they are present. Whereas some would-be terrorists may self-radicalize and even attempt criminal acts, more threatening terrorists have been linked to radical networks in Kashmir and Pakistan. The concluding section will summarize the key finding of this chapter and will seek to answer the question of why Muslim communities in London could not prevent radicalization of a small number of individuals.

Conclusion: Street Protests, Terrorism, and Anti-War Mobilization

The Rushdie Affair of 1988 was the first time that British Muslims of South Asian background protested on a mass scale. They protested in a similar manner to how they would have protested in their home countries—with much passion, burning of flags, and some violence. In the years to follow, there was little Muslim mobilization until the Iraq War of 2003. The anti-Iraq War protests were very different: Major Muslim and Pakistani groups organized orderly street protests and built alliances with groups on the political left.

Pakistani communities in the Greater London area have been active in voicing their opposition to the wars in Afghanistan and Iraq. Groups with a significant presence of British Pakistanis, ranging from the mainstream Muslim Council of Britain to the radical Hizb ut-Tahrir, have organized some of the protests; some other expressions of mobilization have led to repulsive terrorist acts.

Despite the denunciation of violence by the vast majority of community leaders, British Pakistanis and individuals with links to radical groups in Pakistan have been involved in a significant portion of terrorist plots, allegedly in reaction to British foreign policy and conflicts abroad. Overall, migration and security policies allowing inflow of violent radicals, the presence of radical groups, and transnational links with violent radical abroad, are all factors that contributed to the occurrence of reactive conflict spillover. Although poor Muslim economic integration, discrimination, and inadequate political representation do not cause political violence alone, they do add to the creation of an environment where some Muslims are more open to listening to radical ideas.

Nevertheless, it should be questioned why Muslim communities in London (and the United Kingdom) could not prevent the radicalization of a handful of misguided individuals and groups. First, radicals that were inclined towards violence were already present within London and the United Kingdom. In fact, immigration of violent radicals was not seen as a security threat to the UK until 9/11/2001 (or even 7/7/2005). Many such radicals were members of opposition movements in their home countries or members of terrorist groups. The very presence (and agitation) of such individuals served as a structural factor that made political violence by the said radicals—and radicalization of some other British Muslims—more likely. Additionally, the lack of economic integration and the existing discrimination served as additional factors that helped the radical voices gain additional followers. Pupcenoks and McCabe (2013) show how radical Muslim groups in the UK appeal to the existing socioeconomic problems in British Muslim communities to gain followers. In such contexts, some individuals self-radicalize and even attempt to conduct acts of terror. Fortunately, such so-called lone wolf terrorists have been quite amateurish and incompetent in the past (e.g., see Mueller and Stewart 2012).

Likewise, the presence of radical groups within communities, and connections with radical networks abroad, create conditions conducive to radicalization for some individuals. Protests and other political activities organized by radical, non-violent groups, such as Al-Muhajiroun or Islam4UK, can lead to violence. Furthermore, some former members of Al-Muhajiroun have later joined terrorist cells. Connections with radical networks abroad are particularly perilous, as through such ties would-be terrorists can receive paramilitary training and ideological guidance that may enable a few of them to attempt to commit terrorist attacks. Such extremists present greater threat than the lone wolves.

The next chapter will turn to community activism among Detroit Arab Muslims, another comparable, politically mobilized, yet largely peaceful Muslim community. How to explain a relative lack of foreign policy-inspired political violence in Detroit?

Notes

1 Giry 2006; Saggar 2006.
2 Peter Bergen and Paul Cruickshank, "Al Qaeda-on-Thames: UK Plotters Connected," *The Washington Post*, Guest Analysis, April 30, 2007.
3 E.g., see O'Duffy 2008, 41.
4 Mustafa 2015, 137.
5 The Irish Times, "Islamic Leaders Call on Muslims to Demonstrate," October 12, 2001.
6 The Ottawa Citizen, "People Worldwide Protest Bombings: Tens of Thousands Demonstrate in European Cities," October 14, 2001.
7 Graham Johnson, "350,000 Say No To War; London Protest Blasts PM's Saddam Plan," *Sunday Mirror*, September 29, 2002, 19.
8 " 'Million' march against Iraq war," *BBC News*, February 16, 2003; Birt 2005, 104.
9 " 'Million' march against Iraq war," *BBC News*, February 16, 2003.
10 Rowan Walker, "News Briefing: Protest Thousands Take Part in Anti-War Rallies," *The Observer*, February 25, 2007.
11 Michael Seamark and David Wilkes, "Prophet Cartoon Protest Leader is Found Guilty of Inciting Murder," *Daily Mail*, January 6, 207.
12 Stewart Tendler, "Cartoon Protester Stirred Race Hate," *The Times*, November 10, 2006.
13 The English Defence League (EDL) was created in response to an Islam4UK protest march on March 10, 2009. It is a social organization promising to defend the English working class from the alleged dual threats of elite-led policies of multiculturalism and the Islamization of Britain. The group itself is composed of a patchwork of discontented citizens, football club supporters, and former members of far-right political parties like the British National Party (BNP).
14 John F Burns, "Britain Moves to Ban Islamic Group," *The New York Times*, January 13, 2010.
15 It is believed that Islam4UK has since resurfaced under the name Muslims Versus Crusades.

16 As compiled by the author in summer of 2010.
17 The same individuals were also convicted of another failed attempt to carry out a similar attack on the Glasgow airport on June 30, 2007.
18 Schwartz 2008.
19 Leiken 2009, 187.
20 Kirby 2007.
21 O'Duffy 2008, 38.
22 O'Duffy 2008, 38.
23 O'Duffy 2008, 41.
24 Shipman 2009.
25 Gannon 2010.
26 www.telegraph.co.uk/news/worldnews/asia/pakistan/8042774/US-drone-strike-kills-five-German-militants-in-Pakistan.html
27 MSNBC 2010b.
28 Express Tribune 2010; The 2005 London metro bombers were also connected to Luton.
29 Abrams 2008.
30 Pargeter 2008, 146–152.
31 Haubrich 2010, 191.
32 Hellyer 2007, 249.
33 Leiken 2005.
34 Segell 2006, 46.
35 Peter Bergen and Paul Cruickshank, "Al Qaeda-on-Thames: UK Plotters Connected," *The Washington Post*, Guest Analysis, April 30, 2007.
36 Alan Cowell and Douglass Jehl, "Police Ask Public to Help Trace Suspect; Homemade Explosive Now Suspected," *The New York Times International*, July 15, 2005.
37 Elaine Sciolino and Don Van Natta Jr., "2004 British Raid Sounded Alert on Pakistani Militants," *New York Times International*, July 14, 2005.
38 "Three guilty of airline bomb plot," *BBC News*, September 7, 2009.
39 Boisre 2006.
40 E.g., see Clarke 2007; Pargeter 2008.
41 Kaye and Charlton 1990; Schuster and Solomos 2004.
42 Bloch 2000.
43 Hatton 2011, 45.
44 Migration Watch UK 2004.
45 Hatton 2011, 94.
46 Peter Wilkinson, "UK's 'Broken' Asylum System Remains Battleground," *CNN*. November 21, 2010.
47 Schuster and Solomos 2004.
48 Hatton 2011, 45.
49 Hatton (2011, 67) quotes the UK Immigration Minister, Liam Byrne, proclaiming in November 2006 that "asylum applications for the year to date are at their lowest level since 1993 and we intend to build on this progress."
50 Hatton 2011, 48–9.
51 Pargeter 2008, 158.
52 Baxter 2007.
53 Gerges 2005; Kepel 2002.
54 Harvey 2000, 370.
55 Clarke 2007, 3.
56 Cesari 2004, 106.
57 Pargeter 2006, 734; also see Sageman 2004, 144–145.
58 Clarke 2007, 4.
59 Hakeem, Haberfeld and Verma 2012, 23–40.

60 Bonino 2012.
61 Klausen 2009a, 9.
62 Klausen 2009a, 14.
63 Klausen 2009a; UK Home Office 2012.
64 Klausen 2009a.
65 Mayor's Office for Policing and Crime 2013; UK CONTEST 2011.
66 Bonino 2012, 15.
67 Mumisa 2010.
68 Bonino 2012, 16
69 Briggs 2010, 7.
70 Briggs 2010, 8.
71 Gelb 2009, 5.
72 Quotations in the original. Source: Brighton 2007, 4.
73 Engage 2009.
74 Engage 2011.
75 Spalek 2005.
76 Spalek 2005.
77 Tom Morgan, "Police Could Face Legal Action over 'Unfair' Searches." *Independent*. March 15, 2010.
78 Ansari 2006; Islamic Human Rights Commission 2009; Majeed 2010.
79 Economist 2011b.
80 E.g., see Ansari 2006.
81 Briggs 2010.
82 UK PREVENT Strategy 2011; Klausen 2009.
83 Anwar and Bakhsh 2003; Cesari 2004, 23; Dancygier 2010, 16; Gillian-Ray 2014, 71–72; Office of the Deputy Prime Minister 2006; Saggar 2009.
84 Gilliat-Ray 2014, 72.
85 E.g., see Dancygier 2010, 62–101.
86 Heath and Demireva 2014, 177.
87 Heath and Demireva 2014, 169.
88 Open Society Institute 2004.
89 O'Duffy 2008, 40.
90 Daily Mail 2007.
91 Jackson and Doerschler 2012, 143–167.
92 Cesari 2004, 23.
93 Regeneration and Renewal Organization 2003.
94 O'Duffy 2008, 40.
95 Office of the Mayor of London 2006, 41.
96 Ballard 1990, 228.
97 Vidino 2010, 10.
98 Change Institute 2009; Economist 2006.
99 Amnesty International 2012; Jackson and Doerschler 2012; Open Society Institute 2010.
100 E.g., see Modood and Calhoun 2005; Weller 2006; Jackson and Doerschler 2012, 105–120.
101 Jackson and Doerschler 2012, 109, 111.
102 Andrew McCcorkell, "Muslims Call for Action against Hate Crimes," *The Independent*, June 12, 2011.
103 Jackson and Doerschler 2012, 111.
104 Pew 2006, 5.
105 Pew 2006, 8–9.
106 Lambert and Githens-Mazer 2010.
107 Lambert and Githens-Mazer 2010, 32–33.
108 See Convay 1997; Allen 2010; Esposito and Kalin 2011.

109 Greenslade 2005.
110 Abbas 2001, 245.
111 Meer and Modood 2009.
112 Pew 2006, pages 6, 8 and 2.
113 Pew 2006, 7.
114 However, the TUC has lost much of its influence in the Labour Parties following the reforms within Labour in the 1990s.
115 Trades Union Congress 2006.
116 Purdam 2001, 148.
117 Purdam 2001, 149.
118 Joly 1995, 91.
119 Ibid.
120 Joly 1995, 111.
121 Mustafa 2015, 125.
122 Cohen and Layton-Henry 1997.
123 Purdam 2001, 154.
124 Gilliat-Ray 2014, 86.
125 E.g., see Cesari 2011.
126 Lambert 2011, 67.
127 UK Communities and Local Government 2009, 47.
128 E.g., see Pew 2006, Gallup 2011, 25.
129 Shamiul Joarder, interview, August 19, 2009.
130 Abbas 2007, 9; UK Communities and Local Government 2009, 47.
131 Gilliat-Ray 2015, 65.
132 Yvonne Riddley interview, August 5, 2009.
133 Yvonne Riddley, interview, August 5, 2009.
134 Anjem Choudary interview, August 10, 2009.
135 Abbas 2007, 224; Sageman 2008.
136 UK Foreign and Commonwealth Office/Home Office 2004; Mogahed and Nyiri 2007; However, some studies warns that there remains a worrying level of support for radicalism among British Muslims—see Brachman 2009; O'Duffy 2008.
137 Yvonne Riddley, interview, August 5, 2009.
138 Tehmina Kazi interview, August 12, 2009.
139 Tehmina Kazi, interview, August 12, 2009.
140 Anjem Choudary interview, August 10, 2009.
141 Anjem Choudary, interview, August 10, 2009.
142 Anjem Choudary, interview, August 10, 2009.
143 Peter Neumann, personal communication, August 5, 2009.
144 Yvonne Ridley, interview, August 5, 2009.
145 Chris Doyle interview, August 18, 2009.
146 Shamiul Joarder interview, August 19, 2009.
147 Ambrogi 2010.
148 Chris Doyle, interview, August 18, 2009.
149 Shamiul Joarder interview, August 19, 2009.
150 Shamiul Joarder, interview, August 19, 2009.
151 Pargeter 2008.
152 Pargeter 2008, 4.
153 Leiken 2004, 64.
154 Pargeter 2008, 14.
155 For an authoritative study on Hizb Ut-Tahrir, endorsed by the group's own leadership, see Taji-Farouki 1996.
156 Mehmood Naqshbandi, interview, August 31, 2009.
157 Baxter 2007.

158 Supporters of both of these groups predominately consist of Pakistanis; for conveyor belt to terrorism, see Baran 2004; Hamid 2007; Husain 2007; for how only small minorities of British Pakistanis sympathize with extremist ideology, see Nachmani 2009, 77.
159 Diane Macedo, "Radical Islamist Group is Returning to Chicago for Major Recruitment Drive," FoxNews.com, June 16, 2010.
160 However, Gruen (2011) disturbingly reports that in 2010 Hizb Ut-Tahrir's branches in several countries (including the UK) issued calls for Muslims to engage in armed conflict with Israel and the Coalition troops in Afghanistan. This exemplifies a significant change in the Hizb Ut-Tahrir-UK's rhetoric and its impacts are yet to be seen.
161 Moazzam Begg interview, August 24, 2009.
162 Moazzam Begg, interview, August 24, 2009.
163 Bhatt 2010.
164 Githens-Mazer 2008.
165 Lambert and Githens-Mazer 2010, 899.
166 Weaver 2015.

7 Generally Peaceful Protest
Arab Muslims in Detroit

For decades, sizeable and active Arab and Muslim communities have inhabited the metropolitan Detroit area. Much has been written about the development of increasingly influential Detroit Arab institutions, and their participation in local politics and affairs in former homelands. Scholars and activists have been debating whether Detroit's Arab community is exceptional or representative of Arab communities in America.[1]

This chapter shows that Detroit Arab Muslim protest politics, in reaction to events abroad, have been eclectic and peculiar. As opposed to many Muslim communities in the West, the community in Detroit[2] has often shown its opposition through cooperation and, for the most part, supported the American-led Iraq War 2003-2011. Christian Arabs from Iraq, known as Chaldeans, constitute half of the Arab population in Michigan; they also strongly supported the 2003 invasion of Iraq.[3] Local Shia Muslims, particularly of Iraqi background, constituted another bastion of support for the war. Despite notable political activism and mobilization, the community has not experienced reactive conflict spillover, and Detroit Arab Muslims have not been involved in terror plots elsewhere. In fact, this chapter provides further evidence that transnational political mobilization by Western Muslims is not necessarily related to extremism and radicalization.

Interestingly, even at moments when War on Terror conflicts abroad escalated, the community remained relatively uninvolved in political protest. This chapter will argue that the lack of activism in relation to Afghanistan and Iraq is largely due to benefits the conflicts have brought to the community in Detroit, and due to the support that the local Shia community and large segments of the Iraqi-American community expressed for the occupation of Iraq. The empirical evidence implies that it is easier to mobilize members of a community when a community is united on an issue. The strong and deep cleavage on the Iraq War has led to (1) apathy and (2) opposition to anti-American mobilization. Second, the Shia and Christian Iraqi Americans played a role similar to Cuban Americans and Soviet Jewish Americans—they belonged to a rare class of diasporas that was hostile to their state of origin, or, more precisely, hostile to the regime in that state, and were therefore supportive of aggressive US policy against their former home state.

This chapter describes and assesses Detroit's Arab and Muslim community's peaceful reactions to the wars in Afghanistan and Iraq. It assesses community activism on other key Middle Eastern conflicts to provide evidence that, in contrast to the tepid activism on the Iraq War, Detroit Muslims are capable of impressive mobilization. Furthermore, this chapter shows that Detroit has only experienced a quite limited reactive conflict spillover from wars in Afghanistan and Iraq due to the implementation of refugee and asylum policies aiming to prevent inflow of violent radicals, the lack of radical groups at home, and the absence of notable connections with radical networks abroad. Finally, despite economic deprivation, Detroit has eschewed radical politics largely due to extensive inter-group ties, and Muslim interests have been represented reasonably well through alliances between elected leaders and local Arab and Muslim representatives.

Detroit Arab Muslim Reactions to Conflicts in the Middle East, 2001–2010

American Arabs and Muslims have expressed concerns about Western involvement in the wars in Afghanistan and Iraq. American Muslim organizations have condemned the Iraq War, while vocal Detroit Muslim segments have supported it. Although there has been little activism in reaction to the situation in Afghanistan, Iraq is quite important to Detroit Muslims for several reasons. More visible, active, and influential segments of Detroit Muslims are Arabs who—in foreign policy matters, above all—care about developments in Arab countries. Furthermore, Detroit is home to a large and growing Iraqi American population, which for obvious reasons is expected to be more concerned about developments in Iraq.

Forty-nine thousand Iraqis came to the US in the 1990s as refugees from Saddam Hussein's regime, and their migration continued following the US-led invasion of Iraq in 2003.[4] In 2000, there were 31,927 Iraqi-born residents in Michigan, and 30,569 of them resided in Detroit.[5] An additional 41,000 Iraqi refugees, a large number of whom settled in Detroit, arrived in the US between 2000 and 2009.[6] However, religious and ethnic divisions within the Iraqi diaspora worldwide make it "inappropriate to invoke the term 'Iraqi' in describing it."[7] Community tensions were particularly notable after significant galvanizing events abroad.

Trigger events can be episodes associated with escalation of conflicts abroad, such as the American government's decision to go to war in Iraq in 2003, or the escalation of violence in Iraq from 2003–2006. Some specific triggers include the execution of Saddam Hussein and the bombing of the Samarra mosque, both in 2006. Triggers can be generated by intensified media coverage of a conflict or significant events (such as a meeting of certain world leaders, or attacks on significant religious or political landmarks). Reactions to conflicts abroad and reactive conflict spillover can also occur as a result of a build-up of certain events and situations.

London and Detroit both responded to the same conflicts abroad. However, responses to the same triggers were somewhat different. Similar to London, intensification of certain conflicts abroad brought many street protests in Detroit. More recently, Arab, Muslim, and local leftist organizations organized sizeable protest marches when conflicts escalated in Lebanon or Palestine. Unlike London, anti-Iraq War protests have been negligible and almost non-existent, due to a significant segment of Detroit Muslims who endorsed the war. More importantly, except for instances of vandalism following the execution of Saddam Hussein, no Detroit Muslims have been involved in political violence or terrorist plots.

The bombing of the mosque in Samarra and Saddam Hussein's execution served as major triggers for the escalation of tensions between Sunnis and Shias in the community. Otherwise, Detroit Muslims remained largely politically inactive regarding Afghanistan and Iraq. Political activism did not intensify in the 2003–2006 period, when it appeared that the coalition could lose the war, or during other points of escalation. Abed Hammoud, a Shia Arab Muslim of Lebanese descent, and a secular community leader involved with several local Arab organizations including the CONGRESS and AAPAC, explained the common perception that any anti-war activism was usually perceived as an endorsement of Saddam Hussein:

> Troops there [in Iraq], the policy of Bush administration was totally bad. Yet if I stand up and criticize that policy, some Iraqi refugees from Saddam, Saddam killed their family, are not willing to listen to the details of my argument, to see nuances and semantics of my argument. They say, "you're defending Saddam."[8]

As a result, Detroit's Arab and Muslim community remained deeply divided and inactive regarding the Iraq war.[9] In contrast to London, reactive conflict spillover in forms of violent protest and attempted terrorist acts has not taken place in Detroit. Nationally, 35.5 percent of Muslims had participated in a protest and 44.6 percent attended a rally.[10] Locally, Detroit's Muslims tend to be quite politically mobilized and active; however, visible reactions to the Iraq War and occupation include only two street protests. However, Detroit's Arab Muslims have been more involved in activism regarding two other key conflicts during the decade following 9/11: the 2006 Israel-Hezbollah war, and the 2008–2009 Israeli incursion into the Gaza Strip. Subsequently, this chapter provides evidence that the community is capable of being passionate and active about conflicts abroad, even if the Iraq War did not generate noteworthy activism.

Detroit has a long history of activism in opposition to American policy. Some have even suggested that challenging the direction of American foreign policy has been the status quo in the community.[11] The preferred way of expressing opinions, street protest, is slowly giving way to nascent lobbying attempts by Arab and Muslim groups, and online protest. Even in instances of sizable street protests, community activism has remained passionate yet self-constrained and always within the boundaries of the law.

A bulk of community activism concerning foreign causes has been reactive. Detroit's Arabs and Muslims have organized protests and rallies on certain foreign policy issues that are of concern to many Muslims, including the 2005 controversy over reports of a Koran being flushed down the toilet by American soldiers at the Guantanamo Bay detention facility, and Danish newspaper *Jyllands-Posten's* September 30, 2005 publication of cartoons ridiculing Prophet Muhammad.[12] Due to community pressures, local legislatures have taken largely symbolic measures in support of Muslim causes. The City of Dearborn's Council passed a resolution condemning Israeli attacks on civilians during the Gaza War in 2009.[13]

Street protests have been common in Detroit in instances when certain conflicts in the Middle East escalate (see Tables 7.1, 7.2, and 7.3). They are often organized by the CAAO, the Palestine Office-Michigan, MECAWI, and American organizations and individuals. The Palestine Office-Michigan, which actively supports the Palestinian cause, was created during the decade following 9/11. The CAIR and the ADC seek government support for Palestine and other foreign policy issues deemed important to American Muslims.

A popular venue that has hosted some of the most populous and well-known protests is Warren Avenue in Dearborn. Activities have taken place in numerous other venues in nearby towns and mosques as well. Protests tend to be planned ahead of time, and then advertised in mosques and Arab media sources, including the Arab News and popular local portal arabdetroit.com. Similar to recent protests elsewhere in the Western world, text messages and online networking tools have been widely used.

Table 7.1 Protests in Reaction to the Iraq War, 2001–2010[1]

Total Protest Count	Organizers of Protests	Themes of Protests	Key Demands of Protests
• two major protests supporting Iraq War (10/17/2002, 04/05/2003) • two major protests opposing Iraq War (10/17/2002, 04/05/2003)	• Wealthy Iraqi-Americans, Detroit Shia religious leaders • Mainstream Detroit anti-war group (MECAWI)	• Pro-war • Anti-war	• Remove Saddam Hussein • Do not invade Iraq • Withdraw from Iraq

Source:
1 Compiled by the author using the Lexis-Nexis Academic database and internet research (November 2010).

Table 7.2 Protests against Israel's Incursion into Lebanon, July–August 2006[1]

Total Protest Count	Organizers of Protests	Themes of Protests	Key Demands of Protests
• 30+ major anti-Israel protests (that is, daily protests during the duration of the conflict)	• Mainstream Detroit anti-war group (MECAWI) • Muslim and Arab groups (CAAO, AAPAC, ADC; Palestinian and Lebanese organizations)	• Anti-Israel	• Cessation of Israel's bombardment of Southern Lebanon • Demands that the US places pressure on Israel to stop the bombardment

Source:
1 Compiled by the author using the Lexis-Nexis Academic database and internet research (November 2010).

Table 7.3 Protests against Israel's Shelling of Gaza, Winter 2009[1]

Total Protest Count	Organizers of Protests	Themes of Protests	Key Demands of Protests
• Four major protests against Israel (12/2008–01/2009)	• Arab Muslim umbrella group (CAAO)	• Anti-Israel	• Stop Israel's bombardment of Gaza • Calls for the US to place pressure on Israel • Demands that the US stops providing financial and military aid to Israel • Demands that Egypt stops cooperation with Israel

Source:
1 Compiled by the author using the Lexis-Nexis Academic database and internet research (November 2010).

In addition to protests, the community holds regular awareness-raising events in the form of dinners, lectures, and cultural activities. Nevertheless, in recognition that street protests can have little impact on governmental foreign policy-making, in recent years Detroit Arabs and Muslims have paid increasing attention to awareness-raising activities and lobbying.

Many of the interviewees reflected on the evolution of community activism into more sophisticated forms of protest, such as lobbying. A Palestinian Muslim second-generation student activist at the UM-Dearborn explained:

> Besides raising funds for needy and getting food and medicines out there in Iraq, Afghanistan, Palestine, Lebanon, Pakistan . . . at the

beginning we were doing a mistake. At first, we only sent to the Middle East and Asia. Then we realized that we need to talk to our Congressmen, our senators.

A number of the interviewees suggested that protest politics have become less vocal following 9/11. In contrast to the past, the 2000s demonstrations did not resemble broad community events. Before 9/11, you could see families reuniting, whereas in the post 9/11 era protests have been less attended and public events have been visibly under more surveillance by the authorities.[14] Some of the interviewees expressed their reluctance to take part in public protest in the post-9/11 environment, where Muslim political activism is often viewed with suspicion by the government and mainstream media.

Arab and Muslim organizations and their leaders play a major role in organizing collective responses on foreign policy issues. Abed Hammoud is skeptical that street protests can influence foreign policy decision-making in the US. Yet he is quick to acknowledge that, under certain circumstances, everyday Muslims may call for a protest, and then it is the responsibility of the community leadership to organize one.[15] Hammoud was a key organizer of a 10,000 person-strong protest against the Israel-Hezbollah War in 2006. He agreed to take a lead role in the organization of the protest in response to public demands, and due to a concern that, without elite leadership, spontaneous protests could become disorderly, provocative, and violent.[16]

During the post-9/11 period, the largest expressions of political protest in Arabic Detroit focused on Palestine and Lebanon. Yet, by 2010, support for such activities had declined. Imad Hamad, the director of a local ADC office, and several other community leaders interviewed, noted that political activism and attendance at pro-Palestinian events had noticeably decreased following 9/11.[17] Interviewees identified two major factors for the drop in pro-Palestinian activism: lack of progress in Palestine despite years of activism for the cause, and post-9/11 American suspicion regarding any pro-Palestinian activism. Yet the decline of support for Palestine seems surprising because public opinion polls show that Detroit Arabs strongly care about the resolution of Arab-Israeli conflict,[18] and that issues surrounding Palestine are simultaneously advocated from humanitarian and Islamic points of view. In addition, the overall pro-Israel sentiment in the US makes it harder to gather support for anti-Israel activities, whereas comparatively more overt British anti-Israel sentiment makes such actions more likely in the UK.[19]

Those who perceive the Arab-Israeli conflict through religious lenses seek to promote the cause of fellow Muslims in Palestine or campaign for protection of holy mosques in Jerusalem. All interviewed local Shia Imams stated that they address the issue of Palestine in their sermons. Other Detroit Muslims condemned the miserable humanitarian situation of Palestinians. Several of the interviewees highlighted the importance of building interfaith coalitions to effectively counter human rights violations in Palestine. The community came together strongly during the Israel-Hezbollah War protests of 2006. Meanwhile, the Iraq occupation has remained a sensitive and important, yet divisive, issue.

Until recently, American Muslims have shown few signs of radicalization in the post 9/11 era.[20] The recruitment of Minneapolis-area Somalis into the Somali *al-Shabaab* militia, perceived as a terrorist organization by the US, served as a vivid wake-up call. Regardless, journalists, practitioners, and scholars have expressed concerns about the implications of homegrown radicalization.[21] Schanzer, Kurzman, and Moosa (2010) explain lack of radicalization among American Muslims due to the following five reasons: (1) relative financial success; (2) self-policing; (3) community-building by mosques and other community institutions; (4) political mobilization and participation; and (5) ongoing Americanization while preserving Islamic identity.

Nevertheless, a top-ranking Obama administration security official pronounced that, in 2009, the US counterterrorism efforts shifted from international to domestic terrorism.[22] By mid-2010, a third of all charged terrorist suspects have been American citizens.[23] Despite close government surveillance, there has been virtually no violent or illegal activism in Detroit in reaction to conflicts abroad.[24]

The extent of counter-terrorism measures undertaken by the US government has been limited to the investigation of a few area charities, and prosecution and deportation of a few individuals with alleged terrorist ties.[25] For example, in 2004, two Detroit Arab men were convicted "of conspiring to provide material support and resources to terrorists;" however, this conviction was overturned a few months later, and the charges were later thrown out altogether.[26] As of 2011, six Arab Americans with Detroit connections were found guilty "on charges related to providing material support for terrorism," and all of these cases involved support for Hezbollah.[27]

Muslim perpetrators targeted by law enforcement agencies in Detroit have been petty criminals, not Islamic would-be terrorists. In a notorious case, the FBI shot to death local Imam Luqman A. Abdullah during a raid on a Dearborn warehouse on October 28, 2009. The mission of FBI was to arrest Imam Abdullah and 10 of his supporters based on allegations concerning the sale of stolen property.[28] After opening fire on an FBI canine, the Imam was reportedly shot 21 times.

Local Islamic and civil rights groups called for an investigation immediately.[29] Detroit Mayor Dave Bing soon endorsed their appeals and a formal investigation was launched on February 2, 2010.[30] Although a tragic incident, the attention placed on the shooting illustrates that law enforcement agencies do not have higher-profile cases (such as individuals suspected of associations with terrorism) in the area.

Another notorious case involves an attempted aircraft bombing in 2009. On December 25, 2009, Umar Farouk Abdulmutallab, a Nigerian citizen, attempted to detonate plastic explosives hidden in his underwear in the name of Al-Qaeda while on board Northwest Airlines Flight 253 en route from Amsterdam to Detroit. Abdulmutallab spent about 20 minutes in the bathroom as it approached Detroit, and then covered himself with a blanket after returning to his seat. Other passengers then heard popping noises, smelled a foul odor, and some saw Abdulmutallab's trouser leg and the wall of the plane on fire. Fellow passenger Jasper Schuringa, a Dutch film director, subdued Abdulmutallab as flight attendants used fire extinguishers to douse the flames.[31] Nevertheless, while Abdulmutallab's attempted terrorist act placed Detroit in the spotlight, he did not have ties to the local Muslim community. Overall, except for some fundraising for Hezbollah, none of the multiple investigations and arrests have produced evidence that the community has connections with terrorism.[32]

In sum, whereas the war in Iraq was led by the US and the Coalition, the other two conflicts involved Israel and Palestinians. Therefore, it can be argued that American Arabs and Muslims may be more comfortable in showing political opposition in instances where the US is not a leading party to a conflict. However, public opinion polls show that American Muslims overwhelmingly oppose the Iraq War.[33] Additionally, Muslim communities in those European countries who were also members of the Coalition (particularly in the UK) tended to be vocal in their opposition to the War.[34] Instead, Detroit Arab Muslims visibly mobilize and take sides on hostilities abroad if the community holds a common view on the conflict involving one of their sending states, and if key local ethnic groups become actively involved in reactive political activism.

Pro- and Anti-Iraq War Protest Activism, 2001–2010

On the eve of the Iraq War in 2003, the United States as a whole and the Muslim community in Detroit in particular were torn between supporters and opponents of the war. According to mainstream sources, this conflict took the lives of more than 4,400 American soldiers and more than 100,000 Iraqis. The Detroit Arab and Muslim community's internal divisions were most evident during the period leading up to the war in 2002–2003 and during the months following the execution of former Iraqi dictator Saddam Hussein in 2006.

Leading up to the war, the media widely reported on only two protests held by Detroit Muslims. Each time, a larger anti-war protest was met by a smaller, but vocal, counter-protest supporting the war. Additional protests were organized by mainstream American groups, yet based on media reports and interviews with community leaders, only a few Muslims participated in those protests (and therefore they are not referenced

in Table 7.1). Furthermore, it is difficult to locate comprehensive information about the protests, as many of them were poorly covered by the
media.

During President George W. Bush's visit to Dearborn in the fall of
2002, some 500 people demonstrated outside the Ritz-Carlton Hotel in
Dearborn.[35] A number of Arab Americans were among the Michigan
Emergency Coalition against War and Injustice (MECAWI)-organized
protest. One of them criticized the pro-war protest across the street:

> Do I want the killing of thousands of people to get rid of a bully
> they created in the first place? They are blinded by Hussein. They are
> ignorant of what lies ahead. I'll bet in ten years a lot of those people
> will be carrying rifles against the US.[36]

Meanwhile, on the other side of the street, a group of about 100 predominantly Shia Iraqi Americans organized a counter-protest supporting
the war.[37] A number of wealthy Iraqis and Shia religious leaders, many of
them refugees from the Hussein's regime, were among pro-war demonstrators. The demonstrators called for the removal of Saddam Hussein's
regime through military means, and strongly endorsed the war. The second major pro-war protest took place on April 5, 2003. It was organized
by mainstream American groups, but there was a major Muslim contin-
gent among the protesters.[38]

In addition, numerous Bush administration officials traveled to Dearborn to seek and receive support for the Iraq War and the subsequent
occupation from certain segments of Detroit's Arabs and Muslims. Several prominent local religious Shia leaders, including Karbala Center's
Husham al-Husainy and Islamic Center of America's Sayid Hassan
Al-Qazwini, actively endorsed US involvement in Iraq and organized
pro-war events. A picture of President George W. Bush kissing Al-Qazwini
on the cheek at an event in Dearborn in April 2003 was widely circulated
within the local Muslim community in Detroit and in the wider Middle East. Afterwards, as the support for the war and occupation waned,
Al-Qazwini received mounting criticism from constituents for his close
relations with the Bush administration. Thus, largely due to the existing
internal divisions, the community showed little activism regarding the
war even though the Iraq War and subsequent occupation was of the
utmost importance to Detroit Muslims. Yet certain triggering events were
able to bring up tensions and spur the community into action.

The execution of Sunni strongman and former dictator Hussein
briefly intensified Shia-Sunni tensions in the community. Hussein was
captured in 2003 and executed in December 2006. A predominantly
Iraqi-background Shia crowd of more than 150 gathered in Dearborn
expecting Saddam's execution on December 29, 2006.[39] The celebration
continued for the entire day. Following the festivities, two Shia mosques

and several Shia businesses were vandalized in January 2007.[40] In the following weeks, a few other acts of vandalism occurred; all together, four mosques and at least 12 predominantly Iraqi-owned businesses were harmed.[41] No arrests were made, yet allegations centered on a number of local Sunnis.

Community leaders continuously took notice and anticipated minor tensions during periods when violence escalated in Iraq. Arab Sunni and Shia leaders in Michigan started to meet regularly to promote coopera- tion following the February 22, 2006 bombing of the Golden Mosque of Samarra in Iraq, one of the most holy shrines in Shia Islam.[42] On May 10, 2007, a few months after the Saddam Hussein's execution, many of the local religious leaders signed a "Muslim Code of Honor" agreement con- demning sectarian violence and hate speech.[43] The agreement has been on display at visible locations in area mosques ever since. The Council of Islamic Organizations of Michigan (CIOM) initiated the accord, and similar measures were later replicated in Muslim communities in Califor- nia and New York.

Although the Iraq War has stirred emotions in the community, there has been little overt activism. Community leaders were effective in quell- ing tensins when they did arise. Some Arabs and Muslims have lobbied and worked with the US government. Individual Arabs and Muslims have participated in anti-war events organized by American groups such as the MECAWI and Women in Black. More recently, following Barack Obama's election in 2008 and the subsequent withdrawal of American combat troops from Iraq in 2011, protests by American groups have come to a standstill.

Explaining Iraq War Activism

Although segments of Detroit's Arabs and Muslims lobbied the US gov- ernment regarding the situation in Iraq, the scarcity of Iraq-related events in the community was surprising. The lack of activism can be attributed to two main causes: internal divisions regarding the Iraq War (and the dominance of the Shia and Chaldean Christian Arab pro-war position), and the benefits that the war has brought to segments of Arab and Mus- lim communities. Initially, there were some public expressions of anti- and pro-war activism—and, notably, more Iraq-related activities took place on college campuses. Yet, after 2003, community members have participated in anti-war activism (often initiated by American groups) as individuals, not as representatives of organizations. Neither concern about the Iraq War led to radicalization.

However, more activism regarding foreign policy events could be seen on nearby college and university campuses. Henry Ford Community College in Dearborn and the University of Michigan-Dearborn host a number of active Arab and Muslim student groups. Besides staying active on the usual issues surrounding Palestine and Lebanon, student groups organized events on the occupation of Iraq. For example, a University of Michigan-Dearborn Lebanese male student group leader explained how on the fifth anniversary of the American involvement in Iraq, the local Arab Student Union organized an Iraq Awareness Week. The week consisted of a series of seminars and a rally. At one point, the group exhibited 157 crosses, each representing a fallen Michigan soldier. In another instance, during a student-organized candlelight vigil in support of American troops, Arab Student Union representatives passed 500 roses, each symbolizing an alleged 1,000 people who had died in Iraq.

A number of interviewees expressed their surprise about community inattentiveness to the war in Iraq. Steve Elturk, a Lebanese Sunni Imam of the Islamic Organization of North America, commented that he is not sure why there has been little activism concerning Iraq in recent years, but "when Bush decided to go after Iraq, we did rally and we did whatever we could here."[44] An Arab Muslim female activist involved with pro-Palestinian activities expressed her surprise that there had been virtually no activism: "Yes, it's really strange. It's not like the situation in Iraq is non-existent."

Shia Imam Muhammad Ali Elahi explained that there has been little activism concerning Iraq because "local issues are more important. Yet there are concerns about homeland, effects on relatives, and foreign policy. It's natural that local issues are more important, closeness matters and makes [a] difference."[45] An active, long-time community activist and the new director of Dearborn Heights Community and Economic Development Department, Ron Amen, explained the difference between the anti-Iraq War and pro-Palestinian protests: "There were protests . . . against the Iraq War, the invasion of Afghanistan. I attended them, we got very little media coverage. It's not what the administration wanted the media to show . . . the invasion of Iraq certainly didn't generate the emotions in the Arab Muslim population that the issue of Palestine does."[46]

Meanwhile, the Shia (and Iraqi Chaldean) pro-war perspective was the most influential in determining Muslim reactions to the occupation of Iraq in Detroit. The majority of Detroit's Iraqi community came to the area in the 1990s as refugees from Saddam Hussein's regime. Therefore, the Iraqi community in the area has been younger and staunchly anti-Hussein. The community tended to support the Iraq War and the resulting empowerment of the Shia community in Iraq during the occupation. However, the war also created an extraordinary inflow of Iraqi refugees to Detroit, many of whom found it hard to adjust to their new environment.[47] Detroit South Asian scholar Saeed Ahmed Khan explained that "in reacting to the Iraq conflict, the dominant force is the Iraqi Shia perspective, it's hard for Sunnis to get out and protest Iraq."[48]

According to community activist Aoun Jaber, "there has been little on Iraq. Most Iraqis are pro-US, and agree with the US policy because they were attacked by Hussein, they fled to the US."[49] A middle-aged Yemeni community member further elaborated: "Well, Iraqis [in Detroit] wanted the War with Iraq." A Shia religious leader shared his observation that "American interests there go along with Iraqi interests so that everybody there can be happy." Abed Hammoud, a former chairman of the influential Congress of Arab American Organizations and one of the founders of the Arab American Political Action Committee, noted how anti-war protests vanished following the beginning of the Iraq War: "The problem with Iraq is that it's sensitive in different ways. We have a big Iraqi community in Dearborn. . . . in Dearborn, our concerns about the community are . . . they were very anti-Saddam . . . it makes it hard sometimes. You can offend them . . . if I stand up and criticize [government] policy . . . they say, 'you're defending Saddam.' "[50] As a result, activism on the issue of War in Iraq has been relatively minor.

At the same time, many local Sunnis opposed American involvement in the affairs of the Middle East, whereas others sympathized with the former Iraqi strongman Saddam Hussein for his perceived record of active opposition to Western interventions in the Middle East. Some of these tensions were felt following Saddam Hussein's execution. Although some in the community celebrated this event, others perceived the expressions of public joy as hateful. One of the interviewees, a young, Iraqi-born male in his early 20s, remembered that he received hateful comments from some of the nearby Sunnis while he was celebrating the execution on Warren Avenue in Dearborn. Another South Asian male community leader shared an observation that "when Iraq was invaded, Sunni-Shia conflict became more important. There were tensions in Dearborn . . . During the beginning of the Iraq War, communities stopped talking to each other. But then the tension went away, it's always like this."

Furthermore, many Detroit Arabs and Muslims have benefited from the ongoing occupation of Iraq. The Central Intelligence Agency (CIA), other US governmental agencies, and private companies recruited heavily among Detroit Arabs during the Iraq War. Whereas a survey of news media reports provides inconclusive evidence, field research interviews with community leaders and activists provide evidence that the community has been actively working with the government and companies operating in Iraq.

News media reports suggest that the government and private sector actively recruited among Detroit Arabs and Muslims, with questionable results. Numerous news reports describe the CIA's campaigns to recruit in Detroit, whereas local Arabs and Muslims are quick to suggest publically that the CIA's hiring campaign will be unsuccessful.[51] Other reports reveal widely divergent figures of Detroit Muslim involvement with the occupation of Iraq. For example, one article proclaimed that anywhere from a few dozen to 2,000 Detroit Arabs were recruited by the Pentagon as of 2003.[52] Interviewees shared similar views.

Some interviewees spoke of friends and relatives who have been working in Iraq for the government or private companies in professions ranging from translators to truck drivers. Local Shia Imam Husham Al-Husainy disclosed that "this community has been visited by so many people—CIA, FBI, Pentagon—there's a big chunk of them that went with them. You have hundreds of Iraqis, translators, who went with the Pentagon."[53]

Anecdotal evidence suggests that a number of Dearborners are working in the military and as auxiliaries to the military. For example, an Iraqi-background male interviewee in his 20s explained that when his brother started to work for an international company in Iraq, the entire family was initially looked down upon by the community. Now, a few years later, the situation has changed. More local Muslims are starting to take employment with the government and private companies in Iraq, and this practice is becoming increasingly accepted in the local community. Another interviewee stated how his friend is using money earned from work in Iraq to build a new house for his family in Detroit. Therefore, this evidence suggests that many of Detroit's Arabs benefit from being employed by the US government and Western companies operating in Iraq.

In sum, the community failed to take a unified position regarding the Iraq War. Many divisions were evident among Chaldeans, Shia and Sunni Muslims, and different ethnic groups residing in the area. Segments of the Arab community benefited from the war, and a large number of Detroit Iraqis (frequently refugees from the Saddam Hussein regime) firmly endorsed American policies towards Iraq. As a result, internal divisions made the initiation of major political activities impossible, even though different segments of Detroit Arabs and Muslims held strong opinions for and against the war.

Anti-Israel Protests during the Israel-Hezbollah War, Summer 2006

In contrast, the Israel-Hezbollah war mobilized the entire community for more than a month, from July 12 to August 14, 2006. The standoff predominantly involved Hezbollah guerilla forces and the Israeli military. Israel bombarded Hezbollah positions in Southern Lebanon and elsewhere in the country, imposed air and naval blockades, and deployed infantry and tanks in Southern Lebanon. More than 40 Israeli civilians and 100 Israeli soldiers were killed.[54] According to the United Nations, on the Lebanese side at least 1,000 civilians and a greatly disputed number of Hezbollah fighters were killed.[55] The US State Department estimated that some 5,000–7,000 American citizens with connections to metro Detroit's Arab community (and about 25,000 American citizens overall) were in Lebanon at the time of the hostilities with Israel.[56]

During the conflict, anti-Israeli activities took place in Detroit almost daily, and "up to 1000 people have turned out day after day" for protests while the conflict continued.[57] In numerous instances, more than one protest took place on the same day in the metro Detroit area. In Dearborn alone, anywhere from 500 to 10,000 people per event (predominantly Arabs) participated in regular vigils, town hall meetings, and political protests during the summer 2006.[58] The largest protests occurred at the beginning of the conflict, and the activism declined as the conflict progressed. It is impossible to document all protest activities because not all of them were reported by the media. The field research findings corroborate assertions made by other accounts that almost daily protests occurred in the Detroit metropolitan area while the fighting continued.

Media accounts of anti-Israel activism show that the most sizeable protests took place at the beginning of the conflict. Arab and Muslim groups' anti-Israel rally on Warren Avenue attracted 500 participants on July 14, just two days after the outbreak of the hostilities.[59] Protesters demanded cessation of Israel's incursion into Southern Lebanon, and requested that the US place pressure on Israel. Other less-reported events took place in the streets and mosques of metro Detroit, including inner Detroit and the towns of Warren and Flint. A left-leaning news source reports that one protest organized by the MECAWI with the support of the Lebanese and Palestinian communities resulted in a 2,000 person-strong march through downtown Detroit demanding the end of US involvement in the Middle East on August 4.[60]

On July 18, 2006, the largest Arab American rally in 10 years took place in Dearborn.[61] Some 10,000 protesters condemned Israel's incursion into Southern Lebanon and called for a halt to Israel's perceived aggression. They also called for Saudi Arabia to stop fueling Israeli planes conducting the attacks. The rally was organized by Muslim groups, but the frontline of the rally consisted of interfaith groups of rabbis, priests, and Imams.[62] Some of the chants included: "Israel out of Lebanon!" "Down, down Israel!" and "Death to Israel!"[63] A Shia Lebanese religious leader, Husham Al-Husainy of the Karbalaa Center in Dearborn, took a more moderate stance: "I think this is the best way that we walk together as Muslims, Christians, and Jews against injustice. This is the best way to ensure that Muhammed, Jesus and Moses are happy with us."[64] This particular event drew support from a broad variety of groups: Arab Americans (particularly Lebanese, Iraqis, and Yemenis), Latinos, and African Americans.[65]

In the summer of 2006, the Detroit Arab and Muslim community managed to build coalitions with mainstream groups and displayed impressive activism while the Israel-Hezbollah war was taking place. In spite of some angry protester rhetoric, including calls of "Death to Israel," all of the activism came to pass through nonviolent means. As a whole, this episode suggests that the community is capable of mounting significant transnational mobilization.

Anti-Israel Protests during the Gaza War, Winter 2009

Finally, the last major episode of reactive community activism on foreign policy issues during the post 9/11 decade came in 2008–2009, during Israel's incursion into Gaza from December 27, 2008 to January 18, 2009. On December 27, Israel began airstrikes against targets in the Gaza with the stated goal of stopping firing rockets into Israel. The Israeli ground invasion began on January 3, 2009. The six-week conflict brought much suffering and devastation to Palestinians in the Gaza Strip. 13 Israelis and more than 1,000 Palestinians were killed. Over 4,000 homes were destroyed and around $2 billion worth of damage was done to Gaza.[66]

In Detroit, calling for a halt to Israel's actions, the largest demonstration took place in December of 2008. Mainstream national media sources insisted that, despite blistering cold, at least 1,000 people marched through streets of Dearborn in opposition to Israel's incursion into Gaza on December 30.[67] The protesters waved Palestinian flags and shouted anti-Israel epithets as they demanded halt to Israel's bombardment of the Gaza Strip. Some protesters carried "a mock coffin decorated with pictures of dead and injured children and labeled 'U.S. Tax Dollars at Work' and 'Victims of Zionism.'"[68] A young person of Palestinian descent proclaimed that Israel's actions were similar to a holocaust; others blamed the US government for providing sizeable amounts of military aid to Israel.[69] Some other chants included "Gaza, Gaza don't cry, Palestine will never die," "Israel is a terrorist state," "God is great," and "a martyr is beloved by God."[70] Meanwhile, an umbrella organization—the Congress of Arab American Organizations (CAAO), the organizer of the protest—claimed that there were at least 5,000 people in the audience.[71]

Smaller protests were held at University of Michigan-Flint campus and elsewhere in metro Detroit.[72] The CAAO held several other protests in the couple weeks following the protest, and those drew "hundreds" of supporters.[73] During these protests, the demonstrators chanted, chanted "Free, Free, Palestine!" "Israel is a terrorist state!" and "No Justice, No Peace!"[74] The most common sentiments among the demonstrators included disgust with the US, Israel, and the Arab regimes for their complicity regarding the Gaza attacks by Israel. Some protesters held graphic posters of corpses of small children killed by Israeli troops.[75]

It is evident that protests against Israel's incursion into the Gaza Strip during the winter of 2009 also proceeded calmly, despite some radical rhetoric. The Gaza protests were notably less well attended than the Israel-Hezbollah war protests two and a half years earlier. Although varying weather conditions undoubtedly affected the levels of participation at these events, ethnic factors were quite important in explaining attendance. After all, Lebanese-Americans (who played a key role in leading political mobilization during the Israel-Hezbollah war) surpass Palestinian-Americans in terms of population and influence within Detroit's Arab and Muslim communities, where ethnicity-based motives galvanize political action in response to events abroad.

In sum, for the most part Detroit's Arab and Muslim mobilization in response to the wars in Afghanistan and Iraq, and other key Middle Eastern conflicts, has been passionate yet peaceful. Such an outcome was due to certain incentives created by the migration context in the US and Detroit, and the characteristics of the Detroit's Arab Muslim communities.

Context: Careful Screening, and Economic Deprivation yet Inter-Group Ties

The two main contextual factors that have aided in preventing conflict spillover to Detroit are careful screening of asylum seekers and refugees, and extensive inter-group ties involving Detroit Arab Muslims and local authorities—such ties helped to remedy some of the negative effects associated with otherwise economically deprived Muslim communities in Detroit. First, through careful screening and relatively restrictive asylum and refugee policy, the US was largely able to prevent an inflow of migrants intending to escalate violence against other minorities or the state. Second, although Detroit's Arab Muslims—similarly to London's Pakistanis—are economically deprived, Detroit has eschewed radicalization largely due to the mitigating effects of close ties between Muslims, government officials, and law enforcement agencies, and the overall confidence that Detroit Muslims have in American institutions.

The Security-Driven Nature of Asylum and Refugee Admissions

Due to a better screening procedures and more restrictive admission policies, the US did not accept scores of radical asylum seekers with intentions to escalate violence against other migrant communities or the state. Overall, the US is the world's largest receiver of refugees and immigrants for permanent settlement.[76] Historically, the US has granted asylum to individuals seeking to flee from countries with which American had relatively strained relationships. During the Cold War, Hungarian, Cuban, and Vietnamese refugees were granted relatively easy access to immigration to the US through presidential executive orders.[77] Until the passage of the 1980s Refugee Act, the US definition of a "refugee" was restricted to those who fled communist states or countries in the Middle East.[78] The act was codified in response to a surge in refugee admissions at the end of the Vietnam War, and adopted a more humanitarian definition of "refugee." In the 1990s, substantive human rights concerns were important in determining asylum admissions.[79] Between 1975 and 1992, the US admitted some 1.7 million political refugees, predominantly from Asian and the Soviet Union.[80] In 1997 and 1998, the Congress codified bills requiring cessation of prior practices of discrimination against asylum seekers from Nicaragua, El-Salvador, Guatemala, and Haiti. Even though these legislative initiatives encouraged an adoption of a more inclusive conception of "refugee," the US continued its cautious asylum policy through the 1990s. During that time, almost 150,000 asylum applications were filed in the US.[81] However, the vast majority of these asylum claims were rejected.[82]

The US further tightened its asylum and refugee admission policies following the 9/11 terrorist attacks. For example, the USA PATRIOT Act (2001) and the Real ID Act (2006) denied admissions for individuals who had provided support to groups that the US designates as terrorist organizations. More recently, following a US decision to admit more refugees from Iraq, the US increasingly started to screen Iraqi refugees in Iraq, as opposed to screening them upon their arrival to the US.[83] Therefore, the US asylum and refugee policy limited the number of immigrants accepted, while employing careful screening procedures and rejecting the majority of asylum claims.[84] Additionally, by the 1990s, US counterterrorism efforts to a large extent focused on countering the threats from violent religious extremists.

In the aftermath of the 9/11 attacks, there was an increase in attacks against Muslim Americans, and there was an increase of 1,600 percent in hate crimes from 2000–2001.[85] The FBI interrogated 11,000 American-based Iraqis.[86] A poll released in 2007 reflected that 54 percent of Muslims believed that they are profiled by police.[87] There was a stark increase from 23 percent in 2007 to 43 percent in 2011 in the number of Muslims Americans who felt that enough effort to reduce terrorism is occurring.[88]

Arab community-police relations reached their lowest point in the 1990s, but trust has been largely rebuilt since then.[89] In fact, Howell and Jamal (2008) observe that in the post-9/11 period, "the special relationship between Arab Detroit, the media, and law enforcement agencies intensified significantly."[90] In the years immediately after the 9/11 attacks, federal agencies focused on protecting local Arab and Muslim communities. Local Wayne County sheriff's office dispatched officers to protect mosques.

The key may be the close relationship that local police had with their own communities. In the mid- to late 1990's, Dearborn officials increased hiring of Arab American police officers. In the aftermath of 9/11, when other areas were reporting an increase in attacks against Muslim Americans, Dearborn actually recorded a reduction in anti-Arab hate crimes.[91] Even as an increase in distrust of the FBI occurred, more trust in local Detroit and Dearborn policing was occurring as well.[92]

In sum, the security-driven asylum and refugee admissions—and domestic counterterrorism policies—enabled the US to limit the acceptance of radicals, and to swiftly remove those with violent dispositions toward other migrant groups or the American institutions.[93] Such actions contributed to the creation of an environment which favored orderly mobilization in response to important foreign policy events.

Economic Deprivation but Extensive Inter-Group Ties

In many ways the Detroit Muslim community does not resemble a typical American Muslim community. It is characterized by the presence of poverty, poor education, and discrimination. Sixty percent of American Muslims surveyed in a Gallup poll felt that Americans are prejudiced against American Muslims, and 48 percent of American Muslims had experienced discrimination in 2010.[94] It is remarkable that despite these obstacles the community has avoided reactive conflict spillovers—largely the outcome of a creation of an institutionalized peace system involving the different ethnic communities and the government. Additionally, although Arab and Muslims are underrepresented in local elected offices, their interests are relatively well-represented through alliances between elected leaders and Arab and Muslim leaders.

Detroit Muslims do not fit a common perception of a typical American Muslim community. American Muslims are primarily descendants of college and university students. They tend to be notably more affluent and empowered than their counterparts in Europe.[95] Immigrant-background Muslims tend to make either the same or even higher average income—and to be better educated—than an average American overall. Although there certainly are local success stories of Arab Muslim immigrant-background entrepreneurs who in recent decades have started local businesses, such as gas stations and ethnic restaurants, the majority of Detroit's inhabitants struggle with gloomy economic prospects.[96]

Detroit is among the most segregated American cities.[97] Annual FBI crime statistics repeatedly portray the cities of Detroit and Flint as among the most dangerous in the US. The Detroit metropolitan area has been struggling economically since the 1990s, largely due to the deteriorating market position of the American automobile manufacturers based in the Motor City. In 2007, 34 percent of the city residents lived below the poverty line. The Detroit public school system has been struggling to provide quality education to the city's declining population. Therefore, the daily realities of the Detroit Arab Muslim community do not coincide with the overall image of American Muslims.

Furthermore, Shryock and Lin (2009) observe the following paradox: Although Detroit Muslims are poor and segregated, similar to a typical European Muslim community, unlike a European Muslim community, they simultaneously display a perplexing confidence in American institutions:

> [in Detroit] political opposition is sometimes linked to affluence and integration; poverty linked to confidence in institutions; residence in Arab-majority enclaves seems not to increase or diminish levels of social capital; and . . . the most influential and politically integrated Arab American organizations are located in the Arab Muslim enclave of Dearborn, where oppositional politics and confidence in American institutions are fully on display.[98]

How to account for such a paradox? The evidence suggests that Detroit's Muslim community has eschewed radicalism because the various Arab and Muslim groups have built close relations with the media and law enforcement agencies, effectively establishing an institutionalized peace system.[99] This system in Detroit consists of various Muslim organizations, a rich civil society, the Muslim Code of Honor initiative, and the BRIDGES program. Nabeel Abraham (2011) argues that there exists a "Containment System" in the Arab Detroit. This system consists of Arab organizations, local schools, municipalities, and law enforcement agencies, which "monitor and contain conflicts and passions linked ideologically to the terror decade."[100] As a result, poverty and marginalization has not led to radicalization, and Muslim trust in American institutions and the government remains high despite economic woes. This is consistent with Varshney's (2002) observations about the causes of political violence in cities in India, where poor and marginalized communities avoid political violence if they develop extensive civil society inter-group ties.

For example, major Arab organizations, including ACCESS and ADC, work closely with the government, as well as providing many socioeconomic services to local residents.[101] Following 9/11, ADC initiated the Building Respect in Diverse Groups to Enhance Sensitivity (BRIDGES) program, which hosts regular meetings between community leaders and authorities to discuss issues pertaining to Arabs. The project became a national model for community-law enforcement relations.[102] Another, similar establishment, Advocates and Leaders for Police and Community Trust (ALPACT), similarly aims to promote communication between the government and Detroit Arabs and Muslims.[103] Together with local government officials, ADC also hosts an annual US citizenship ceremony to swear in new citizens. In the 2010 ceremony, 200 new citizens were sworn in. Additionally, the community has developed well-established rapport with law enforcement agencies.

Furthermore, the federal government's military and intelligence arms recruited heavily among Detroit's Arabs and Muslims.[104] FBI officials worked closely with the community, and the CIA attempted to recruit extensively from Detroit.[105] During the week following 9/11, 4,000 Arabs from Detroit contacted the FBI and CIA to volunteer as translators.[106] Anecdotal stories suggest that a number of Detroit's Arabs work for the agency, which is consistent with the CIA's general pattern of recruiting foreigners living outside their countries of birth for purposes of subverting their homeland governments.[107]

Meanwhile, also since the 1990s, the community has created a "guestroom" for outsiders willing to engage with it. This "guestroom" is a semi-public domain consisting of community organizations including ACCESS, the famous New Yasmeen Bakery on Warren Avenue in Dearborn, the Arab American National Museum, the Islamic Center of America, and other, bigger mosques.[108] Through this guestroom and extensive interfaith work, the community projects a positive image to outsiders and informs insiders (including new immigrant Muslims) that the way to success is through integration.

On a broader level, public opinion polls similarly show that American Muslims see themselves to be generally economically integrated and optimistic about the future. In fact, American Muslims are generally satisfied with their lives and are more optimistic than other faith groups in the US that things are getting better.[109] Eighty-two percent were satisfied with "the way things are going in their lives," 79 percent rated their communities as "very positive places to live," and 66 percent stated that "the quality of life for Muslims in the U.S. is better than in most Muslim countries."[110] Top problems identified by American Muslims are: negative views about Muslims (29 percent), discrimination/prejudice/not treated fairly (20 percent), and ignorance about Islam (15 percent); only 4 percent selected the option jobs/financial problems.[111] Thus, while some problems remain, an average American Muslim perceives him- or herself to be relatively well-integrated and hopeful about the years to come.

Furthermore, Detroit Muslim interests are represented through several potent organizations and elected political officials. Nevertheless, despite recent gains made in terms of the increase of political participation and organization, Muslim electoral power remains limited. Since the 1980s, scholars and journalists have written about the emergence and evolution of influential Arab and Muslim organizations such as the Arab Community Center for Economic and Social Services (ACCESS), the American Arab Anti-Discrimination Committee (ADC), and the Council of American-Islamic Relations (CAIR). Some critics have referred to CAIR as a "Hamas Terrorist Front Group" and "Muslim Mafia," in recognition of the organization's support for the Palestinian cause and its growing influence in Detroit and Washington DC.[112] Furthermore, 90 percent of cases received by the local ADC in 2008 came from Muslim Arabs.[113] Thus, local community organizations are representative, potent, influential, and command notable grassroots support. Additionally, since the 1990s, Detroit Muslims and Arabs have also made inroads into local politics.

The number of registered Arab voters in Dearborn has grown steadily, from 1,200 in 1990 to 9,800 for the 2000 election and 12,000 for the 2004 national election.[114] Arab Americans constituted 5 percent of Michigan's overall voters in the close 2004 election.[115] Almost 70 percent of Dearborn's Arabs voted in the 2008 election and 65 percent voted in the 2012 election.[116] Nevertheless, although the level of the community's political participation is increasing, there are still very few elected officials of Arab and Muslim background, and Muslim electoral power remains limited. In 2014, three of Dearborn's seven councilors and nine of its elected officials were Arab Americans; however, there were neither Arab nor Muslim representatives serving in the Detroit City Council proper. Two Arab Americans (a Christian and a Muslim) serve in Michigan's House of Representatives; however, no Muslim Americans represent Michigan in the US Congress.

Tellingly, one study found that although Arabs and Muslims are underrepresented in local political offices, their interests are advanced through existing alliances between elected leaders and community leaders.[117] Thus, Arabs and Muslims are well-represented by elected officials who are not from these communities. The study also found that "the combination of single-district city elections, Muslim and Arab demographic minority status, and hostile attitudes by non-Arab and non-Muslim voters" hinders chances for candidates from these communities to get elected.[118]

However, as on the national level, Detroit Arab Americans are an "unreliable" constituency.[119] In 1988, Arab Americans in Michigan showed strong support for Jesse Jackson, a liberal Democrat, in the presidential race, and two years later they endorsed John Engler, a conservative Republican, in the Governor's race.[120] Due to such "unreliability," Arab voters have compromised their ability to gain influence in one of the two major established parties. In sum, Detroit Arab Muslim interests are represented by Islamic organizations and certain elected officials, but the community lacks influence within the two dominant national parties.

To conclude, Detroit Muslims reject radical politics, even though the community is poor and marginalized. This is mainly achieved due to the existing institutionalized peace system in Detroit, consisting of exceptional cooperation between capable Arab and Muslim organizations and local and national law enforcement and governmental authorities. Although Arab and Muslim politicians are still underrepresented, coalitions between elected officials and Arab and Muslims representatives help to voice and address Muslims concerns.

Migrant Communities: Moderate Leaders, No Ties to Radicals Abroad

Although many Muslim leaders and groups contend to represent American Muslims nationally, there is no clear organization that would represent a significant portion of American Muslims nationally. Radical Muslim organizations commanding notable support among everyday Muslims exist neither nationally nor in Detroit. Furthermore, Muslims are well-represented by moderate leaders on the local level in Detroit—and these leaders encourage and promote non-violent political participation regarding the wars in Afghanistan and Iraq. Thus, the non-violent character of Detroit's Arab Muslim protest politics is largely due to the absence of radical groups, and absence of transnational connections with violent-radical networks abroad.

The Moderate Leaders and Their Views on Conflicts in Afghanistan, Iraq

Detroit's Arab Muslim community's leadership is represented by local Muslim and Arab organizations, as well as Imams and certain significant individuals in the community. Additionally, there exist a number of national Muslim organizations, but their representativeness can be questioned. On the local level, Detroit's Arab Muslim community is characterized by the presence of strong and capable community leadership. Detroit leaders are vocal in expressing their opposition to American involvement in the Middle East and certain other aspects of American foreign policy and counterterrorism efforts. The community has remained politically active and orderly during times when emotions rise high. Regular, numerous political protests in reaction to conflicts abroad have often taken place in Detroit. Yet aside from occasional minor scuffles with police during protests, there has not been political violence. Community activism in relation to Palestine, Lebanon, and Iraq tends to be intertwined because similar organizations and individuals tend to participate in activities concerning these countries. Meanwhile, many of these leaders are concerned about the possibility of outsiders coming into their community to spread messages of intolerance and violence, and to promote violent interpretations of Islam.

Nationally, Muslims are represented by numerous religious and civil rights groups. The most influential Islamic organization is the Islamic Society of North America (ISNA), founded in 1981 for the purpose of serving as an umbrella group for Islamic organizations. However, ISNA also has been criticized for being overly conservative. The most capable Muslim civil rights organization is the Council on American-Islamic Relations (CAIR), founded in 1994. However, it is worth asking how much following such groups command. A national poll of American Muslims by Gallup (2011, 25) asked, "Which National Muslim American organization, if any, do you feel most represents your interests?" The most-frequently mentioned group, CAIR, was mentioned by only 12 percent of males and 11 percent of females. ISNA was listed by 4 percent of males and 7 percent of females. Other organizations listed, including the Muslims Public Affairs Council, the Muslims American Society, the Imam Warith Deen Mohammed Group, and the Islamic Circle of North America, were supported by somewhere between 0 and 6 percent of respondents. Arguably, the most significant finding of this survey is that 55 percent of males and 42 percent of females listed "None" to the question of which Muslim organization represents them. Thus, as in in the UK, there are many organizations and individuals that claim to represent American Muslims, but such organizations tend to have little grassroots support. Unlike the UK, no radical Muslim organizations (e.g., Hizb ut-Tahrir) command much support from large segments of American Muslims.

On the local level, there are two general kinds of community leaders: ethnic and Islamic. Some of the main Arab leaders are Osama Siblani, the publisher of local Arab American News; David Warren, the creator of the popular portal www.arabdetroit.com; Hassan Jaber, who helped to build the Arab Community Center for Economic and Social Services (ACCESS) into a major local organization; and Imad Hamad, who for many years held leadership positions within the American-Arab Anti-Discrimination Committee. Some of the religious leaders are the Sunni Imam and public speaker Dawud Walid, who leads the local Michigan CAIR branch; Victor Ghalib Begg, a South Asian Muslim and former leader of the Council of the Islamic Organizations of Michigan, an umbrella group that merged with the Islamic Shura Council of Michigan and now operates under the name of Michigan Muslim Community Council; and Shia Imams Hassan Al-Qazwini, Mohammad Ali Elahi, and others. However, many divisions remain, as the different mosques commonly cater to either Shias or Sunnis, individuals of different ethnic backgrounds (e.g., Lebanese or Yemenis), or even different socioeconomic classes.

Furthermore, local political, community, advocacy, and research organizations play major roles in community leadership. Some of the main political Arab and Muslim organizations include the Muslims Political Action Committee (MPAC), the Arab American Political Action Committee (AAPAC), the Yemeni American Political Action Committee (YAPAC), the Pakistani-American Public Affairs Committee (PAKPAC), the Bangladeshi Political Action Committee (BAPAC), and the Michigan Muslim Democratic Caucus (MMDC). Key community and advocacy organizations include the Arab Community Center for Economic and Social Services (ACCESS), the Council for American Islamic Relations-Michigan (CAIR-MI), the American-Arab Anti-Discrimination Committee-Michigan (ADC-MI), and the Institute for Social Policy and Understanding (ISPU). Additionally, there also a number of influential individuals in the community. For example, the ADC's Imad Hamad stated that community leaders are significant leaders and businesspeople with commercial, engineering, bar, and other community associations, of which there are plenty. At the same time, he admitted that there is not a coherent "Arab American" plan of action, yet community leaders are moving towards creating one.[121] Some other community leaders mentioned in interviews in Detroit include: Najaf Bazi, an active feminist leader; Ali Dagher, a South African activist; Khadigah Alasry, a *hijabi* Yemeni Arab youth leader with the conservative, Muslim Brotherhood-affiliated Muslim American Society; and Aoun Jaber, a middle-aged community leader from a Lebanese background.

In sum, there are many Muslim and Arab organizations and self-proclaimed leaders both nationally and in Detroit. While it is questionable to what extent national Muslim organizations command grassroots support, various local Muslim and Arab organizations tend to be perceived rather positively by Muslims who live in the area.

Furthermore, Detroit Muslim leaders expressed their regret that there was a lack of community leadership concerning the conflict in Afghanistan. With regards to engagements in response to the Iraq War, Detroit leaders and activists prescribed democratic, peaceful means for action, mainly focusing on education, political participation, and lobbying.

Some of the leaders and activists noted that the situation in Afghanistan should be viewed as a humanitarian issue. Khadigah Alasry thought that one should pay particular attention to the situation in Afghanistan only if one is concerned about humanitarian issues. She did not expect that extra attention should be paid because it happens to be a predominantly Muslim country.[122] However, for her, just like for many of the interviewees, the main causes dealt with Detroit, and the main issues dealt with clarifying misrepresentation and misconceptions about Islam.

Sofia Latif, a young South Asian woman, reflected on what community activism should be regarding War on Terror conflicts. "I think that in an ideal world the role of every Muslim is to stand up to injustice. And it's regardless of the injustice being done in Iraq or Palestine or in parts of the world where very few Muslims are."[123] According to her, the best way to do this is through building strong Muslim organizations. South Asian Muslim activist Abdullateef Muhiuddin voiced a similar opinion when discussing political activism regarding conflicts abroad in the community, "I'll attend the events . . . be there to show my support . . . but people who're planning them are usually of Arab descent . . . whether they're from Lebanon, from Iraq, Palestine . . . they're all unified in their movement to support each other."[124]

A lifetime Palestinian cause activist and secular middle-aged male noted that there has been a lack of leadership concerning Afghanistan because it is a non-Arab country. If there had been individuals who took a stance on Afghanistan, Palestinians would have followed. He further reflected that Arabs and Iraqis from the area took part in anti-war activism as individuals, not organizations.

A number of interviewees suggested that political engagement is the best method for Muslims and Arabs to utilize when addressing conflicts abroad. For example, Imam Elahi is one of the best-known Shia activist Imams in the area. He insisted that, in reaction to conflicts abroad, the community needs more education, more promotion of awareness; community members need to strive to influence elected officials.[125] Similarly, Lebanese community activist Aoun Jaber suggested that the best ways to voice a position on foreign policy issues, including Afghanistan and Iraq, are through participation in the system, voting as a political bloc, and funneling candidates into elections.[126] Ron Amen, a middle-aged community leader of Lebanese background, a Shia Muslim, illustrated how public protests can serve as a pressure valve in the community:

> You can put thousands of people out on the streets, protest, and make a lot of noise, jump up and down. And then may get some media attention, it helps to vent some of the passions that are building in people. You know, it's very difficult to watch news every night like people were doing in 2006 and seeing very close relatives, in some case brothers, mothers, sisters being bombed with weapons from America. . . . But like I said, we've learned how to control and channel that emotion.[127]

Sunni Imam Steve Mustapha Elturk encouraged lobbying the government:

> They do affect Muslims in our community. Because we do have Iraqis live with us. We have Afghanis, Pakistanis who live with us. Whenever there is an opportunity to speak or write to congressmen to stop or do whatever, we take an active role. I don't know politically what the Muslim communities do in DC, for example. But I do know that ADC, CAIR national lobby quite a bit in DC for particular issues.[128]

A female Arab non-*hijabi* youth human rights activist in her 20s emphasized the importance of educating the community about conflicts and other events of significance in the Middle East. She expressed fears that, whereas first-generation migrants tend to have firsthand knowledge of and interest in events in the Middle East, second and subsequent generations are notably less knowledgeable.

A middle-aged male Shia religious leader expressed his frustration with the lack of activism concerning Palestine, Afghanistan, and Iraq: "We need to lobby, put pressure. But I don't see that happening, Muslims are too weak." Abed Hammoud suggested that in the long term, the Arab community should work to swing public opinion in the US because "our battle in this country is a battle of public opinion. Years ago, we lost the battle of public opinion. When you lose the battle of public opinion, you lose the public officials."[129] In sum, interviews revealed a near universal acceptance of democratic political attitudes and tactics overall, which is consistent with the track record of Detroit's Muslim political activism regarding foreign policy events in general. In stark contrast to London, Detroit Muslims rejected provocative and violent protest.

The Lack of Radical Groups, No Connections with Networks Abroad

None of Detroit's Arab Muslims have been implicated in terrorism. Radical and provocative groups are absent from the community, and they do not organize contentious protests. Detroit has not witnessed terrorist acts, and no Detroit-linked would-be terrorists have attempted to commit violent acts elsewhere. A number of studies show that during the post-9/11 era the US government placed a particular scrutiny on Detroit, which has resulted only in some charges against a few charities.[130] Many of the interviewees mentioned that fear of powerful American law enforcement agencies has played an important role in quieting political activism in the post 9/11 era; however, it can be questioned how much such alleged fears can explain the relative absence of political violence in Detroit, as hostilities in London have taken place despite the comparable policing power that Britain and London have.

Detroit's Arab Muslims are not connected to radical networks abroad. Because most of Detroit's Muslim community consists of first- and second-generation migrants, many of them maintain close relations with their relatives in sending states. For example, Dearborn Yemenis follow developments in Yemen, Shia (and Chaldean Christian) Iraqis stridently opposed Saddam Hussein's regime, and local Lebanese Americans stay in touch with their relatives in the home state. Indeed, some 5,000 Detroit Lebanese Americans were visiting Lebanon when the hostilities commenced between Israel and Hezbollah during the summer of 2006, but Detroit's Arab groups do not have durable ties to radical groups in foreign countries.[131]

Just like in Europe, the government, the press, and hateful individuals have targeted Detroit Arabs throughout the post-9/11 era.[132] Unlike Europe, Detroit lacks a true presence of conservative, angry Islamist groups such as Hizb Ut-Tahrir. In Britain and elsewhere in Europe, such groups have organized occasionally provocative protests such as Islamist Islam4UK's anti-British soldier protest in Luton, UK, in March 2009.[133] In that protest, Islam4UK protesters held signs saying "Anglian soldiers go to hell" and "butchers of Basra," and shouted "terrorists" as British troops from the Second Battalion of the Royal Anglian Regiment were parading in town.[134] None of this has taken place in Detroit.

To a larger extent than the US, Britain and Europe are home to vocal far-right anti-Muslim groups, including the British National Party and

Stop Islamification of Europe. Such groups play important roles in fostering anti-Muslim sentiment within the broader community and add to the Muslim perception that Islam is under siege. Noteworthy far-right groups are absent in Detroit. Additionally, while targeted by law enforcement agencies and by some anti-Islamic individuals,[135] Detroit has not seen right-wing anger generated towards them on the level London has. Despite some tensions, there has been a notable level of cooperation between government authorities, Arabs, and Muslims in Detroit.

There are virtually no incentives for violent protest in the American context. Unlike protests in UK and London, provocative and violent protests are notably less well-received in the US. Groups alike Hizb Ut-Tahrir and Al-Muhajiroun, which at times have organized such protests in London, have disappeared in post-9/11 Detroit. Former members of Al-Muhajiroun have been involved in violent terrorist acts in London in reaction to foreign policy events. Prior to 9/11, HT was fairly active in Detroit. In some instances, their supporters used physical violence to quiet their opposition in Detroit.[136] A male south Asian community leader and professional explained that Salafis, such as HT, tend to recruit in colleges. "In college, students go through identity crises, especially a number of them were questioning identity post-9/11." He strongly insisted that the community rejects political violence and militant interpretations of Islam; and that a core concern was the possibility of an arrival of radicals from outside of Detroit's Muslim communities. Such radicals can become catalysts for conflict, and they widen the sectarian divide. "Unfortunately," the interviewee warned, "such peoples are at times invited to speak at local mosques."

Largely due to the absence of connections with radicals abroad and a lack of radicals within Detroit, the community has not seen reactive conflict spillover. Despite the odds, strong community leadership and potent representative organizations have successfully created an environment unreceptive to political violence.

Conclusion: Passionate yet Nonviolent Protest Politics

The Detroit Arab and Muslim community is known for its political activism and existing effective institutions. Arab Muslims have voiced their opinions on a number of foreign policy issues during the decade following 9/11, most notably the War and Occupation of Iraq, the Israel-Hezbollah War, and the Gaza War. Local political activism is frequently expressed through protests, lobbying, and awareness-raising activities generally initiated by Arab and Muslim groups, while more provocative and violent means of protest (including terrorism) do not hold appeal in Detroit.

With its passionate yet orderly activism on many foreign policy issues, the Detroit Arab Muslim community remains remarkably different from European Muslim settlements. Arab Muslims have opposed many

American policies towards the Middle East on the one hand, yet worked closely with authorities on the other. Many of Detroit's Arab Muslims have benefited from and supported the Iraq War. Lessons from Detroit suggest that the internal composition of Muslim communities matters in their responses to foreign policy events along religious, sectarian lines, and (most importantly) ethnic lines; and that an otherwise mobilized Muslim community, critical of many aspects of US foreign policy, can be largely supportive of American involvement in the Muslim World.

The community is characterized by a strong community identity and potent leadership. Hardline Islamist groups that have organized more provocative protests in London disappeared in Detroit following 9/11. None of the local ethnic Arab communities possess ties with radical networks. During the terror decade, the community has been active regarding Palestine and Lebanon. It has largely remained quiet concerning Afghanistan and Iraq, largely due to local Shia and Chaldean support for the US and Coalition in the Iraq War 2003-2011.

In sum, reactive conflict spillover did not occur in Detroit because there were very few radicals present in the city, and the community did not have connections to radical groups and networks. Interestingly, spillover did not occur *despite* a lack of economic integration, due to a presence of an institutionalized peace system in the community. The following chapter outlines the key findings of this study as it draws the book to a conclusion.

Notes

1 Those emphasizing Detroit's exceptionalism argue that in comparison to a typical American Arab and Muslim community Detroit is: more politically active and successful; more poor yet simultaneously also more politically integrated; and that it works more closely with the government than most other communities. See Abraham, Howell and Shryock 2011; Abraham and Shryock 2011; Abraham and Shryock 2000; Howell and Jamal 2008.

2 In recognition of a great internal diversity, this chapter will use terms of Detroit's Arab Muslim "community" and "communities" interchangeably, as appropriate for the issue discussed. Local Arab Muslims come together as a community on some points of concern, while they are divided on others.

3 Shryock, Abraham and Howell 2011, 387.

4 Grieco 2003.

5 Ibid.

6 US Department of Homeland Security 2010.

7 Al-Rasheed 2005, 319.

8 Abed Hammoud, interview, December 14, 2009.

9 Meanwhile, Iraqi-background individuals in London were surprisingly inactive in London during the same time period. This conundrum is further addressed in the book's conclusion.

10 Ayers and Hofstetter 2008.

11 Abraham 1989, 35.

12 Dawud Walid, interview, November 19, 2009.

13 Nick Mayer, "Dearborn City Council Passes Gaza Resolution," *The Arab American News*, January 23, 2009.
14 Sally Howell, personal communication, November 19, 2009.
15 Abed Hammoud, interview, December 14, 2009.
16 Hammoud interview, December 14, 2009.
17 Hamad interview, November 11, 2009.
18 See Stockton 2009.
19 Catrina Stewart, "Peres Accuses Britain of Anti-Israel Sentiment," *The Independent*, August 2, 2010.
20 Max Fisher, "Why Home-Grown Islamic Terrorism Isn't a Threat," *The Atlantic*, November 11, 2009; "Study: Threat of Muslim-American Terrorism in U.S. Exaggerated," *CNN*, January 6, 2010.
21 Myriam Bernaad, "Facing Homegrown Radicalization," *The Washington Institute for Near East Policy*, Policy Watch #1575, September 3, 2009; Craig Whitlock, "Western Terror Recruits on the Rise," *The Washington Post,* October 19, 2009.
22 "Napolitano: Domestic Extremism Top Concern," *MSNBC*, February 22, 2010.
23 "The Times Square Scare," *The Economist*, May 8, 2010.
24 Howell and Shryock 2003; Detroit Arab American Study Team 2009.
25 John Solomon, "Despite Evidence, Man Deported: Case Demonstrates Legal Difficulties of Terrorism Trial," *The Boston Globe,* June 3, 2004; "Documents Suggest Dearborn Men May Be Terror Supporters: Father, Son Convicted on Fraud Charges," *ClickonDetroit.com,* June 16, 2005; Paul Egan, "Feds tie Dearborn Charity to Terror," *The Detroit News,* July 25, 2007.
26 Howell and Jamal 2011, 89–90.
27 Howell and Jamal 2011, 90.
28 Robert Brignall, "Justice Department to Probe Luqman Abdullah Shooting," *Detroit Crime Examiner*, February 3, 2010.
29 Niraj Warikoo, Ben Schmitt, and Robin Erb, "Islamic Leader's Family Urges Investigation into His Death," *Detroit Free Press,* October 31, 2009.
30 Robert Brignall, "Justice Department to Probe Luqman Abdullah Shooting," *Detroit Crime Examiner*, February 3, 2010.
31 Hagar Mizrahi, "Dutch Passenger Thwarted Terror Attack on Plane," *Israel News*, December 27, 2009.
32 Youmans 2011, 270.
33 Pew 2007, 5.
34 Rehman 2007.
35 Shannon Jones, "Protest against Iraq War in Dearborn, Michigan," *World Socialist Web Site*, October 17, 2002.
36 MECAWI is a multi-national, multi-racial coalition of Detroit area activists opposed to the US's involvement in wars. Shannon Jones, "Protest against Iraq War in Dearborn, Michigan," *World Socialist Web Site*, October 17, 2002.
37 Shannon Jones, "Protest against Iraq War in Dearborn, Michigan," *World Socialist Web Site*, October 17, 2002.
38 Matthew Engel, "War in the Gulf," *The Guardian*, April 7, 2003.
39 "Iraqi-Americans Celebrate Saddam's Execution," *MSNBC*, December 29, 2006.
40 Howell 2011, 155; "Iraq War Tests Unity among U.S. Muslims," *Reuters*, February 25, 2007.
41 Cheryl Corley, "Michigan Muslims Feel Sectarian Ripples," *National Public Radio*, February 12, 2007.
42 "Iraq Sectarian Violence Affects American Muslims," *Voice of America*, May 10, 2007.

43 See the Appendix for a copy of the Code.
44 Steve Elturk, interview, Detroit, December 19, 2009.
45 Steve Elturk, interview, Detroit, December 19, 2009.
46 Elturk interview.
47 Strum 2007.
48 Saeed Ahmed Khan, interview, Detroit, November 18, 2009.
49 Aoun Jaber, interview, Detroit, November 20, 2009.
50 Abed Hammoud, interview, Detroit, December 14, 2009.
51 Mlive.com, "CIA Commercials to Recruit US Arabs, Iranians," November 9, 2009.
52 Matthew Engel, "War in the Gulf," *The Guardian*, April 7, 2003.
53 Husham Al-Husainy, interview, Detroit, December 1, 2009.
54 "PM 'Says Israel Pre-Planned War,'" *BBC News*, March 8, 2007.
55 Report of the Commission of Inquiry on Lebanon pursuant to Human Rights Council resolution S-2/1," November 23, 2006.
56 Andrew Dietderich, "Mideast Conflict Brings Fear to Local Businesspeople," *Crain's Detroit Business*, July 24, 2006; Ajrouch 2011, 193.
57 Andrew Gumbel, "Stars, Stripes, and the Star of David." *The Independent*, August 15, 2006.
58 While the largest single protest was estimated to involve 10,000 participants, common protests included less than 1,000 individuals (Naber 2009, 149).
59 Niraj Warikoo, "Hundreds in Metro Detroit Protest Israeli Attacks," *Arab American Institute*, July 14, 2006.
60 Monica Moorehead, "U.S. Out of the Middle East!," *Workers World*, August 9, 2006.
61 Aatif Bokhari, "Michigan: 10,000 March to Protest Israeli Attacks," *The Arab American News*, July 24, 2006.
62 Aatif Bokhari, "Michigan."
63 Aatif Bokhari, "Michigan."
64 Al-Hushainy interview.
65 Bokhari, "Michigan: 10,000 March."
66 "Gaza: Humanitarian Situation," *BBC News*, January 30, 2009.
67 "Hundreds in US Protest Strikes in Gaza," *USA Today*, December 30, 2008.
68 Ibid.
69 Tom Eley, "Protests in Dearborn, Michigan Denounces Israeli Attack on Gaza" *Watan*, December 30, 2008.
70 The New Zealand Herald, "Protests Erupt in US Over Gaza Attacks," *The New Zealand Herald*, December 31, 2008.
71 Eley, "Protests in Dearborn."
72 "Hundreds in US Protest Strikes on Gaza," *USA Today*, December 30, 2008.
73 Tom Eley, "Detroit: Hundreds Rally Against Israel Atrocities," *World Socialist Web Site*, January 9, 2009.
74 Ibid.
75 Ibid.
76 Lejeune-Kaba 2010; Teitelbaum 1980, 24.
77 Salehyan and Rosenblum 2008, 107.
78 Salehyan and Rosenblum 2008, 106.
79 Rosenblum and Salehyan 2004.
80 US Committee for Refugees and Immigrants 1992.
81 Salehyan and Rosenblum 2008, 104.
82 Barnett 2002.
83 Charley Keyes, "U.S. Admits More Iraqi Refugees," *CNN Online*, June 04, 2008.

84 Price 2009.
85 Oswald 2005, 1776.
86 Howell and Shryock 2011, 83.
87 Morreale 2004.
88 Pew 2011.
89 Youmans 2011.
90 Howell and Jamal 2008, 47.
91 Youmans 2011, 275.
92 Ibid 276.
93 However, in some rare instances the US refugee policy could not prevent radical incitement to violence, or the radicalization of refugees (such as a number of Somali refugees in Minnesota during the decade following 9/11 or a few Chechen refugees in Boston in 2013).
94 Gallup 2011, 39–40.
95 Leiken 2004, 59; Skerry 2003, 40.
96 Bobby Ghosh, "Arab Americans: Detroit's Unlikely Saviors," *Time*, November 13, 2010.
97 Farley et. al 1994; Walid interview 2009.
98 Shryock and Lin 2009, 278.
99 For institutionalized peace systems, see Varshney 2002. For the "special relationship" between Arab Detroit, the media and law enforcement agencies, see Jamal 2008.
100 Abraham 2011, 348–9.
101 Howell and Jamal 2008, 65–70.
102 Bakalian and Bozormergh 2009, 154.
103 Howell, 2011b, 153.
104 Youmans 2011, 277.
105 Steven Stanek, "CIA in Recruitment Pitch to Arab-Americans," *The National*, November 20, 2009.
106 Howell and Jamal 2011, 94; "Arabic Speakers Answer U.S. Need," *Detroit Free Press*, September 19, 2001, 7A.
107 Weiner 2007.
108 Andrew Shryock, personal communication, November 23, 2009.
109 Gallup 2011, 5.
110 Pew 2011b, 3.
111 Pew 2011b, 46.
112 Gaubatz and Sperry 2009.
113 Imad Hamad, interview, November 11, 2009.
114 Cruiel 2004; Rose 2001.
115 Ibid.
116 Pupcenoks and Senzai 2016.
117 Sinno and Tatari, 2011.
118 Ibid.
119 In the past, American Arab and Muslim voter allegiance has swung back and forth between endorsing Republican and Democrat candidates.
120 Holmes 1996.
121 Imad Hamad, interview, November 11, 2009.
122 Khadigah Alasry, interview, December 13, 2009.
123 Sofia Latif, interview, December 9, 2009.
124 Abdullateef Muhiuddin, interview, December 5, 2009.
125 Mohammad Ali Elahi, interview, November 21, 2009.
126 Aoun Jaber, interview, November 20, 2009.
127 Ron Amen, interview, November 24, 2009.

128 Steve Mustapha Elturk, interview, December 19, 2009.

129 Abed Hammoud, interview, December 14, 2009.

130 Howell and Shryock 2003; Howell and Jamal 2009.

131 The extent of Detroit Muslim connections to terrorism is limited to a few allegations of individual monetary support for charities including Hezbollah and Hamas.

132 Howell and Shryock 2003; Howell and Jamal 2009.

133 Matthew Taylor et al., "Muslim Groups Pledges More Protests against UK Soldiers," *The Guardian*, March 11, 2009.

134 Ibid.

135 Howell and Shryock 2003.

136 Abdo 2006.

8 Similar Communities, Different Outcomes

On May 4, 2010, Faisal Shahzad, a naturalized American citizen from Pakistan, was detained on terrorism charges as he was preparing to leave the US for Dubai from a New York City airport. Following the arrest, Shahzad readily admitted to being the sole perpetrator of the failed attempt to detonate a car bomb in Times Square a few days earlier, on May 1. It soon became clear that the perpetrator had ties with the Pakistani Taliban and other radical groups in Pakistan, and that he had received prior training in the development of explosives in Waziristan, Pakistan. Similar to other would-be terrorists,[1] his actions were inspired by a transnational motivation to punish the US for perceived wrongdoings against the Muslim *ummah*, but he was enabled to physically carry out this terrorist plot due to relevant training and guidance received from his connections with violent extremist networks abroad. Years later, this act remains the largest post-9/11 terrorist scare in the country.

The 2010 Time Square car bombing attempt is a recent instance of reactive conflict spillover. However, reactions to conflicts abroad in Muslim diasporic communities unfold on a spectrum, ranging from minor peaceful protest actions to terrorist plots. Furthermore, for the purpose of mobilization in response to conflicts abroad, with the exception of select major conflicts such as the Arab-Israeli conflict, Western Muslims frequently mobilize on the basis of their ethnic background and sectarian divisions.

Indeed, it is misguided to study Islam and Muslim communities in the West as a monolith. There are notable divisions between the Islam preached and lived by the elites and the daily realities of ordinary Muslims. Muslim scholars and scholars of Islam in the West frequently write about Western Muslims as a group, or generalize their findings from studying certain ethnic Muslim communities, rather than studying Muslims as a whole. Western governments and private foundations similarly encourage research on "Muslims" in Europe and the US. Major Muslim organizations compete with each other as they strive to represent their envisioned Muslim communities. Western governments frequently encourage such actions, as they are eager to find a national

Muslim organization that could be the spokesperson for domestic Muslims.

This popular emphasis on religious identity is indeed puzzling, especially because such an approach is usually not used when studying migrants from other religions. For example, scholars of Latin American diasporas do not study Latin Americans as Catholics, but as representatives of their ethnic and linguistic communities.[2] Even when Latin Americans are lumped together as "Latinos," they are usually not primarily defined by their religiosity. What is problematic with perceptions of Muslims in the West is that they are now mostly defined and perceived as a relatively cohesive religious group. Furthermore, it is telling how the focus of British discourse on minorities has shifted over the last few decades: discourse of "color" was used in the 1950s and 1960s, "race" in the 1960s, 1970s, and 1980s, "ethnicity" in the 1990s, and religion from the 1990s on.[3] This cautions that the current emphasis on religion may be just a passing trend, not unlike the other ones that came before.

The experiences from London and Detroit reveal that strong divisions exist in Muslim communities. As noticed by Mandaville (2001), diasporic Muslims in the West experience religion quite differently than Muslims in sending states. Ordinary Muslims tend to associate with other individuals who share their ethnicity, language, culture, or ethnic cuisine. Mosques and Muslim umbrella groups are usually led by representatives of a certain ethnicity. In everyday life, ethnic and sectarian divisions are more important than commonalities presented by Islam. *Asabiyyah*—social and ethnic solidarity—frequently trumps religious solidarity in Islamic communities.[4]

On the individual level, Muslims in the West tend to be more religious than non-Muslims, and their religiosity has increased in the post-9/11 period. Authoritative sources claim that somewhere between 20 and 40 percent of American Muslims attend mosques regularly.[5] Studies about mosque attendance in Western Europe similarly place mosque attendance at about 20 percent.[6] Islamist groups, like Hizb ut-Tahrir, frequently proclaim loudly that there is worldwide unity in the Muslim *ummah*. However, such groups are a fringe minority. Meanwhile, mainstream Muslim organizations, such as the Muslim Council of Britain or the Council for American-Islamic Relations, tend to lack grassroots support. Additionally, ethnic background frequently determines what mosque or social circle Muslim individuals will join.[7] Mosque boards frequently are controlled by representatives of a certain ethnicity. Additionally, whereas a significant number of migrant-background Muslims follow the dominant form of Islam practiced in their sending state, some change their religious sect of Islam. It is also significant—and frequently overlooked—that significant portions of Western Muslims do not practice regularly and do not think that any religious institution can represent their views and needs.

In addition, social and ethnic solidarity influences Muslim community reactions to conflicts abroad. Often, such mobilization occurs following a trigger event abroad. Triggers are particularly important to Detroit's Muslim community. A number of Detroit's Arab Muslims stated that virtually all of the community's foreign policy-focused political activism is in response to events abroad; in other words, without triggers there would not be Detroit Muslim activism in response to foreign events and conflicts.

Moreover, the level of mobilization that a certain trigger will generate depends on strategic framing of the importance of triggers. In this process, certain ethnic factors will once again be important: Triggers associated with conflicts in sending states will be of particular interest to migrant-background Muslims, and so will triggers associated with conflicts in the Middle East involving Israel.[8] Meanwhile, humanitarian catastrophes in Muslim countries in Africa and Muslim-on-Muslim conflicts (e.g., Hamas-Fatah, or the discriminatory treatment of Palestinians in refugee camps across the Middle East) are frequently overlooked. Thus, significant galvanizing events affecting Muslim countries do not inherently trigger reactive activism. Instead, only triggers and major events that are framed as significant by community leaders generate activism. Finally, instances of non-spontaneous hostile spillovers (e.g., terrorist acts) frequently occur without immediate prior triggers.

Furthermore, it is misguided to question why Muslims radicalize or participate in terrorist plots, as such radicalization on the individual level is influenced by varied pathways, mechanisms, and processes. Islam as a religion matters for the daily lives of many Muslims; however, Islam closely interlinked with ethnic identity markers matters more in the process of political mobilization to foreign policy events. However, there are also a few major and long-lasting conflicts—such as the ongoing Arab-Israeli conflict—that are viewed through Islamic lenses.

From Political Mobilization to Reactive Conflict Spillover

Why do similar communities react differently to the same conflicts abroad? Why do some conflicts spill over to some migrant-background communities, but not to others? Furthermore, what is the relationship between the immigration context and characteristics of the communities—and opportunities for individual radicalization? Although it is beyond the scope of this research to explain why diasporic Muslims—or members of other minority communities in the West—join extremist groups abroad, the findings do point to the importance of structural conditions, state policies, and characteristics of migrant communities in creating an environment that either is or is not conducive to various forms of political mobilization and, potentially, radicalization.

This study finds that trigger events frequently galvanize minority communities into action in response to events abroad, especially if triggers are promoted as important by the community leaders. Such triggers are quite important for peaceful mobilization, but are frequently not that important in leading to pre-mediated political violence. Muslim communities frequently tend to react to foreign policy events based on their ethnic identities and sectarian divisions, which is quite different from mobilization in response to domestic problems such as Islamophobia or discrimination (when the same communities are frequently unified under a common Islamic identity).

Reactive conflict spillover, or political violence in diasporic communities in response to conflicts abroad, occurs in communities with strong ethnic identities, often following a trigger event framed as important by community leaders. In such communities, a combination of different opportunities provided by varied migration contexts and characteristics of the migrants themselves determine whether the initial mobilization remains peaceful or if it will lead to reactive conflict spillover. Certain migration contexts and characteristics of diasporic communities create environments that make the radicalization of individuals more likely. Thus, it is hard for Muslim leaders to prevent the radicalization of individual Muslims unless the structural conditions promoting radicalization are properly understood and ameliorated. Key findings suggest that spillovers are likely to occur in already mobilized minority communities, which are characterized by one or more of the following three factors:

1. Policies Allowing Inflow of Violent Radicals

Even though it pursued restrictive asylum and refugee policies, mainly due to economic reasons, the UK did accept notable numbers of violent radicals. Prior to 9/11 and 7/7, the UK accepted hundreds of violent recidivists, as the key government officials commonly believed that such radicals did not constitute a security threat to the UK. The presence of such individuals created an environment that enabled a spillover of violence from conflicts abroad. However, security considerations have played a prominent role in more recent British regulations on migration, and Britain is currently screening incoming migrants for connections with extreme violence, as well as using the existing counterterrorism laws to remove violent radicals already present. In the long term, such policies will decrease the possibility of spillovers of violence.

Meanwhile, for the US, security considerations (and screening to exclude violent radicals), have influenced the shaping of the country's asylum and refugee policies since at least the 1990s. The US has admitted large numbers of anti-Communist refugees, especially during the Reagan administration, whereas the admission of refugees declined significantly after 9/11.[9] These findings underline the significance of closer screenings of immigrants to detect extremists and prevent their admission. They also warn to be vigilant towards the security threats represented by Western

Muslims fighting for extremist groups in the Middle East, as a number of them are expected to return to the West at a later date.

2. Presence of Well-Established Radical Groups

Communities with operational, well-established radical groups are more likely to experience instances of provocative political activism with a potential for hostilities. In London, angry conservative Muslim groups (including Hizb ut-Tahrir, and various reincarnations of Al-Muhajiroun) were particularly active regarding the Western military presence in the Muslim world. Additionally, London's Muslim fringe groups were able to attract a number of supporters by presenting themselves as an alternative to the mainstream British organizations, which were frequently perceived to be ineffective by the majority of British Muslims. In particular, the Al-Muhajiroun protests tended to attract protesters who engaged in confrontation, as well as angry and confrontational counter-protests by radical right groups, including the English Defence League.[10] In several instances, anti-war protests that were primarily organized by these groups resulted in violence, which was initiated either by one of the members of the group or by the opponents of conservative Islamist groups.

Meanwhile, such conservative and radical groups have been absent in Detroit. Instead, protests in Detroit are usually carefully organized by mainstream Muslim and Arab groups such as the CAIR and CAAO. The absence of Islamist and radical groups in the community has ensured the lack of major provocative or violent activism.

3. Ties with Radical Networks Abroad

Finally, communities with connections with radical networks abroad are likely to experience reactive conflict spillover. Although various reasons can lead individuals to radicalize and even participate in violent terrorist acts, the more dangerous violent radicals tend to receive guidance, and practical or paramilitary training, through their connections with radical networks abroad. In the UK, virtually all major post-9/11 terrorist plots have had connections either to British Pakistanis or to radical networks in Pakistan.

Meanwhile, despite numerous investigations and much law enforcement attention, connections with extremist networks abroad have not been discovered in Detroit. The community members do keep ties with their friends and relatives in former home countries, but there is no evidence of noteworthy community connections to radicals abroad.

This research also provided some surprises. Contrary to the initial expectation, poverty and marginalization does not necessarily lead to radicalization in communities where there are institutionalized inter-group social relationships. Thus, whereas the lack of economic integration (as well as institutionalized discrimination) may have contributed to radicalization of some individuals in London, in Detroit economic deprivation did not lead to radicalization, largely due to extensive inter-group ties. In a related finding, Varshney (2002) found that Indian cities with "institutionalized peace systems" did not experience ethnic riots. In Detroit, such institutionalized inter-group initiatives include the BRIDGES program, close ties among the Muslim community leaders and local government representatives, the Muslim Code of Honor initiative, and the presence of various Muslim civil society groups. Collectively, they have created an environment that prevents radicalization and political violence despite overall poverty and marginalization.[11]

Future research should focus on whether the theoretical assertions about reactive conflict spillover could be replicated in other cases. It would be particularly interesting to see if the developed explanatory framework could be applied to non-Muslim cases, as this research is grounded in the broader social science literature, and the findings are not intended to be specific only to Muslim communities in the West. Future research should also seek to better understand how different internal and external structures, processes, and pathways lead to Islamist radicalization on the individual level.

This book also raises further, specific questions: (1) Until recently, why have London's Bangladeshis been so apolitical and uninvolved with radical activism? (2) Where are Iraqis in London? Just like fellow Muslim Pakistanis, Bangladeshis constitute a major minority community in London. Until recently, Bangladeshis have been peculiarly apolitical and uninvolved, neither with political activism nor violent extremist activism—quite unlike the Pakistanis.

According to the 2001 UK Census, there are more than 170,000 Bangladeshis in London, where they constitute more than 2 percent of the city's population—a population comparable to their fellow South Asian British Pakistanis. The Bangladeshi community is particularly concentrated in East London. Bangladeshis constitute 33 percent of the population in the borough of Tower Hamlets, and 10 percent in the borough of Newham. Nevertheless, whereas Pakistani Britons have been associated with a large number of terrorist plots, only a handful of Bangladeshis have been implicated in involvement with terrorism. Bangladeshi criminal activism in London has been generally limited to participation in street gangs.[12] In fact, there were no Bangladeshis among the 48 people charged, convicted, or suicided in the UK between 2001 and 2008.[13] Even though the situation changed in 2009 and 2010, when more than 10 British Bangladeshis were indicted on charges related to terrorism,[14] the radicalization among British Bangladeshis has been relatively miniscule. How do we account for such divergent outcomes in these two similar communities?

There are at least two possible explanations for these outcomes: the impact of the kind of Sufi-influenced Islam practiced in Bangladesh and the divergent historic and political paths of Pakistan and Bangladesh, but both of these are flawed. First, it may be the case that the forms of Sunni Islam practiced in Bangladesh—such as Barelvism—place more emphasis on spirituality and eschew violence.[15] Thus, Bangladeshis may be more likely to resist radical Islam. However, not all of London's Bangladeshis are Barelvis, as some of them follow a Wahabbi-influenced Deobandi Islam. Furthermore, some of the Bangladeshis have converted to Salafism and, as suggested by Wiktorowicz (2005), Muslims who radicalize tend to denounce the kind of Islamic influences they were raised in.

Second, some argue that "the origins and political history of Bangladesh did not create the type of grievances associated with partition as for those of Pakistani origin."[16] As a result, Bangladeshis are less likely to become violent radicals. This line of reasoning emphasizes that, even though Pakistan and Bangladesh were both partitioned from India in 1947, the creation of Pakistan, and the following tense relationship with India, created an environment more conducive to radicalization in Pakistan. However, this explanation ignores the growth of radical Islam within Bangladesh since at least the 1990s.[17] Following the end of the Afghan-Soviet War in 1989, many Bangladeshis who fought in the war returned home to spread a more militaristic brand of Islam. Furthermore, the militarization of Bangladeshi Islamists has further increased as a result of the return of former Taliban fighters since the early 2000s.[18] Thus, there is no clear answer explaining the relative lack of radicalization among London's Bangladeshis.

Also, where are British Iraqis and why were they not publicly supportive of the War in Iraq, similar to Iraqis in Detroit? Estimates of the Iraqi population in the UK vary greatly, yet a credible mid-range assessment by the International Organization of Migration estimates the population of Iraqis in London to be around 125,000 as of 2007.[19] Therefore, a sizeable Iraqi population is present in London—and is largely composed of Kurds, an Iraqi ethnic group oppressed under the Saddam Hussein regime, which was the key target in the Iraq War of 2003. Nevertheless, the Iraqi diaspora in Britain was not a major player in recent anti-war political activism—which is inconsistent with their pre-9/11 political participation.

Prior to 9/11, London served as the main location for anti-Saddam resistance outside Iraq.[20] British Iraqi groups opposed to Saddam Hussein's regime were occasionally vocal in London in the late 1980s. For example, on January 18, 1988, a group of 70 Iraqi migrants opposing Saddam Hussein's regime initiated a fight in the Iraqi government's Cultural Centre in London.[21] Nevertheless, contrary to Iraqis in Detroit, London's Iraqis did not express visible support for the Iraq War. Even more surprisingly, very little information about the Iraqi diaspora in the UK during the last decade is available. Regardless of the reasons, the diverging nature of political activism of London's ethnic Muslim communities further suggests that ethnicity is a key variable leading to differing mobilization patterns when it comes to foreign policy events.

Implications for International Relations and Political Science

First of all, this book dispels any remaining doubts on whether international migration matters for the study of international relations and political science. As political actors, migrants affect politics in the homeland and in the land of immigration. Increasing minority political participation and representation has been particularly evident in the post-9/11 period.[22] This research provides several suggestions for the study of British and American politics, political activism, the intersection between religion and politics, and the impact of radical groups on political mobilization.

This study highlights the existence of radical non-electoral politics in Britain and suggests that the US retains its ability to integrate immigrants and minorities. Most scholarship on politics in Britain regards British politics as highly consensual, with a broad agreement on the institutional framework, leaving little space for extremist views, either on the left or right (except for the Irish Question). However, such accounts fail to adequately explain an existence of a broad spectrum of fringe groups adhering to more provocative and occasionally violent tactics. To some extent, immigration has contributed to the emergence of such groups, as it has changed the landscape of European politics, making them more contentious.[23] On the whole, however, this book does not challenge the big picture of the effects of immigration politics in the UK, nor the effects of immigrants on American politics. Additionally, because many Americans see their country as a land of immigration, they are more welcoming towards immigrants—and this popularly held belief further facilitates minority integration and prevents radicalization.

Furthermore, this project contributes to our understanding of conflict in migrant and minority communities. For example, Dancygier (2010) looks at domestic migrant-background communities and argues that conflicts in minority communities are caused by economic and electoral forces. This project, however, highlights the importance of ethnic identity in reactive politics, specifically in response to foreign policy events. Political mobilization in Muslim communities frequently occurs along sectarian and, most importantly, ethnic lines, but Islam also helps to define different ethnic identities. Nevertheless, Muslims come together as Muslims (frequently joined by other minorities, such as Christian Arabs, or by sympathetic Christian groups) to tackle important domestic problems, such as Islamophobia and discrimination. These findings suggest that Samuel Huntington's "Clash of Civilizations" thesis is more wishful thinking than reality—there is no one united Islamic civilization and divisions among Muslims are often more important than their religious commonalities.

Consistent with Wiktorowicz's (2005) findings, this study finds that very religious Muslims do not become involved with terrorism. Muslim political activism and Islamism does not necessarily lead to violent extremism.

Whereas Detroit Imams and religious leaders have taken strong stances on foreign policy issues—and even led public demonstrations—none of Detroit's Muslims and Arabs have been implicated in terrorism offences. Furthermore, there are different shades of Islamism, and instead of steering to violent radicalization, some Islamist groups can instead serve as a "pressure valves" through which disenchanted Muslims can express their anger.

Indeed, the effect of Islamist groups will likely depend on the nature of their messages. Some former British Al-Muhajiroun members have participated in terror plots globally. Additionally, whereas Hizb ut-Tahrir UK's branch frequently boasts that none of their members have been implicated with terrorism, some former members of the Hizb in other countries have been associated with violent extremism. How do we account for such differences? Perhaps the differences can be found in their rhetoric—Hizb branches operating in Asia and the Middle East tend to utilize rhetoric that is similar to the now defunct British Al-Muhajiroun—which supports political violence and oppose democracy. Furthermore, individuals are likely to join radical and potentially violent movements as a result of radicalization following significant shocks in their personal life, not due to increasing levels of religiosity.[24]

Policy Recommendations

This study implies several suggestions for state threat assessment, security policy, and integration efforts. In the past, government officials have speculated under what conditions escalation of conflicts abroad could lead to hostilities in their migrant-background communities. The framework for understanding the process of transnational mobilization and reactive conflict spillover could be of use to policy-makers and government officials in determining threat assessment from internal migrant-background communities. This research suggests that minority reactive transnational mobilization can take various forms, and it does not have to lead to violence, even though the "the risk of overreaction to violence by a handful of immigrants appears quite high."[25] Additionally, as radical networks abroad can pose national security threats, it is important to carefully screen incoming migrants; build institutionalized working relationships among the government, law enforcement, and Muslim community leaders; and not to overlook the significance of proper Islamic education.

The threat represented by violent Muslim radicals has been exaggerated. Indeed, less than 100,000 Muslims—or less than one 15,000th of the world's Muslim population—have been involved with Islamic terrorist organizations over the last quarter-century.[26] Since 9/11, no terrorist has managed to detonate a bomb in the US, and only one successful instance has occurred in the UK.[27] The thousands of alleged, existing Al-Qaeda operatives in the US were never found, and the chances of an American perishing in a terrorist attack are 1 in 3.5 million per year (which falls within the scope of "acceptable risk").[28] To a great extent, such alarmism is due to the sensational media coverage of violent radicalism.

The disproportionate media attention on the few existing violent radicals create an exaggerated sense of insecurity, and it inadvertently assists some radical groups. By paying notable attention to violent extremism, the media provides the publicity that is sought after by the perpetrators—and this publicity may encourage some to embrace extremism. Furthermore, without the constant media attention, radical groups—like Al-Muhajiroun and Islam4UK—would likely lose their relevance to the public discourse and would naturally disintegrate. Nevertheless, it is likely that the appeal of extremist groups will steadily decline unless unpredictable disastrous events take place in the Middle East (which cannot be ruled out), or if the violent backlash from the far right continues and intensifies. Still, vigilance is required, as religious violent radicals have wreaked havoc in the past, even if there are very few of them.

This study also warns of security threats that radical networks present to the national security. Most of the major terrorist plots in the UK have displayed connections to radical networks in Pakistan. As exemplified by the failed 2010 Time Square car bombing attempt, ties with violent radicals in Pakistan constitute a security threat to the US as well. Therefore, continued involvement with counterterrorism efforts and aid aimed at governmental capacity-building in Pakistan (and other countries where the existing government weakness leads to the creation of safe havens for violent radicals) should be a high priority for the United States.

The findings highlight the significance of a closer screening of immigrants to detect radicals and prevent their admission. Such screening efforts are difficult, as they should ensure that violent radicals are not admitted, while avoiding the trap of stigmatizing those who have in the past unintentionally aided (either unknowingly or due to coercion) groups that the US designates as terrorist organizations.[29] This objective will be difficult to accomplish, as it would involve extensive background-checking.

Even more difficult tasks will consist of dealing with violent radicalization of moderate Muslims following their arrival to the West,[30] and with challenges represented by returning Western Muslims who have fought for extremist groups in areas such as Syria and Iraq. Success in containing threat associated with radicalized Muslims at home can be most effectively achieved through joint efforts of government, law enforcement agencies, and Muslim community leaders. Meanwhile, political protest politics in minority communities will not lead to hostilities if the government and community leaders work together to marginalize the role of conservative

Islamist groups, ensure that community members do not cultivate ties with radical networks abroad, and avoid provocative policing.

To prevent the radicalization of homegrown and convert would-be terrorists, the government and community leaders should promote initiatives aiming to build institutional ties between the government, law enforcement organizations, and communities themselves. Such projects would reduce the likelihood of reactive conflict spillovers in the future and prevent radicalization. The Building Respect in Diverse Groups to Enhance Sensitivity (BRIDGES) program, which hosts regular meetings between community leaders and government authorities in Detroit, has been remarkably successful. Therefore, similar bottom-up programs should be promoted in other migrant and minority communities.

However, the British PREVENT program has been less successful. In the framework of the program, the British government offered funding to British Muslim organizations claiming to work on de-radicalization projects. Seventy-seven million British pounds were spent in the framework of the program between 2007 and 2011. Nevertheless, in 2010, a committee of the British Members of Parliament warned that the program has "stigmatized and alienated" participating Muslims.[31] In 2011, Britain's government publically admitted that the program had failed to reduce domestic radicalization—and pledged that the UK's approach from now on will focus on actively identifying extremist threats.[32] More broadly, the fate of PREVENT suggests that government-initiated top-down civil society programs are not likely to be successful in Muslim communities in the West.

Indeed, since the program's inception in 2007, British Muslims have been debating the merits of accepting the government's funds. Some British Muslims and Pakistanis assert that the Muslim think tank Quilliam lost its grassroots credibility after accepting one million pounds from the government. Overall, the dubious record of the PREVENT program contrasted the spectacular successes of BRIDGES, suggests that in attempts to prevent violent radicalization, it is more effective to build "bridges" between law enforcement officials and Muslim leaders, than to fund de-radicalization groups.

In addition, there are numerous steps that Muslim and migrant leaders can take to prevent the spillover of hostilities. The Muslim Code of Honor agreement (see Appendix) is another successful Detroit Muslim initiative that could be replicated elsewhere. This agreement was institutionalized by a number of local Detroit area Muslim leaders following Saddam Hussein's execution in 2006. The initiative aims to prevent reactive conflict spillovers in the local Muslim community, as it condemns sectarian violence and hate speech and calls for closer relationships between local Sunnis and Shias. British Muslim and Pakistani leaders are promoting similar initiatives on a less formal level. For example, Moulana Muhammad Shadid Raza, the former president of the UK's Mosques and Imams National Advisory Board (MINAB), has regularly encouraged Muslim religious leaders to reflect in their public prayers on the similarities that all Muslim sects share. However, the London Muslim and Pakistani community would be more likely to avoid future instances of hostile spillover if they would adopt more institutionalized forms of intergroup interactions, such as BRIDGES or the Muslim Code of Honor.

Finally, research about migrant-background individuals involved in terrorist plots shows that such individuals tend *not* to be knowledgeable about the religion which supposedly inspires their extreme actions.[33] Instead, such would-be terrorists are increasingly radicalized through their membership in a group of like-minded individuals; they come to accept the violent religious interpretations of the group's leaders as the only correct interpretation (oftentimes without knowing that there are alternate credible interpretations of Islam). Muslim community leaders in London and Detroit are well aware about the dangers presented by the potential arrival of charismatic, violent extremist preachers.

Several Muslim community representatives, especially in Detroit, expressed their fears that if the members of local Muslim communities are not adequately informed about the mainstream interpretations of Islam, some outside extremist agitators may be able to convince segments of the local Muslim community about the validity of their extremist interpretations. In recognition of this problem presented by charismatic, outside extremists, several Muslim groups in each location are engaged in educating Muslims about the mainstream interpretations of Islam. One such group is the Muslim American Society in Detroit. The continued work of such groups is particularly important to Muslim communities in the West because it is not Islam, but rather an ignorance of credible mainstream interpretations of Islam, that contributes to creation of extremists. Indeed, formal Islamic education—provided by reputable Islamic educational establishments that present mainstream views on Islam thoroughly—prevents radicalization.[34] Key initiatives for Muslim community leaders should focus on standing up to extremists, continuing self-policing efforts, becoming more engaged in politics, and providing proper religious teachings.[35] At the end, a key challenge for governments and Muslim community leaders is to learn through trial and error. They must determine which programs work better than others, and then replicate them elsewhere.

A Future Outlook

The United Nations estimates that migrant populations in the West will increase significantly during the next decade. Sixty million migrants, or 1.2 million per year, are expected to arrive in Europe between 2010 and 2060.[36] As the new migrants arrive, they will bring along their language, religion, culture, and politics. The demographic trends suggest that many of the new arrivals will come from volatile regions in Africa, Asia, and the Middle East. It is almost unavoidable that there will be concerns about the possibility of conflict spillovers in migrant-origin groups. Fortunately, hostile spillovers occur only under certain circumstances, and there are numerous initiatives that governments and migrant community leaders can employ to diffuse and prevent hostile mobilization in reaction to conflicts abroad.

Meanwhile, Muslim communities in the West, such as the Pakistanis in London and the Arab Muslims in Detroit, will continue to grow and mature. A 2011 study estimates that the number of Muslims in the US will increase from 2.6 million in 2010 to 6.2 million in 2030, and the Muslim population in certain parts of Western Europe will exceed 10 percent of the total population.[37] Ethnic politics will likely become more important.

In the decade following 9/11, different Muslim communities, to a large extent, were brought together by common opposition to discriminatory laws and Islamophobia. Western Muslims were unified on many domestic issues. Meanwhile, similar to their home countries' practice of different forms of Islam, Western Muslim communities will continue to remain divided among their sectarian and ethnic lines.[38] They will continue reacting to conflicts abroad based on these ethno-national lines, especially in instances where community leaders will articulate certain foreign events and triggers as particularly important.

There is also a growing amount of evidence that the potential for violent spillovers will greatly decrease in years to come. Western countries are increasingly taking security into considerations when developing their asylum and refugee policies. Muslim communities are increasingly integrating into Western societies, and to a greater extent than frequently noticed.[39] Unless we experience another major terrorist attack with a Muslim involvement, comparable to 9/11—or unless the anti-Muslim backlash from the far right intensifies—integration trends will continue.[40] Indeed, a threat presented by radical networks abroad remains, but can be dealt with through the careful screening of immigrants, effective policing, reasonable counterterrorism actions, and provisions of aid—aimed at institutional capacity-building—to governments in areas from which such threats emanate.

In response to foreign policy events, it is likely that some provocative protests, clashes between predominately Muslim protesters and police, or Muslims and far-right groups, will remain. However, such encounters are not likely to differ substantially from the level of violence encountered in recent anti-globalization protests. Furthermore, while integration challenges remain, the historical pattern in the transatlantic area suggests that Muslims of immigrant-heritage will likely become unproblematic Britons, Europeans, and Americans.[41]

Notes

1 Although Shahzad's attempt to detonate a car bomb in New York City was unsuccessful, he did succeed in leaving explosives on a car in Time Square without catching the attention of the authorities. In other words, the authorities did not foil his plan, and a major tragedy was averted predominantly due to a fortunate coincidence (the explosives did not explode as intended).

2 The majority of Latin Americans are Catholics, even though Protestantism has gained a considerable following since the 1980s. According the US State Department, Protestants constitute significant and growing minorities in Salvador, Honduras, Belize, and Nicaragua (The Economist, "Going Forth and Multiplying," February 5, 2011, 49).

3 For an overview, see Peach 2006, 353; for "color" see Banton 1955, Rose 1969; "race" Rex and Moore 1967, Smith 1989; "ethnicity" Modood et al. 1997, Bonnett and Carrington 2000; and "religion" Runnymede Trust 1997.

4 Khan S. 2011.

5 Both Haddad and Lummis (1987, 8), and Leonard (2003, 17) mention that only 20 percent of American Muslims attend mosque regularly, whereas a Pew (2007) public opinion poll shows that as many as 40 percent of American Muslims attend mosque at least once a week.

6 Nielsen 2004, 54.

7 Cesari 2004.

8 Many Muslims idealize matters pertaining to the Middle East, the birthplace of Islam.

9 Nevertheless, some radicalized Muslim migrants have been admitted to the US. Furthermore, an additional problem is presented by the fact that some migrants radicalize after their arrival in the receiving states.

10 E.g., see Pupcenoks and McCabe 2013.

11 Meanwhile, perhaps due to the mutual suspicion—which has historically defined much of the interactions between the British state and its Muslim minorities—such an institutionalized peace system seems not to have developed in London.

12 Mehmood Naqshbandi, interview, August 31, 2009.

13 O'Duffy 2008, 41.

14 E.g., see Dodds 2010; Stobart 2010.

15 O'Duffy 2008, 41.

16 O'Duffy 2008, 41.

17 Khan S. 2010b; Scheurer 2008.

18 Scheurer 2008.

19 International Organization for Migration 2007. Other estimates include: 65,000 Iraqis in the UK as of 2009 according to the UK's Office of National Statistics; 350,000–450,000 Iraqis in the UK according to the Iraqi embassy (International Organization for Migration 2007).

20 Al-Rasheed 1994.

21 Michael Simmons, "Iraqis Held After A Brawl," *The Guardian*, January 19, 1988.

22 Bird, Saalfeld and Wust 2011.

23 Messina 2007.

24 E.g., see Silber and Bhatt 2007.

25 Castles and Miller 2003, 275.

26 Kurzman 2011, 27.

27 Mueller and Stewart 2012, 88.

28 Mueller and Stewart 2012, 101, 96.

29 Spiegel et al. 2012, 444.

30 Most violent Muslim extremists radicalize after their arrival to Europe (Al Qaeda's New Front 2005).
31 Dominic Casciani, "Prevent Extremism Strategy 'Stigmatising,' Warn MPs," *BBCNews*, March 30, 2010.
32 HM Government 2011.
33 Abrams 2008; Husain 2007; Stern 2010.
34 Ibrahim 2010.
35 Khan, Chehab and Qassim 2010.
36 Migration News 2011.
37 Michelle Boorstein, "Global Muslim Population Gains Will Outstrip Non-Muslim Growth Over the Next 20 Years," *The Washington Post*. January 27, 2011.
38 Laurence 2012.
39 Jackson and Doerschler 2012.
40 Laurence 2012.
41 Jackson and Doerschler 2012; Laurence 2012.

References

Abbas, Tahir. 2001. "Media Capital and the Representation of South Asian Muslims in the British Press: An Ideological Analysis." Journal of Muslim Minority Affairs 21(2): 245–257.

Abbas, Tahir, ed. 2005. Muslim Britain: Communities under Pressure. London: Zed Books.

Abbas, Tahir, ed. 2007. Islamic Political Radicalism: A European Perspective. Edinburgh: Edinburgh University Press.

Abbas, Tahir. 2011. Islamic Radicalism and Multicultural Politics: The British Experience. London and New York: Routledge.

Abbas, Tahir, and Fran Reeves, eds. 2007. Immigration and Race Relations: Sociological Theory and John Rex. London, New York: I.B. Tauris.

Abdo, Genevieve. 2006. Mecca and Main Street: Muslim Life in America after 9/11. Oxford: Oxford University Press.

Abiri, Elisabeth. 2000. "Migration and Security from a North-South Perspective: Sweden and Malawi." In Migration, Globalization and Human Security, eds. David Graham and Nana Poku. London: Routledge, 70–92.

Abraham, Nabeel. 1989. "Arab-American Marginality: Mythos and Praxis." In Arab Americans: Continuity and Change, eds. Baha Abu-Laban and Michael W. Suleiman. Belmont, MA: Association of Arab-American University Graduates, Inc., 17–45.

Abraham, Nabeel. 1994. "Anti-Arab Racism and Violence in the United States." In The Development of Arab-American Identity, ed. Ernest McCarus. Ann Arbor, MI: The University of Michigan Press, 155–214.

Abraham, Nabeel. 2009. Personal Communication. November 16.

Abraham, Nabeel. 2011. "Arabs Behaving Badly." In Arab Detroit 9/11: Life in the Terror Decade, eds. Nabeel Abraham, Sally Howell, and Andrew Shryock. Detroit, MI: Wayne University Press, 347–377.

Abraham, Nabeel, and Andrew Shryock, eds. 2000. Arab Detroit: From Margin to Mainstream. Detroit, MI: Wayne University Press.

Abraham, Sameer, and Nabeel Abraham, eds. 1983. Arabs in the New World: Studies on Arab American Communities. Detroit, MI: Wayne State University Press.

Abrams, Max. 2008. "What Terrorists Really Want: Terrorist Motives and Counterterrorism Strategy." International Security 32(4): 78–105.

Adamson, Fiona. 2006. "Crossing Borders." International Security 31(1): 165–199.

Ahmad, Waqar I. U., and Venetia Evergeti. 2010. "The Making and Representation of Muslim Identity in Britain: Conversations with British Muslim 'Elites.' " Ethnic and Racial Studies 33(10): 1697–1717.

Ahmed, Akbar. 2010. Journey into America: The Challenge of Islam. Washington DC: Brookings Institution Press.

Ajami, Fouad. 1993. "The Summoning." Foreign Affairs. September/October.

Ajrouch, Kristine J. 2011. "Detroit Transnational: The Interchange Experience in Lebanon and the United States." In Arab Detroit 9/11, eds. Nabeel Abraham, Sally Howell, and Andrew Shryock. Detroit, MI: Wayne University Press, 186–209.

Al Qaeda's New Front. 2005. Frontline PBS Documentary.

Alashry, Khadigah. 2009. Interview with Juris Pupcenoks. Detroit, MI, December 13.

Alexiev, Alex. 2005. "Violent Extremists in the UK and Europe." IP Global. Published by German Council on Foreign Relations. Winter. Available at: www.ip-global.org/archiv/volumes/2005/winter2005/violent-islamists-in-the-uk-and-europe—the-british-government—s-complacency-is-not-warranted.html

Alexseev, Mikhail. 2005. Immigration Phobia and the Security Dilemma. Cambridge, UK: Cambridge University Press.

Al-Husainy, Husham. 2009. Interview with Juris Pupcenoks. Detroit, MI, December 1.

Ali, Sundas. 2008. "Second and Third Generation Muslims in Britain: A Socially Excluded Group?" University of Oxford, Working Paper. Available at: www.wjh.harvard.edu/~hos/papers/Sundas%20Ali.pdf

Allen, Christopher. 2010. Islamophobia. Surrey, UK: Ashgate.

Al-Rasheed, Madawi. 1994. "The Myth of Return: Iraqi Arab and Assyrian Refugees in London." Journal of Refugee Studies, 7:2/3, p. 199–219.

Al-Rasheed, Madawi. 2005. "Iraqi Diaspora." In Immigration and Asylum: From 1900 to the Present, Entries A to I, Volume 1, eds. Matthew J. Gibney and Randall Hansen. Santa Barbara, CA: ABC-CLIO, Inc.

Ambrogi, Stefano. 2010. "Far Right Marches 'Drive Muslims to Militancy.' " Reuters, November 19. Available at: http://uk.reuters.com/article/2010/11/19/uk-britain-edl-militancy-idUKTRE6AI2H420101119

Ameli, Saied R., Manzur Elahi, and Arzu Merali. 2004. British Muslims' Expectations of the Government. Social Discrimination: Across the Muslim Divide. London: Islamic Human Rights Commission.

Amen, Ron. 2009. Interview with Juris Pupcenoks. Detroit, MI, November 24.

Amnesty International. 2012. Choice and Prejudice: Discrimination against Muslims in Europe. London: Amnesty International.

Ansari, Fahad. 2006. British Anti-Terrorism: A Modern Day Witch-Hunt. Updated 2006. London: Islamic Human Rights Commission Report.

Anwar, Muhammad, and Qudir Bakhsh. 2003. "British Muslims and State Policies." Coventry, UK: CRER, University of Warwick.

Arab American Institute. 2003. "Arab Americans-Michigan." Available at: www.aaiusa.org/page/file/f6bf1bfae54f0224af_3dtmvyj4h.pdf/MIdemographics.pdf

Arab Detroit Website. Available at: www.arabdetroit.com/arabamericans.php

Archer, Toby. 2009. "Welcome to the Umma: British State and Its Muslim Citizens since 9/11." Cooperation and Conflict 44(3): 329–347.

Archick, Kristin, John Rollins, and Steven Woehrel. 2005. "Islamist Extremism in Europe." Congressional Research Service (CRS) Report for Congress. July 29.

Available at: www.dtic.mil/cgi-bin/GetTRDoc?Location=U2&doc=GetTRDoc.
pdf&AD=ADA444807

Armstrong, John. 1976. "Mobilized and Proletarian Diasporas." American Political Science Review 70(2): 393–408.

Asad, Talal. 2003. Formations of the Secular: Christianity, Islam, Modernity.
Stanford, CA: Stanford University Press.

Aswad, Barbara. 1992. "The Lebanese Muslim Community in Dearborn, Michi-
gan." In The Lebanese in the World: A Century of Emigration, eds. Albert
Hourani and Nadim Shehadi. London: Center for Lebanese Studies and
I. B. Tauris, 167–187.

Ayers, John, and Richard C. Hofstetter. 2008. "American Muslim Political Participation Following 9/11: Religious Belief, Political Resources, Social Structures and Political Awareness." Politics and Religion 1: 3–26.

Ayoob, Mohammed. 1991. "Third World Security Problematic." World Politics
43(2): 257–283.

B'Tselem, The Israeli Information Center for Human Rights in the Occupied Territories. 2008. Statistics, Casualties. Available at: www.btselem.org/English/
Statistics/Casualties.asp

Bagby, Ihsan. 2004. "A Portrait of Detroit Mosques: Muslim Views on Policy,
Politics and Religion." ISPU Report. Available at: http://ispu.org/files/PDFs/
detriot_mosque_2.pdf

Bagby, Ihsan. 2010. "The American Mosque in Transition: Assimilation, Acculturation and Isolation." In Muslims and the State in the Post-9/11 West, ed.
Erik Bleich. London and New York: Routledge, 120–137.

Bagby, Ihsan, Paul M. Perl, and Bryan T. Froehle. 2001. "The Mosque in America: A National Portrait." Report. Washington DC: Council on American
Islamic Relations.

Bakalian, Anny and Mehdi Bozorgmehr. 2009. Backlash 9/11: Middle Eastern
and Muslims Americans Respond. Berkley, Los Angeles, London: University
of California Press.

Baker, Wayne, and Andrew Shryock. 2009. "Citizenship and Crisis." In Citizenship and Crisis: Arab Detroit After 9/11, ed. the Detroit Arab American Study
Team. New York: Russell Sage Foundation.

Balgamis, Deniz A., and Kemal H. Karpat, eds. 2008. Turkish Migration to the
United States; From Ottoman Times to the Present, Publications of the Center
for Turkish Studies, Volume 5. Madison, WI: University of Wisconsin Press.

Ballard, Roger. 1990. "Migration and Kinship: The Differential Effect of Marriage Rules on the Process of Punjabi Migration to Britain." In South Asians
Overseas: Contexts and Communities, eds. Colin Clarke, Ceri Peach, and Steven Vertovec. Cambridge, UK: Cambridge University Press, 219–249.

Banta, Benjamin. 2008. "Just War Theory and the 2003 Iraq War Forced Dis-
placement." Journal of Refugee Studies 21(3): 261–284.

Banton, Michael. 1955. The Coloured Quarter: Negro Immigrants in an English
City. London: Cape.

Baran, Zeno. 2004. Hizb Ut-Tahrir: Islam's Political Insurgency. Washington
DC: The Nixon Center Monograph. Available at: www.nixoncenter.org/
Monographs/HizbutahrirIslamsPoliticalInsurgency.pdf

Baran, Zeno. 2005. "Fighting the War of Ideas." Foreign Affairs 84(6): 68–78.

Barnett, Don. 2002. The Coming Conflict over Asylum: Does America Need a New Asylum Policy? The Center for Immigration Studies Backgrounder. Available at: www.cis.org/ConflictOverAsylumPolicy

Barreto, Matt A., and Dino Bozonelos. 2009. "Democrat, Republican, or None of the Above? The Role of Religiosity in Muslim American Party Identification." Politics and Religion 2(2): 200–229.

Basham, Patrick. 2006. "Many British Muslims Put Islam First." CBS News. August 14. Available at: www.cbsnews.com/news/many-british-muslims-put-islam-first/ (Reprinted with permission from National Review Online).

Bassiri, Kambiz Ghanea. 1997. Competing Visions of Islam in the United States: A Study of Los Angeles. Westport, CN: Greenwood Press.

Bawardi, Hani. 2009a. Arab Immigrant Political Organization from 1515 to 1951: Transnationalism as a Marker of Arab-American Identity Development. Ph.D. Book, Wayne State University, United States.

Bawardi, Hani. 2009b. Personal Communication. Detroit, MI, December 4.

Baxter, Kylie. 2007. British Muslims and the Call to Global Jihad. Clayton, Australia: Mohash University Press.

Baydoun, Rashid. 2009. Interview with Juris Pupcenoks. Detroit, MI, December 11.

BBC News. 2002. "Short History of Immigration." Available at: http://news.bbc.co.uk/hi/english/static/in_depth/uk/2002/race/short_history_of_immigration.stm#1972

BBC News. 2003. "'Million' march against Iraq war," February 16. Available at: http://news.bbc.co.uk/2/hi/2765041.stm

BBC News. 2007. "PM 'Says Israel Pre-Planned War.'" March 8. Available at: http://news.bbc.co.uk/2/hi/middle_east/6431637.stm

BBC News. 2009a. "Gaza: Humanitarian Situation." January 30. Available at: http://news.bbc.co.uk/2/hi/middle_east/7845428.stm

BBC News. 2009b. "Three Guilty of Airline Bomb Plot." September 7. Available at http://news.bbc.co.uk/1/hi/uk/8242238.stm

Beckford, James A., Daniele Joly, and Farhad Khosrokhavar, eds. 2005. Muslims in Prison: Challenges and Change in Britain and France. Basingstoke: Palgrave Macmillan.

Begg, Moazzam. 2006. Enemy Combatant: My Imprisonment at Guantanamo, Bagram, and Kahdahar. With Victoria Brittain. New York, London: The New Press.

Begg, Moazzam. 2009. Interview with Juris Pupcenoks. Birmingham, August 24.

Behdad, Ali. 2005. A Forgetful Nation: On Immigration and Cultural Identity in the United States. Durham, NC and London: Duke University Press.

Bell, Stewart. 2000. "8,000 Tamil Guerillas in Toronto: Police." National Post, June 17. Available at: www.spur.asn.au/extra/national_post.htm000617–1.htm

Bell, Stewart. 2002. "Gangs Linked to Terrorism, Study Finds: Members, Tactics Overlap." National Post, March 5. Pg. A4.

Belton, Patrick. 2003. "In the Way of Prophet: Ideologies and Institutions in Dearborn, Michigan, America's Muslim Capital." Next American City. October. Available at: http://americancity.org/magazine/article/in-the-way-of-the-prophet-ideologies-and-institutions-belton/

Benjamin, Daniel, and Steven Simon. 2003. The Age of Sacred Terror. New York: Random House.

Benjamin, Daniel, and Steven Simon. 2005. The Next Attack: The Failure of the War on Terror and a Strategy for Getting it Right. New York: Times Books.

Benraad, Myriam. 2009. "Facing Homegrown Radicalization." The Washington Institute for Near East Policy. Policy Watch #1575. September 3. Available at: www.peace-process.org/pdf.php?template=C05&CID=3113

Benyon, John. 1986. "Spiral of Decline: Race and Policing." In Race, Government and Politics in Britain, eds. Zig Layton-Henry and Paul B. Rich. London: Macmillan: 227–277.

Bergen, Peter, and Paul Cruickshank. 2007. "Al Qaeda-on-Thames: UK Plotters Connected." The Washington Post. Guest Analysis, April 30. Available at: http://newsweek.washingtonpost.com/postglobal/needtoknow/2007/04/al_qaedaonthames_plotters_well.html

Berkovitch, Jacob. 2007. "A Neglected Relationship: Diasporas and Conflict Resolution." In Diasporas in Conflict: Peacemakers or Peace Wreckers? eds. Hazel Smith and Paul Stares. Tokyo: United Nations University Press, 17–38.

Berman, Paul. 2003. Terror and Liberalism. New York and London: W.W. Norton.

Bhatt, Chetan. 2010. "The 'British Jihad' and the Curves of Religious Violence." Ethnic and Racial Studies 33(January): 39–59.

Bigo, Didier. 2001. "Migration and Security." In Controlling a New Migration World, eds. Virginie Guiraudon, and Christian Joppke. London: Routledge, 121–149.

Bird, Karen, Thomas Saalfeld, and Andreas M. Wust, eds. 2011. The Political Representation of Immigrants and Minorities: Voters, Parties and Parliaments in Liberal Democracies. London and New York: Routledge.

Birt, Jonathan. 2005. "Lobbying and Marching: British Muslims and the State." In Muslim Britain: Communities under Pressure, ed. Tahir Abas. London and New York: Zed Books, 92–106.

Blaise, Clark, and Bharati Mukherjee. 1987. The Sorrow and the Terror: The Haunting Legacy of the Air India Tragedy. New York: Viking.

Blassingham, John. 1979. The Slave Community: Plantation Life in the Antebellum South. Oxford: Oxford University Press.

Bleich, Erik. 2009. "Where Do Muslims Stand on Ethno-Racial Hierarchies in Britain and France? Evidence from Public Opinions Surveys, 1988–2008." Patterns of Prejudice 43(3–4): 379–400.

Bleich, Erik, ed. 2010. Muslims and the State in the Post-9/11 West. London and New York: Routledge.

Bloch, Alice. 2000. "A New Era or More of the Same? Asylum Policy in the UK." Journal of Refugee Studies. 113(1): 29–42.

Bokhari, Aatif Ali. 2006. "Michigan: 10,000 March to Protest Israeli Attacks." The Arab American News, July 24. Available at: http://news.newamericamedia.org/news/view_article.html?article_id=26c3ba97c33914fe777719631c2d4535

Bolognani, Marta. 2009. Crime and Muslim Britain. London: Tauris.

Bonino, Stefano. 2012. "Policing Strategies against Islamic Terrorism in the UK after 9/11: The Socio-Political Realities for British Muslims." Journal of Muslim Minority Affairs 32(1): 5–31.

Bonnett, Alastair and Bruce Carrington. 2000. "Fitting into Categories or Falling between Them? Rethinking Ethnic Classification." British Journal of Sociology of Education 21: 487–500.

Boorstein, Michelle. 2011. "Global Muslim Population Gains Will Outstrip Non-Muslim Growth Over the Next 20 Years." The Washington Post. January 27.

Available at: www.washingtonpost.com/wp-dyn/content/article/2011/01/27/AR2011012700012.html?referrer=emailarticle

Borgeson, Kevin, and Robin Valeri, eds. 2009. Terrorism in America. Sudbury, MA: Jones and Bartlett Publishers.

Bosire, Richard Moegi. 2006. Compliance with International Human Rights Standards: Treatment of African Migrants and Asylum Seekers in Britain. Ph.D. Book, University of Delaware, United States.

Boswell, Christina. 2000. "European Values and the Asylum Crisis." International Affairs 76(3): 537–557.

Bowen, John R. 2009. Can Islam Be French? Pluralism and Pragmatism in a Secular State. Princeton, NJ: Princeton University Press.

Brachman, Jarret M. 2009. Global Jihadism: Theory and Practice. New York: Routledge.

Brandon, James. 2009. "Unlocking Al-Qaeda: Islamist Extremism in British Prisons." Quilliam Foundation Report. November. Available at: www.quilliamfoundation.org/images/stories/pdfs/unlocking_al_qaeda.pdf

Brass, Paul. 1997. Theft of an Idol. Princeton, NJ: Princeton University Press.

Brettell, Caroline, and James Hollifield, eds. 2008. Migration Theory. New York and London: Routledge.

Briggs, Rachel. 2010. "Community Engagement for Counterterrorism: Lessons from the United Kingdom." International Affairs 86(4): 971–81.

Brighton, Shane. 2007. "British Muslims, Multiculturalism and UK Foreign Policy: 'Integration' and 'Cohesion' in and Beyond the State." International Affairs 83(1): 1–17.

Brignall, Robert. 2010. "Justice Department to Probe Luqman Abdullah Shooting." Detroit Crime Examiner, February 3. Available at: www.examiner.com/x-19336-Detroit-Crime-Examiner~y2010m2d3-Justice-Department-to-probe-Luqman-Abdullah-shooting

Bristol Evening Post. 2006. "Anti-War Protesters Criticize BBC." April 5, pg. 3.

British Muslims for Secular Democracy (BMSD). 2010. "Think Global, Act Local: A Study of the Political Choices of British Muslim Students." Report, April. Available at: www.bmsd.org.uk/pdfs/think%20global%20act%20local.pdf

Brown, Gregory S. 2004. Coping with Long-distance Nationalism: Inter-Ethnic Conflict in a Diaspora Context. Doctoral Dissertation, the University of Texas at Austin. Available at: www.library.utexas.edu/etd/d/2004/browng58501/browng58501.pdf

Brown, Judith. 2006. Global South Asians. Cambridge, UK: Cambridge University Press.

Buckley, Mary, and Rick Fawn, eds. 2003. Global Responses to Terrorism. London and New York: Routledge.

Building Islam in Detroit Exhibit. 2009. University of Michigan-Dearborn, Bertkowitz Library, November.

Bunglawala, Inayat. 2010. "UK Government and MCB Restore Relations." Islamonline.net, February 8. Available at: www.islamonline.net/servlet/Satellite?c=Article_C&cid=1265523803530&pagename=Zone-English-Euro_Muslims/EMELayout

Bunting, Madeleine. 2005. "Muslim Voices Have Been Lost in the Rush to Make Headlines." The Guardian, October 10. Available at: www.guardian.co.uk/politics/2005/oct/10/religion.politicalcolumnists

Burns, John F. 2009. "Terror Inquiry Looks at Suspect's Time in Britain." The New York Times, December 29. Available at: www.nytimes.com/2009/12/30/world/europe/30nigerian.html?pagewanted=all&_r=0

Burns, John F. 2010. "Britain Moves to Ban Islamic Group." The New York Times. January 12. Available at: www.nytimes.com/2010/01/13/world/europe/13britain.html

Buzan, Barry. 1991. People, States and Fear, London: Longman.

Buzan, Barry, and Ole Wæver. 2003. Regions and Powers. Cambridge, UK: Cambridge University Press.

Byman, Daniel L., and Kenneth M. Pollack. 2007. Things Fall Apart: Containing the Spillover from an Iraqi Civil War. Washington DC: Brookings Institution Press.

Cainkar, Louise A. 2009. Homeland Insecurity. New York: Russell Sage.

Caldwell, Christopher. 2009. Reflections on the Revolution in Europe: Immigration, Islam and the West. New York, London, Toronto, Sydney, Auckland: Doubleday.

Camarota, Steven A. 2002. The Open Door: How Militant Islamic Terrorists Entered and Remained in the United States, 1993–2001. Center for Immigration Studies Backgrounder. Available at: www.cis.org/articles/2002/theopendoor.pdf

Carr, Matthew. 2010. Blood and Faith: The Purging of Muslim Spain 1492–1614. London: Hurst.

Casciani, Dominic. 2007. "The Battle Over Mosque Reform." BBC News, November 29. Available at: http://news.bbc.co.uk/2/hi/uk_news/magazine/7118503.stm

Casciani, Dominic. 2010. "Prevent Extremism Strategy 'Stigmatising,' Warn MPs." BBCNews, March 30. Available: http://news.bbc.co.uk/2/hi/8593862.stm

Castles, Stephen and Mark J. Miller. 1993. The Age of Migration: International Population Movements in the Modern World. London: MacMillan.

Castles, Stephen and Mark J. Miller. 1998. The Age of Migration: International Population Movements in the Modern World, 2nd Edition. New York: Palgrave.

Castles, Stephen, and Mark J. Miller. 2003. The Age of Migration: International Population Movements in the Modern World, 3rd Edition. New York: Palgrave Macmillan.

Castles, Stephen, and Mark J. Miller. 2009. The Age of Migration: International Population Movements in the Modern World,. 4th Edition. New York: Guilford Press.

Cesari, Jocelyne. 2004. When Islam and Democracy Meet: Muslims in Europe and in the United States. New York: Palgrave McMillan.

Cesari, Jocelyne. 2011. "Muslims in Europe and the US: A Shared but Overrated Risks of Radicalism." In Jihadi Terrorism and the Radicalization Challenge: European and American Experiences, 2nd Edition, ed. Rik Coolsaet. Surrey, UK: Ashgate, 101–116.

Cesari, Jocelyne, ed. 2010. Muslims in the West after 9/11: Religion, Politics and Law. London and New York: Routledge.

Cesari, Jocelyne. 2013. Why the West Fears Islam: An Exploration of Muslims in Liberal Democracies. Palgrave Macmillan: New York.

Change Institute, Department for Communities and Local Government. 2009. The Pakistani Muslim Community in England. Online Publication, March. Available at: www.communities.gov.uk/documents/communities/pdf/1170952.pdf

Chebel d'Appollonia, Ariane. 2008. "Immigration, Security, and integration in the European Union." In Immigration, Integration, and Security: America and Europe in Comparative Perspective, eds. Ariane Chebel d'Appollonia and Simon Reich. Pittsburgh, PA: University of Pittsburgh Press, 203–228.

Chebel d'Appollonia, Ariane. 2012. Frontiers of Fear: Immigration and Insecurity in the United States and Europe. Ithaca, NY: Cornell University Press.

Chebel d'Appollonia, Ariane. 2015. Migrant Mobilization and Securitization in the US and Europe: How Does It Feel to Be a Threat? New York: Palgrave MacMillan.

Chebel d'Appollonia, Arriane, and Simon Reich, eds. 2008. Immigration, Integration, and Security: America and Europe in Comparative Perspective. Pittsburgh, PA: University of Pittsburgh Press.

Choudary, Anjem. 2009. Interview with Juris Pupcenoks. London, August 10.

Clarke, Peter. 2007. "Learning from Experience—Counter Terrorism in the UK since 9/11." The Colin Cramphorn Memorial Lecture. April 24. Available at: www.gees.org/documentos/Documen-02228.pdf

Clements, Ben. 2015. Religion and Public Opinion in Britain: Continuity and Change. New York: Palgrave.

ClickonDetroit.com. 2005. "Documents Suggest Dearborn Men May Be Terror Supporters: Father, Son Convicted on Fraud Charges." June 16. Available at: www.clickondetroit.com/news/4617596/detail.html

CNN. 2010. "Study: Threat of Muslim-American Terrorism in U.S. Exaggerated." January 6. Available at: http://edition.cnn.com/2010/US/01/06/muslim.radicalization.study/index.html

CNN Law Center Online. 2003. "Reid: 'I Am at War with Your Country.'" January 31. Available at: www.cnn.com/2003/LAW/01/31/reid.transcript/

Cohen, Robin. 1997. Global Diasporas. London: UCL Press.

Cohen, Robin. 2008. Global Diasporas, 2nd Edition. New York: Routledge.

Cohen, Robin, and Zig Layton-Henry, eds. 1997. The Politics of Migration. Cheltenham, UK and Northampton, MA: An Elgar Reference Collection.

Cole, David. 2003. Enemy Aliens: Double Standards and Constitutional Freedoms in the War on Terror. New York: New Press.

Coleman, Doriane Lambelet. 1996. "Individualizing Justice through Multiculturalism: the Liberals' Dilemma." Columbia Law Review 96: 1093.

Collier, David, and James Mahon. 1993. "Conceptual "Stretching" Revisited: Adapting Categories in Comparative Analysis." American Political Science Review 87(December):

Connor, Phillip. 2010. "Contexts of Immigrant Receptivity and Immigrant Religious Outcomes: the Case of Muslims in Western Europe." Ethnic and Racial Studies 33(March): 376–403.

Constanza, Stephen E., John C. Kilburn Jr., and Ronald Helms. 2009. "Counterterrorism." In Terrorism in America, eds. Kevin Borgeson and Robin Valeri. Sudbury, MA: Jones and Bartlett Publishers, 91–115.

Convay, Gordon. 1997. "Islamophobia: Its Features and Dangers." Runnymede Trust Consultation Paper.

Cooper, Robert. 2003. The Breaking of Nations. London: Atlantic Books.

Corley, Cheryl. 2007. "Michigan Muslims Feel Sectarian Ripples." National Public Radio, February 12. Available at: www.npr.org/templates/story/story.php?storyId=7371776

Council for Foreign Relations, The. 1996. The Clash of Civilizations? The Debate. New York and London: W. W. Norton.

Council for Foreign Relations, The. 2010. The Clash of Civilizations? The Debate, 2nd Edition. New York and London: W.W. Norton.

Cowan, Rosie, and Richard Norton-Taylor. 2006. "Britain Now No 1 al-Qaeda Target—Anti-Terror Chiefs." The Guardian, October 19. Available at: www. theguardian.com/politics/2006/oct/19/alqaida.terrorism

Cowell, Alan. 2007. "4 Guilty in Failed 2005 London Bombing." The New York Times, July 9. Available at: www.nytimes.com/2007/07/09/world/europe/09cnd-london.html

Cowell, Alan, and Douglass Jehl. 2005. "Police Ask Public to Help Trace Suspect; Homemade Explosive Now Suspected." The New York Times International, July 15. Available at: www.nytimes.com/2005/07/15/world/europe/police-ask-public-to-help-trace-a-bomber-homemade-explosive-is-now-hinted.html

Crenshaw, Martha, ed. 2010. The Consequences of Counterterrorism. New York: Russell Sage.

Cronin, Audrey K. 2009. How Terrorism Ends. Princeton, NJ: Princeton University Press.

Cross, Gary S. 1983. Immigrant Workers in Industrial France: The Making of a New Laboring Class. Philadelphia, PA: Temple University Press.

Cruickshank, Paul. 2010. "The Growing Danger from Radical Islamist Groups in the United States." CTC Sentinel 3(August): 4–10.

Crul, Maurice, and Hans Vermeulen, eds. 2003. "The Future of the Second Generation: The Integration of Migrant Youth in Six European Countries." Special Issue of International Migration Review 37(4): 965–1371.

Crul, Maurice, and Jens Schneider. 2010. "Comparative Integration Context Theory: Participation and Belonging in New Diverse European Cities," Ethnic and Racial Studies 33(7): 1249–1268.

Curiel, Jonathan. 2004. "Arab Americans Could Help Sway Crucial States." Chronicle. Available at: http://articles.sfgate.com/2004–10–28/news/17448462_1_arab-american-institute-muslim-voters-muslim-americans

Dahlberg-Acton, John. 1967. Essay in the Liberal Interpretation of History. Chicago and London: University of Chicago Press.

Daily Mail. 2007. "Ethnic Minorities 'Have Double Poverty Rate.'" April 30. Available at: www.dailymail.co.uk/news/article-451589/Ethnic-minorities-double-poverty-rate.html April 30.

Dancygier, Rafaela. 2010. Immigration and Conflict in Europe. Cambridge: Cambridge University Press.

della Porta, Donatella. 1998. "Police Knowledge and Protest Policing: Some Reflections on the Italian Case." In Policing Protest: The Control of Mass Demonstrations in Western Democracies, eds. Donatella della Porta and Herbert Reiter. Minneapolis, MN: University of Minneapolis Press, 228–252.

della Porta, Donatella, Abby Peterson, and Herbert Reiter. 2006. "Policing Transnational Protest: An Introduction." In The Policing of Transnational Protest, eds. Donatella della Porta, Abby Peterson, and Herbert Reiter. Burlington, VT: Ashgate, 1–12.

della Porta, Donatella, and Olivier Fillieule. 2004. "Policing Social Movements." In The Blackwell Companion to Social Movements, eds. David A. Snow, Sarah A. Soule, and Hanspeter Kriesi. Blackwell: Oxford, 217–241.

Denemark, Robert A. 2008. "Fundamentalisms as Global Social Movement." Globalizations 5(4): 571–82.

Detroit Arab American Study Team, eds. 2009. Citizenship and Crisis: Arab Detroit After 9/11. New York: Russell Sage Foundation.

Detroit Free Press. 2001. "Arabic Speakers Answer U.S. Need," September 19, 7A.

Dhillon, Simrat. 2007. "The Sikh Diaspora and the Quest for Khanistan: A Search for Statehood or for Self-preservation?" Institute of Peace and Conflict Studies, New Delhi, India. Available at: www.ipcs.org/pdf_file/issue/1787132181IPCS-ResearchPaper12-SimratDhillon.pdf

Diehl, Claudia, and Rainer Schnell 2006. " 'Reactive Ethnicity' or 'Assimilation'? Statements, Arguments, and First Empirical Evidence for Labor Migrants in Germany." International Migration Review 40:4: 786–816.

Dietderich, Andrew. 2006. "Mideast Conflict Brings Fear to Local Businesspeople." Crain's Detroit Business, July 24, p. 1.

Diouf, Sylviane. 1998. Servants of Allah: African Muslims Enslaved in the Americas. New York: New York University Press.

Docobo, Jose. 2005. "Community Policing as the Primary Prevention Strategy for Homeland Security at the Local Law Enforcement Level." Homeland Security Affairs 1(1): 1–12.

Dodds, Paisley. 2010. "UK Terror Plot Aimed British Landmarks, Shopping." Associated Press, December 20. Available at: www.boston.com/news/world/europe/articles/2010/12/21/uk_terror_plot_aimed_british_landmarks_shopping/

Doyle, Chris. 2009. Interview with Juris Pupcenoks. London, August 18.

Dreyfus, Jean-Marc, and Jonathan Laurence. 2002. "Anti-Semitism in France." The Brookings Institution, Analysis. Available at: www.brookings.edu/fp/cusf/analysis/dreyfus.pdf

Duran, Khalid, and Daniel Pipes. 2002. "Muslim Immigrants in the United States." Center for Immigration Studies Backgrounder. August. Available at: www.cis.org/USMuslimImmigrants

Eatwell, Roger. 2006. "Community Cohesion and Cumulative Extremism in Contemporary Britain." Political Quarterly 77(2): 204–216.

Economist, The. 2005. "Islam, America and Europe." Special Report. June 24.

Economist, The. 2006. "Who Speaks for British Muslims?" June 15.

Economist, The. 2008. "Hockey and Hijab." December 4.

Economist, The. 2010. "The Times Square Scare." May 8, 32.

Economist, The. 2011a. "Going Forth and Multiplying." February 5, 49.

Economist, The. 2011b. "Second Life." March 5, 17.

Edmunds, June. 2000. "The Evolution of British Labour Party Policy on Israel from 1967 to the Intifada." Twentieth Century British History 11(1): 23–41.

Egan, Paul. 2007. "Feds tie Dearborn Charity to Terror." The Detroit News. July 25. Available at: http://detnews.com/article/20070725/METRO/707250395/Feds-tie-Dearborn-charity-to-terror

Elahi, Mohammad Ali. 2009. Interview with Juris Pupcenoks. Detroit, MI, November 21.

Eley, Tom. 2008. "Protests in Dearborn, Michigan Denounces Israeli Attack on Gaza." Watan, Arab American National Newspaper, December 30. Available at: www.watan.com/en/the-community/221-tom-eley-.html

Eley, Tom. 2009. "Detroit: Hundreds Rally Against Israel Atrocities." World Socialist Web Site, January 9. Available at: www.wsws.org/articles/2009/jan2009/demo-j09.shtml

Elturk, Steve. 2009. Interview with Juris Pupcenoks. Detroit, MI, December 19.

Engage. 2009. "Figures for Government Funding of Muslim Organisations Revealed." March 27. Available at: www.iengage.org.uk/component/

content/article/290-figures-for-government-funding-of-muslim-organisations-revealed

Engage. 2011. "Quilliam Criticizes Home Office for Cutting Funding." 24 March. Available at: www.iengage.org.uk/component/content/article/1292-quilliam-criticises-home-office-for-cutting-funding

Engel, Matthew. 2003. "War in the Gulf: Iraqi Exiles in America Outnumbered by Arab Anti-War Protesters: Tensions Rise in Divided Suburb of US City Which Houses Hundreds of Thousands of Arabic Speakers." The Guardian. April 7, p. 9.

Ernst, Card, ed. 2013. Islamophobia in America: The Anatomy of Intolerance. New York: Palgrave MacMillan.

Ernst, Carl W. 2013b. "Introduction: The Problem of Islamophobia." In Islamophobia in America: The Anatomy of Intolerance. New York: Palgrave, 1–19.

Esposito, John L., and Dalia Mogahed. 2007. Who Speaks for Islam? New York: Gallup Press.

Esposito, John L., and Ibrahim Kalin. 2011. Islamophobia: The Challenge of Pluralism in the 21st Century. Oxford: Oxford University Press.

Ewing, Katherine Pratt, ed. 2008. Being and Belonging: Muslims in the United States since 9/11. New York: Russell Sage.

Express Tribune. 2010. "Luton: A Town Becoming Synonymous with Extremism." December 19. Available at: http://tribune.com.pk/story/91795/luton-a-town-becoming-synonymous-with-extremism

ExressIndia.com. 2007. "Sikh Extremism Spread Fast in Canada." May 23. Available at: www.expressindia.com/news/fullstory.php?newsid=86965.

Faist, Thomas. 2006. "International Migration and Security Before and After 11 September 2001." In The Immigration Reader, eds. Anthony Messina and Gallya Lahav. Boulder, CO: Lynne Rienner Publishers, 609–617.

Farley, Reynolds, et al. 1994. "Stereotypes and Segregation: Neighborhoods in the Detroit Area." The American Journal of Sociology 100(3): 750–780.

Ferjani, Said. 2009. Interview with Juris Pupcenoks. London, August 11.

Field, Clive. D. 2012. "Revisiting Islamophobia in Contemporary Britain: Opinion Poll Findings for 2007–10. In Islamophobia in the West: Measuring and Explaining Individual, ed. Marc Helbling. London: Routledge, 147–161.

Finlan, Alastair. 2004. The Collapse of Yugoslavia 1991–1999. Oxford: Osprey.

Fisher, Max. 2009. "Why Home-Grown Islamic Terrorism Isn't a Threat." The Atlantic, November 11. Available at: www.theatlantic.com/politics/archive/2009/11/why-home-grown-islamic-terrorism-isnt-a-threat/29993/

Fletcher, Richard. 2006. Moorish Spain. Berkeley and Los Angeles: University of California Press.

Franz, Barbara. 2007. "Europe's Muslim Youth: An Inquiry into the Politics of Discrimination, Relative Deprivation, and Identity Formation." Mediterranean Quarterly 18(1): 89–112.

Freeman, Gary. 1979. Immigrant Labor and Racial Conflict in Industrial Societies: The French and British Experience, 1945–1975. Princeton, NJ: Princeton University Press.

Freeman, Gary. 2005. "Political Science and Comparative Immigration Politics." In International Migration Research: Constructions, Omissions and the Promises of Interdiciplinarity, eds. Michael Bommes and Ewa Morawska. Aldershot, UK and Burlington, VT: Ashgate, 111–128.

Frontline. 2005. Al-Qaeda's New Front. Documentary.

Gallup. 2011. "Muslim Americans: Faith, Freedom, and the Future." Report.

Gannon, Kathy. 2010. "Pakistani Terrorism Training: Dozens of Europeans Visiting." Huffington Post. October 3. Available at: www.huffingtonpost.com/2010/10/03/pakistan-terrorism-traini_n_748642.html

Gaubatz, David P., and Paul Sperry. 2009. Muslim Mafia: Inside the Secret Underworld That's Conspiring to Islamize America. Los Angeles: WND Books.

Geddes, Andrew. 2003. The Politics of Migration and Immigration in Europe. London: Sage.

Gelb, Norman. 2009. "Battling Jihadism in Britain." The New Leader, September/October: 5–6.

George, Alexander, and Andrew Bennett. 2005. Case Studies and Theory Development in the Social Sciences. Cambridge, MA, and London: MIT Press.

Gerges, Fawaz. 2005. The Far Enemy. Cambridge, UK: Cambridge University Press.

Gest, Justin. 2010. Apart: Alienated and Engaged Muslim in the West. New York: Columbia University Press.

Ghayur, Arif. 1984. "Demographic Evolution of Pakistanis in America: A Case Study of a Muslim Subgroup." American Journal of Islamic Social Sciences 1: 113.

Ghosh, Bobby. 2010. "Arab Americans: Detroit's Unlikely Saviors." Time, November 13. Available at: www.time.com/time/magazine/article/0,9171,2028057,00.html

Gieco, Elizabeth. 2003. "Iraqi Immigrants in the United States." Migration Policy Institute Report. Available at: www.migrationinformation.org/usfocus/display.cfm?ID=113#7

Gilliat-Ray, Sophie. 2015. "The United Kingdom." In The Oxford Handbook of European Islam, ed. Jocelyne Cesari. Oxford: Oxford University Press, 64–103.

Giry, Stephanie. 2006. "France and Its Muslims." Foreign Affairs 85(September/October), 87–104.

Githens-Mazer, Jonathan. 2008. "Variations on a Theme: Radical Violent Islamism and European North African Radicalization," PS: Political Science and Politics 41(1): 19–24.

Githens-Mazer, Jonathan, and Robert Lambert. 2010. "Why Conventional Wisdom on Radicalization Fails: The Persistence of a Failed Discourse." International Affairs 86(4): 889–901.

Giugni, Marco. 2002. "Explaining Cross-National Similarities among Social Movements." In Globalization and Resistance: Transnational Dimensions of Social Movements, eds. Jackie Smith and Hank Johnson. Lahan, Boulder, New York: Rowman and Littlefield Publishers, Inc., 13–29.

Givens, Terri, Gary P. Freeman, and David L. Leal, eds. 2008. Immigration Policy and Security. New York and London: Routledge.

Glazer, Sara. 2010. "Radical Islam in Europe." In Issues in Terrorism and Homeland Security: Selections from CQ Researcher, ed. CQ Researcher. Thousand Oaks, CA: Sage Publications, 155–186.

Goertz, Gary. 2006. Social Science Concepts. Princeton, NJ: Princeton University Press.

Gomez, Michael. 1994. "Muslims in Early America." The Journal of Southern History 60 (November): 671.

Goodwin, Matthew. 2008. "Backlash in the 'Hood: Determinants of Support for the British National Party (BNP) at the Local Level." Journal of Contemporary European Studies 16(3): 347–361.

Gourevitch, Peter. 1978. "Second Image Reversed: The International Sources of Domestic Politics." International Organization 32(Autumn): 881–912.

Graham, David, and Nana Poku, eds. 2000. Migration, Globalization and Human Security. London: Routledge.

Grant, Peter. R. 2010. "The Protest Intentions of Skilled Immigrants with Credentialing Problems: A Test of a Model Integrating Relative Deprivation Theory with Social Identity Theory." British Journal of Social Psychology 47(4): 687–705.

Greene, Toby. 2013. Blair, Labour, and Palestine: Conflicting Views on Middle East Peace After 9/11. New York: Bloomsbury Academic.

Greenhill, Kelly M. 2010. Weapons of Mass Migration. Ithaca, NY: Cornell University Press.

Greenslade, Roy. 2005. Seeking Scapegoats: The Coverage of Asylum in the UK Press. Asylum and Migration Working Paper #5. Institute for Public Policy Research. Available at: www.ippr.org/publications/seeking-scapegoats-the-coverage-of-asylum-in-the-uk-pressworking-paper-5-of-the-asylum-and-migration-series

Grigorova-Mincheva, Lyubov. 2000. Ethnoterritorial Separatist Movements and Spillover Crises: The Balkans in the 1900s. Ph.D. Thesis, University of Maryland College Park, United States.

Gruen, Madeleine. 2011. "The Violent Shift in Hizb al-Tahrir's Rhetoric." Combating Terrorism Center at West Point Sentinel 4(2): 11–13.

Guibernau, Montserrat, and John Hutchinson, eds. 2004. National Destiny. Oxford: Blackwell.

Guild, Elizabeth. 2009. Security and Migration in the 21st Century. Cambridge, UK and Malden, MA: Polity.

Guiraudon, Virginie, and Christian Joppke, eds. 2001. Controlling a New Migration World. London: Routledge.

Gumbel, Andrew. 2006. "Stars, Stripes, and the Star of David." The Independent, August 15, p. 23.

Gurr, Ted. 1970. Why Men Rebel. Princeton, NJ: Princeton University Press.

Gurr, Ted R. 1993. Minorities at Risk. Washington DC: United States Institute of Peace.

Gurr, Ted R. 2000. Peoples versus States: Minorities at Risk in the New Century. Washington DC: United States Institute of Peace Press.

Haddad, Yvonne and Adair Lummis. 1987. Islamic Values in the United States. New York: Oxford University Press.

Hakeem, Farrukh B., M. R. Haberfeld, and Arvind Verma. 2012. Policing Muslim Communities: Comparative International Context. New York: Springer.

Hamad, Imad. 2009. Interview with Juris Pupcenoks. Detroit, MI, November 11.

Hamid, Saddek. 2007. "Islamic Political Radicalism in Britain: The Case of Hizb-Ut-Tahrir." In Islamic Political Radicalism: A European Perspective, ed. Tahir Abbas. Edinburgh: Edinburgh University Press, 145–59.

Hamid, Sadek. 2014. "Muslim Association of Britain." In Islamic Movements of Europe: Public Religion and Islamophobia in the Modern World, eds. Frank Peter and Rafael Ortega. New York and London: IB Taurus, 112–114.

Hammar, Thomas. 1985. European Immigration Policy: A Comparative Study Cambridge, UK: Cambridge University Press.

Hammoud, Abed. 2009. Interview with Juris Pupcenoks. Detroit, MI, December 14.

Hanagan, Michael. 2002. "Irish Transnational Social Movement, Migrants, and the State System." In Globalization and Resistance: Transnational Dimensions of Social Movements, eds. Jackie Smith and Hank Johnston. Laham, Boulder, New York, and Oxford: Rowman & Littlefield Publishers, Inc.

Hanson, Victor Davis. 2001. Why the West Has Won: Carnage and Culture from Salamis to Vietnam. New York: Faber and Faber.

Harden, Blaine. 1992. 'Turkish Kurds' Revolt Sparks Wide Violence." The Washington Post, March 25, A25.

Harff, Barbara, and Ted R. Gurr. 2004. Ethnic Conflict in World Politics, 2nd Edition. Boulder, CO: Westview Press.

Harris, Hermione. 2004. The Somali Community in the UK: What We Know and How We Know It. Commissioned and published by the Information Centre about Asylum and Refugees in the UK. Available at: www.icar.org.uk/somali communityreport.pdf

Harvey, Colin J. 2000. "Dissident Voices: Refugees, Human Rights and Asylum in Europe." Social & Legal Studies 9(3): 367–396.

Harvey, L. P. 1990. Islamic Spain 1250 to 1500. Chicago and London: University of Chicago Press.

Hassoun, Rosina J. 2005. Arab Americans in Michigan. East Lansing, MI: Michigan State University Press.

Hastings, Adrian. 1997. The Construction of Nationhood. Cambridge, UK: Cambridge University Press.

Hatton, Timothy J. 2011. Seeking Asylum: Trends and Policies in the OECD. London: Centre for Economic Policy Research.

Hatton, Timothy, and Jeffrey Williamson. 2005. Global Migration and the World Economy: Two Centuries of Policy and Performance. Cambridge, MA and London: The MIT Press.

Haubrich, Dirk. 2010. "The Social Contract and the Three Types of Terrorism: Democratic Society in the United Kingdom after 9/11 and 7/7." In The Consequences of Counterterrorism, ed. Martha Crenshaw. New York: Russell Sage Foundation, 179–212.

Heath, Anthony F., Steven D. Fisher, David Sanders, and Maria Sobolewska. 2011. "Ethnic Heterogeneity in the Social Bases of Voting at the 2010 British General Election." Journal of Elections, Public Opinion and Parties 21(2): 255–277.

Heath, Anthony, and Neli Demireva. 2014. "Has Multiculturalism Failed in Britain?" Ethnic and Racial Studies 37(1): 161–180.

Heather, Peter. 2010. Empires and Barbarians: The Fall of Rome and the Birth of Europe. Oxford: Oxford University Press.

Hellyer, H. A. 2007. "British Muslims and Islam Post-7/7." In Islamic Political Radicalism: A European Perspective, ed. Tahir Abbas. Edinburgh: Edinburgh University Press, 247–262.

Hellyer, H. A. 2010. "For Some MPs the Muslim Vote Will Be Vital." The Guardian, April 20. Available at: www.theguardian.com/commentisfree/2010/apr/20/some-mps-muslim-vote-vital

Hertel, Shareen, Matthew M. Singer, and Donna Lee Van Cott. 2009. "Field Research in Developing Countries: Hitting the Road Running." PS (April): 305–309.

Hewitt, Christopher. 2005. Political Violence and Terrorism in Modern America: A Chronology. Westport, CT and London: Praeger Security International.

Hewitt, Steve. 2008. The British War on Terror: Terrorism and Counter-terrorism on the Home Front Since 9/11. London and New York: Continuum.

Hill, Stuart, and Donald Rothchild. 1986. "The Contagion of Political Conflict in Africa and the World." Journal of Conflict Resolution 30(4): 716–735.

Hizb Ut-Tahrir Britain. 2007. "Radicalisation, Extremism, and 'Islamism:' Realities and Myths in the 'War on Terror'." Report. Available at: www.hizb.org.uk/wp-content/uploads/2007/07/radicalisation_extremism_islamism.pdf

Hizb-Ut Tahrir. 2009. "Struggle for Islam and the Call for Khilafah." Conference, Birmingham, UK, August 2.

HM Government. 2011. Prevent Strategy. Available at: www.homeoffice.gov.uk/publications/counter-terrorism/prevent/prevent-strategy/prevent-strategy-review?view=Binary

Hockenos, Paul. 2003. Homeland Calling: Exile Patriotism & the Balkan Wars. Ithaca, NY and London: Cornell University Press.

Hoffman, Bruce. 2006. Inside Terrorism. New York: Columbia University Press.

Holmes, Steven A. 1996. "Influx of Immigrants is Changing Electorate." The New York Times, October 30. Available at: www.nytimes.com/1996/10/30/us/influx-of-immigrants-is-changing-electorate.html

Home Office. 2004. "Briefing on British Muslims: Socio-Economic Data and Attitudes." Unpublished.

Hooper, Simon. 2015. "Could the Muslim Vote Sway the UK's General Election?" Al Jazeera, 13 March. Available at: www.aljazeera.com/indepth/features/2015/03/muslim-vote-sway-uk-general-election-150311055142181.html

Hopkins, Daniel J. 2010. "Politicized Places: Explaining Where and When Immigrants Provoke Local Opposition." American Political Science Review 104(1): 40–60.

Horowitz, Donald. 1985. Ethnic Groups in Conflict. Berkeley, CA, Los Angeles, and London: University of California Press.

Horowitz, Donald. 2001. The Deadly Ethnic Riot. Berkeley, CA, Los Angeles, and London: University of California Press.

Howell, Sally. 2009. Personal Communication. Detroit, MI, November 19.

Howell, Sally. 2011. "Muslims as Moving Targets: External Security and Internal Critique in Detroit's Mosques." In Arab Detroit 9/11: Life in the Terror Decade, eds. Nabeel Abraham, Sally Howell, and Andrew Shryock, Detroit, MI: Wayne University Press, 151–185.

Howell, Sally, and Amaney Jamal. 2008. "Detroit Exceptionalism and the Limits of Political Incorporation." In Being and Belonging: Muslims in the United States since 9/11, ed. Katherine Pratt Ewing. New York: Russell Sage Foundation.

Howell, Sally, and Amaney Jamal. 2009. "The Aftermath of the 9/11 Attacks." In Citizenship and Crisis: Arab Detroit after 9/11, ed. the Detroit Arab American Study Team. New York: Russell Sage Foundation.

Howell, Sally and Amaney Jamal. 2011. "Backlash, Part 2: The Federal Law Enforcement Agenda." In Arab Detroit 9/11: Life in the Terror Decade, eds. Nabeel Abraham, Sally Howell, and Andrew Shryock. Detroit, MI: Wayne University Press, 87–101.

Howell, Sally, and Andrew Shryock. 2003. "Cracking Down on Diaspora: Arab Detroit and America's "War on Terror." Anthropological Quarterly 76(3): 443–462.

Howell, Sally and Andrew Shryock. 2011. "Cracking Down on Diaspora: Arab Detroit and America's War on Terror." In Arab Detroit 9/11: Life in the Terror Decade, eds. Nabeel Abraham, Sally Howell, and Andrew Shryock. Detroit, MI: Wayne University Press, 67–86.

Huliq. 2007. "Turkish Grey Wolves Hold Violent Rallies in Europe." October 27. Available at: www.huliq.com/39786/turkish-grey-wolves-hold-violent-rallies-in-europe

Huntington, Samuel P. 1993. "The Clash of Civilizations?" Foreign Affairs (Summer), 22–49.

Huntington, Samuel P. 1998. The Clash of Civilizations and the Remaking of World Order. New York: Simon and Shuster.

Hurriyet. 2008. "Bir Dönemin Acı Bilançosu." July 16. Available at: www. hurriyet.com.tr/gundem/9914612.asp?gid=0&srid=0&oid=0&l=1

Husain, Ed. 2007. Islamist: Why I Joined Radical Islam in Britain, What I Saw Inside and Why I Left. London: Penguin.

Husain, Ed. 2009. "Ed Husain: Where is the Muslim Anger over Darfur?" The Independent, August 10. Available at: www.independent.co.uk/opinion/commentators/ed-husain-where-is-the-muslim-anger-over-darfur-1769962.html

Iain Walker, and Heather J. Smith. 2001. Relative Deprivation: Specification, Development, and Integration. Cambridge, UK: Cambridge University Press.

Ibrahim, Azeem. 2010. "Tackling Muslim Radicalization: Lessons from Scotland." The Institute for Social Policy and Understanding Report. Available at: http://ispu.org/GetReports/35/1882/Publications.aspx

Ignatiev, Noel. 1996. How the Irish Became White. London and New York: Routledge.

International Crisis Group. 2006. "La France Face à Ses Musulmans: Émeutes, Jihadisme et Dépolitisation." March 9. Available at: www.crisisgroup.org/~/media/Files/europe/172_la_france_face_a_ses_musulmans_emeutes__jihad isme_amended.

International Organization for Migration. 2007. "Iraq Mapping Exercise." Available at: www.iomlondon.org/doc/mapping/IOM_IRAQ.pdf Irish Times. 2001. "Islamic Leaders Call on Muslims to Demonstrate." October 12, p. 11.

Irvin, Cynthia. 1999. Militant Nationalism: Between Movement and Party in Ireland and the Basque Country. Minneapolis, MN: University of Minnesota Press.

Isikoff, Michael. 2003. "Investigators: The FBI Says, Count the Mosques." Newsweek, February 3. Available at: www.highbeam.com/doc/1G1-96968295.html

Islamic Human Rights Commission. 2009 (reprint of 2002 report). Muslim Profiling. London: Islamic Human Rights Commission.

Jaber, Aoun. 2009. Interview with Juris Pupcenoks. Detroit, MI, November 20.

Jackson, Pamela I., and Peter Doerschler. 2012. Benchmarking Muslim Well-Being in Europe: Reducing Disparities and Polarizations. Bristol, UK: Policy Press.

Jacobson, Jessica. 1998. Islam in Transition: Religion and Identity among British Pakistani Youth. London and New York: Routledge.

Jamal, Amaney, and Nadine Naber, eds. 2008. Race and Arab Americans Before and After 9/11: From Invisible Citizens to Visible Subjects. Syracuse, NY: Syracuse University Press.

Joarder, Shamiul. 2009. Interview with Juris Pupcenoks. London, August 19.

Johnson, Graham. 2002. "350,000 Say No To War; London Protest Blasts PM's Saddam Plan." Sunday Mirror, September 29, p. 19.

Joly, Daniele. 1995. Britannia's Crescent: Making a Place for Muslims in British Society. Avenbury: Aldershot.

Jones, Shannon. 2002. "Protest against Iraq War in Dearborn, Michigan." World Socialist Web Site, October 17. Available at: www.wsws.org/articles/2002/oct2002/dear-o17.shtml

Joppke, Christian. 2010. "Limits of Integration Policy: Britain and Her Muslims." In Muslims and the State in the Post-9/11 West, ed. Erik Bleich. London and New York: Routledge, 100–119.

Kapiszewski, Diana. 2010. "Conceptualizing and Preparing for Fieldwork." Presentation at the American Political Science Association Annual Meeting, Designing and Conducting Field Research in the Social Sciences Panel. Washington, DC. September 4.

Kaplan, David. 2005. "Nuclear Monitoring of Muslims Done without Search Warrants." US News and World Report, December 22. Available at: www.informationclearinghouse.info/article11369.htm

Kassab, Joseph. 2009. Interview with Juris Pupcenoks. Detroit, MI, November 30.

Kaufman, Stuart J. 2001. Modern Hatreds: the Symbolic Politics of Ethnic War. Ithaca, NY and London: Cornell University Press.

Kaufman, Stuart J. 2006. "Symbolic Politics or Rational Choice?" International Security 30(Spring): 45–86.

Kaye, Ronald, and Roger Charlton. 1990. "United Kingdom Admission Policy and the Politically Active Refugee." Research Paper in Ethnic Relations No. 13. Centre for Research in Ethnic Relations, University of Warwick, UK. Available at: www.warwick.ac.uk/fac/soc/CRER_RC/publications/pdfs/Research%20Papers%20in%20Ethnic%20Relations/RP%20No.13.pdf

Kazi, Tehmina. 2009. Interview with Juris Pupcenoks. London, August 12.

Kempe, Frederick. 2006. "U.S. Sees Europe as Front against Radical Islam; Senior Bush Aides Conclude Continent's Extremists Pose a Rising Security Threat." Wall Street Journal (Eastern edition), New York, April 11. Available at: www.wsj.com/articles/SB114470634808922206

Kennedy, Hugh. 1996. Muslim Spain and Portugal: A Political History of Al-Andalus. London and New York: Longman.

Keohane, Robert O., and Helen V. Milner, eds. 1996. Internationalization and Domestic Politics. Cambridge, UK: Cambridge University Press.

Kepel, Gilles. 2002. Jihad: The Trail of Political Islam. London: I.B. Tauris.

Keyes, Charley. 2008. "U.S. Admits More Iraqi Refugees." CNN Online, June 4. Available at: http://articles.cnn.com/2008–06–04/world/iraqi.refugees_1_iraqi-refugees-ambassador-james-foley-syria-and-jordan?_s=PM:WORLD

Khan, Muqtedar M. A. 2002. American Muslims: Bridging Faith and Freedom. Beltsville, Maryland: Amana.

Khan, Muqtedar M. A. 2004. "The Remarkable Moderation of Detroit Muslims." The Detroit News, July 4. Also available on the author's website at: www.ijtihad.org/Moderation%20of%20American%20Muslims.htm.

Khan, Muqtedar M. A. 2011. "The Threat of Islamophobia to American Muslim Civil Rights." Written Statement Submitted to Senate Judiciary Subcommittee on Constitution, Civil Society and Human Rights. March. Available at: http://ispu.org/files/PDFs/580_muqtedar%20khan%20testimony%20version%202.pdf

Khan, Muqtedar M.A., and John Esposito. 2005. "Islam in the West: The Threat of Internal Extremism." Altmuslim.com. February 18. Available at: www.altmuslim.com/a/a/a/2183

Khan, Muqtedar M. A., Sara J. Chehab, and Dima Qassim. 2010. "Understanding and Combating Muslim Radicalism in the United States." Institute for Social Policy and Understanding Policy Brief #43. Available at: www.ispu.org/files/PDFs/428_PB_ISPU-Understanding_and_Combating_Muslim_Radicalism_in_US_-_Khan_-_Chehab_-_Qassim.pdf

Khan, Saeed Ahmed. 2009a. Personal Communication. Detroit, MI, November 18.

Khan, Saeed Ahmed. 2009b. "Muslim Engagement in Public Sphere." A Speech in Building Islam in Detroit Symposium. Mardigan Library, University of Michigan-Dearborn, November 14.

Khan, Shahab Enam. 2009. "In Pursuit of the Causes of Radicalization in the United Kingdom: Exploring the Institutions, Politics and Public Policy Responses." A Working Manuscript.

Khan, Shahab Enam. 2010a. Interview with Juris Pupcenoks. Newark, DE, January 26.

Khan, Shahab Enam. 2010b. "Understanding the Threats from Islamist Terrorism in Bangladesh." Inaugural and Keynote Paper. Presented at ORF-BAI India-Bangladesh Dialogue on Security. New Delhi, India, March 19–20.

Khan, Shahab Enam. 2011. "U.S. Foreign Policy towards Bangladesh: Implications of the Rise of Islamist Terrorism." In National Security Policy in the Obama Administration, eds. Bahram M. Rajaee, and Mark J. Miller. New York: Palgrave McMillan.

King, Gary, Robert Keohane, and Sidney Verba. 1994. Designing Social Inquiry: Scientific Inference in Qualitative Research. Princeton, NJ: Princeton University Press.

Kirby, Aidan. 2007. "The London Bombers as 'Self Starters': A Case Study in Indigenous Radicalization and the emergence of Autonomous Cliques." Studies in Conflict and Terrorism 30(5): 415–428.

Kirshner, Jonathan, ed. 2006. Globalization and National Security. London: Routledge.

Klausen, Jytte. 2009a. "British Counter-Terrorism After 7/7: Adapting Community Policing to the Fight Against Domestic Terrorism." Journal of Ethnic and Migration Studies 35(3): 403–20.

Klausen, Jytte. 2009b. The Cartoons that Shook the World. New Haven, CT and London: Yale University Press.

Koopmans, Ruud. 1995. "The Dynamics of Protest Waves: West Germany, 1965 to 1989." American Sociological Review 58: 637–658.

Koser, Khalid. 2011. "When is Migration a Security Issue?" Brookings Institution. Available at: www.brookings.edu/opinions/2011/0331_libya_migration_koser.aspx

Koslowski, Rey. 2006. International Migration and Globalization of Domestic Politics. New York and London: Routledge.

Krebs, Ronald, and Jack Levy. 2001. "Demographic Change and the Sources of International Conflict." In Demography and National Security, eds. Myron Weiner and Sharon Russell. New York and Oxford: Berghahn Books, 62–105.

Kurzman, Charles. 2011. The Missing Martyrs: Why There Are So Few Muslim Terrorists. Oxford: Oxford University Press.

Kushner, Harvey W. 2003. Encyclopedia of Terrorism. Thousand Oaks, CA: Sage Publications.

Lahav, Gallya. 2010. "Immigration Policy as Counterterrorism: The Effects of Security on Migration and Border Security in the European Union." In The Consequences of Counterterrorism, ed. Martha Crenshaw. New York: Russell Sage Foundation, 130–176.

Laird, Heather. 2009. "Southeastern Michigan is a Great Place for Muslims to Live." SE Michigan Islamic Examiner. October 11. Available at: www.examiner.com/x-26018-SE-Michigan-Islamic-Examiner~y2009m10d11-Southeastern-Michigan-is-a-great-place-for-Muslims-to-live

Laitin, David. 1998. Identity in Formation: The Russian-Speaking Populations in the Near Abroad. Ithaca, NY and London: Cornell University Press.

Lake, David A., and Donald Rothchild. 1998. "Spreading Fear: The Genesis of Transnational Ethnic Conflict." In The International Spread of Ethnic Conflict, eds. David A. Lake and Donald Rothchild. Princeton, NJ: Princeton University Press, 3–32.

Lambert, Robert. 2011. "The Muslim Safety Forum: Senior Police and Muslim Community Engagement During the War on Terror." In Preventing Ideological Violence: Communities, Police and Case Studies of "Successes", eds. P. Daniel Silk, Basia Spalek, and Mary O'Rawe. New York: Palgrave MacMillan: 67–88.

Lambert, Robert, and Jonathan Githens-Mazer. 2010. Islamophobia and Anti-Muslims Hate Crime. Exeter, UK: University of Exeter.

Laqueur, Walter. 1999. The New Terrorism. Oxford and New York: Oxford University Press.

Laqueur, Walter. 2007. The Last Days of Europe: Epitaph for an Old Continent. New York: Thomas Dunne Books/ St. Martin's Press.

Latif, Sofia. 2009. Interview with Juris Pupcenoks. Detroit, MI, December 9.

Laurence, Jonathan. 2012. The Emancipation of Europe's Muslims: The State's Role in Minority Integration. Princeton, NJ: Princeton University Press.

Laurence, Jonathan, and Justin Vaisse. 2006. Integrating Islam: Political and Religious Challenges in Contemporary France. Washington: Brookings Institution Press.

Lavenex, Sandra, and Emek Uçarer, eds. 2003. Migration and the Externalities of European Integration. Lanham, MD: Rowman and Litttlefield.

Layton-Henry, Zig. 1981. A Report on British Immigration Policy Since 1945. Coventry, UK: University of Warwick.

Layton-Henry, Zig. 1992. The Politics of Immigration: Immigration, 'Race' and 'Race' Relations in Post-War Britain. Oxford, UK and Cambridge, MA: Blackwell.

Layton-Henry, Zig, and Paul B. Rich, eds. 1986. Race, Government and Politics in Britain. London: Macmillan.

Leiken, Robert S. 2004. Bearers of Global Jihad? Immigration and National Security after 9/11. Washington: The Nixon Center.

Leiken, Robert S. 2005. "Europe's Angry Muslims." Foreign Affairs (July/August): 120–135.

Leiken, Robert S. 2009. "The Menace in Europe's Midst." Current History (April): 186–188.

Leiken, Robert. 2012. Europe's Angry Muslims: The Revolt of The Second Generation. London and Oxford: Oxford University Press.

Lejeune-Kaba, Fatoumata. 2010. "Number of Asylum-Seekers Remains Stable over 2009, UNHCR Figures Show." UNHCR. March 23. Available at: www.unhcr.org/4ba8d8239.html

Leonard, Karen Isaksen. 2003. Muslims in the United States: The State of Research. New York: Russell Sage Foundation.

Leppard, David. 2010. "Met Allows Islamic Protesters to Throw Shoes." The Sunday Times April 11. Available at: www.timesonline.co.uk/tol/comment/faith/article7094311.ece

Lewis, Philip. 1994, 2002 (updated version). Islamic Britain: Religion, Politics and Identity among British Muslims. London and New York: I.B. Tauris.

Lewis, Philip. 2015. "Imams in Britain: Agents of De-Radicalization?" In Islamic Movements of Europe: Public Religion and Islamophobia in the Modern World, eds. Frank Peter and Rafael Ortega. New York and London: I. B. Tauris, 237–240.

Lucassen, Leo. 2005. The Immigrant Threat. Chicago: University of Illinois Press.

Lyon, Alynna. 1999. International Contributions to the Mobilization of Ethnic Conflict: Sri Lanka, Iraq, and Rwanda. PhD Thesis, Department of Government and International Studies, University of South Carolina, Columbia, SC.

Lyon, Alynna, and Emek Uçarer. 2001. "Mobilizing Ethnic Conflict: Kurdish Separatism in Germany and the PKK." Ethnic and Racial Studies 24(6): 925–948.

Ma'oz, Moshe, and Gabriel Sheffer, eds. 2002. Middle Eastern Minorities and Diasporas. Brighton, Portland: Sussex Academic Press.

Macedo, Diane. 2010. "Radical Islamist Group is Returning to Chicago for Major Recruitment Drive." FoxNews.com, June 16. Available at: www.foxnews.com/us/2010/06/16/radical-islamist-group-set-return-chicago-second-major-recruiting-conference/

Modood, Tariq, Berthoud Richard, Lakey Jane, Nazroo James, Smith Patten, Virdee Satnam and Beishon Sharon, eds. 1997. Ethnic Minorities in Britain. London: Policy Studies Institute.

Modood, Tariq. 2007. Multicultural Politics: Racism, Ethnicity and Muslims in Britain. Edinburgh: Edinburgh University Press.

Modood, Tariq, and Craid Calhoun. 2005. Multicultural Politics: Racism, Ethnicity, and Muslims in Britain. Minneapolis, MN: University of Minnesota Press.

Majeed, Adam. 2010. Policing, Protest and Conflict: A Report into the Policing of the London Gaza Demonstrations 2008–2009. London: Islamic Human Rights Commission.

Malik, Abdul-Rehman. 2009. Interview with Juris Pupcenoks. London, September 4.

Malik, Kenan, From Fatwa to Jihad: the Rushdie Affair and Its Aftermath. Brooklyn: Melville House.

Mandaville, Peter. 2001. Transnational Muslim Politics. London and New York: Routledge.

Marcus, Aliza. 2007. Blood and Belief: The PKK and the Kurdish Fight for Independence. New York and London: New York University Press.

Mayer, Nick. 2009. "Dearborn City Council Passes Gaza Resolution." The Arab American News, January 23. Available at: www.arabamericannews.com/news/index.php?mod=article&cat=Community&article=1883

Mayor's Office for Policing and Crime. 2013. Available at: http://content.met.
police.uk/Site/About

Mazrui, Ali. 2006. "Between the Crescent and the Star-Spangled Banner: American Muslims and US Foreign Policy." International Affairs 72(3): 493–506.

McAdam, Doug. 1982. Political Process and the Development of Black Insurgency 1930–1970. Chicago: University of Chicago Press.

McAdam, Doug. 1996. "Conceptual Origins, Current Problems, Future Directions." In Comparative Structures on Social Movements: Political Opportunities, Mobilizing Structures and Cultural Framings, eds. Doug McAdam, John D. McCarthy, and Mayer N. Zald. Cambridge, UK: Cambridge University Press, 23–40.

McAdam, Doug, Sidney Tarrow, and Charles Tilly. 2001. Dynamics of Contention. Cambridge, UK: Cambridge University Press.

McCarus, Ernest, ed. 1994. The Development of Arab American Identity. Ann Arbor, MI: University of Michigan Press.

McCorkell, Andrew. 2011. "Muslims Call for Action against Hate Crimes." The Independent, June 12. Available at: www.independent.co.uk/news/uk/crime/muslims-call-for-action-against-hate-crimes-2296477.html

McGown, Rima B. 1999. Muslims in the Diaspora: The Somali Communities of London and Toronto. Toronto: University of Toronto Press.

Mearsheimer, John, and Stephen Walt. 2007. The Israel Lobby and U.S. Foreign Policy. New York: Farrar, Straus and Giroux.

Meer, Nasar, and Tariq Modood. 2009. "Refutations of Racism in the "Muslim Question." Patterns of Prejudice 43(3/4): 335–354.

Mehdi, Beverlee T. 1978. The Arabs in America, 1492–1977. New York: Oceana.

Mendick, Robert, and Robert Verkaik. 2014. "Downing Street Set to Crack Down on the Muslim Brotherhood." Telegraph, 19 October. Available at: www.telegraph.co.uk/news/uknews/11171979/Downing-Street-set-to-crackdown-on-the-Muslim-Brotherhood.html

Messina, Anthony. 2007. The Logistics and Politics of Post-WWII Migration to Western Europe. Cambridge, UK: Cambridge University Press.

Michigan Daily, The. 2003. "U.S. Arab Population Doubles Over 20 Years." December 4. Available at: www.michigandaily.com/content/us-arab-population-doubles-over-20-years

Migration News. 2011. V. 18, No1. January. University of California, Davis.

Migration Watch UK. 2004. "The Number of Failed Asylum Seekers Remaining in the UK." Migration Trends 9.14. Available at: www.migrationwatchuk.org/Briefingpaper/document/108

Miller, Mark J. 1978. The Problem of Foreign Worker Participation and Representation in France, Switzerland and the Federal Republic of Germany. Ph.D. Book, University of Wisconsin-Madison United States.

Miller, Mark J. 1981. Foreign Workers in Western Europe: An Emerging Political Force. New York: Praeger.

Miller, Mark J. 1998. "International Migration and Global Security." In Redefining Security, eds. Nana Poku and David Graham. Westport, CT: Praeger, 15–29.

Miller, Mark J. 2000. "A Durable International Migration and Security Nexus: The Problem of the Islamic Periphery in Transatlantic Ties." In Migration, Globalization and Human Security, eds. David Graham and Nana Poku. London: Routledge, 92–109.

Miller, Mark J. 2006a. "Muslim Immigration to Europe." Muslim Public Affairs Journal 1(1): 59–68.

Miller, Mark J. 2006b. "Opportunities and Challenges for Migrant and Migrant-Background Youth in Developed Countries." Short Version Report Submitted to the United Nations Social and Economic Council, July 15. Available at: www.udel.edu/readhistory/resources/2005_2006/summer_06/short.pdf

Miller, Mark J. 2007. "Disquiet on the Western Front: Sleeper Cells, Transatlantic Rift and the War in Iraq." In The War on Terror in Comparative Perspective: U.S. Security and Foreign Policy after 9/11, eds. Mark J. Miller and Boyka Stefanova. New York: Palgrave Macmillan, 111–120.

Miller, Teresa A. 2005. "By Any Means Necessary: Collateral Civil Penalties and the War on Terror." In Civil Penalties, Social Consequences, eds. Christopher Mele and Teresa A. Miller. New York: Routledge, 47–66.

Mirza, Munira, Abi Senthilkumaran, and Zein Ja'far. 2007. "Living Apart Together: British Muslims and the Paradox of Multiculturalism." Report. Available at: www.policyexchange.org.uk/images/publications/living%20apart%20together%20-%20jan%2007.pdf

Mizrahi, Hagar. 2009. "Dutch Passenger Thwarted Terror Attack on Plane." Israel News, December 27. Available at: www.ynetnews.com/articles/0,7340,L-3825447,00.html

Mlive.com. 2009. "CIA Commercials to Recruit US Arabs, Iranians." November 9. Available at: www.mlive.com/news/detroit/index.ssf/2009/11/cia_commercials_to_recruit_us.html

Mlive.com. 2010. "Muslim Group Stages Rally Outside Courthouse." January 8. Available at: www.mlive.com/news/detroit/index.ssf/2010/01/muslim_group_stages_rally_outs.html

Mogahed, Dalia, and Zsolt Nyiri. 2007. "Reinventing Integration: Muslims in the West." Harvard International Review 29(2): 14–18.

Mollenkopf, John and Jennifer Hochschild. 2010. "Immigrant Political Incorporation: Comparing Success in the United States and Western Europe." Ethnic and Racial Studies, January 33(1): 19–38.

Moorehead, Monica. 2006. "U.S. Out of the Middle East!" Workers World, August 9. Available at: www.workers.org/2006/us/anti-war-0817

Moran, Jon, and Mark Phythian, eds. 2008. Intelligence, Security and Policing Post-9/11: The UK's Response to the 'War on Terror.' New York: Palgrave Macmillan.

Morgan, Tom. 2010. "Police Could Face Legal Action over 'Unfair' Searches." The Independent, March 15. Available at: www.independent.co.uk/news/uk/crime/police-could-face-legal-action-over-unfair-searches-1921614.html

Morreale, Stephen. 2004. "Using the Community Policing Model for Approaching Terrorist Threats and Domestic Preparedness." Law Enforcement Executive Forum 4.7: 1–10.

MSNBC. 2006. "Iraqi Americans Celebrate Saddam's Execution." December 29. Available at: www.msnbc.msn.com/id/16400751/

MSNBC. 2010a. "Napolitano: Domestic Extremism Top Concern." February 22. Available at: www.msnbc.msn.com/id/35520031

MSNBC 2010b. "Europe on High Alert over Concern of Terror Attacks." September 28. Available at: www.msnbc.msn.com/id/39406942/ns/world_news-europe/t/europe-high-alert-over-concern-terror-attacks/#.T_8Y3_WuWVo

Mueller, John. 2000. "The Banality of 'Ethnic War'." International Security 25(1): 42–70.

Mueller, John. 2008. "The Iraq Syndrome." In The Domestic Sources of American Foreign Policy, 5th Edition, eds. Eugene Wittkopf and James McCormick. Lanham, MD: Rowman and Littlefield, 115–124.

Mueller, John, and Mark G. Stewart. 2012. "The Terrorism Delusion." International Security 37(1): 81–110.

Muhiuddin, Abdullateef. 2009. Interview with Juris Pupcenoks. Detroit, MI, December 5.

Mumisa, Michael. 2010. "The Civil War among Muslims in Britain." Available at: http://blogs.independent.co.uk/2010/12/01/the-civil-war-among-muslims-in-britain/

Mustafa, Asma. 2015. Identity and Political Participation among Young British Muslims: Believing and Belonging. New York: Palgrave MacMillan.

Mustafa, Taji. 2009. Speech at Hizb-Ut Tahrir "Struggle for Islam and the Call for Khilafah." Conference, Birmingham, UK, August 2.

Naber, Nadine. 2009. "Transnational Families Under Siege: Lebanese Shi'a in Dearborn, Michigan, and the 2006 War on Lebanon." Journal of Middle East Women's Studies 5(3): 145–174.

Nachmani, Amikam. 2009. Europe and Its Muslim Minorities: Aspects of Conflict, Attempts at Accord. Brighton, Portland: Sussex Academic Press.

Naqshbandi, Mehmood. 2008. "Isolating Extremism." Working Draft Online. Available at: http://politics.muslimsinbritain.org/politics2.html

Naqshbandi, Mehmood. 2009. Interview with Juris Pupcenoks. London, August 31.

Nation, Pakistan. 2010. "Muslims in Detroit Denounce Terrorism." January 9. Available at: www.nation.com.pk/pakistan-news-newspaper-daily-english-online/International/09-Jan-2010/Muslims-in-Detroit-denounce-terrorism

NATO HQ Media Operations Centre—Afghanistan. 2010. "ISAF and ANA Strength and Laydown." April 16. Available at: www.isaf.nato.int/images/stories/File/Placemats/Apr-16–2010-placemat.pdf

Navas, Marisol, et al. 2005. "Relative Acculturation Extended Model (RAEM): New Contributions with Regard to the Study of Acculturation." International Journal of Intercultural Relations 29(1): 21–37.

Nesser, Petter. 2006. "Jihadism in Western Europe after the Invasion of Iraq: Tracing Motivational Influences from the Iraq War on Jihadist Terrorism in Western Europe." Studies in Conflict and Terrorism 29(4): 323–342.

Neumann, Peter. 2010. Prisons and Terrorism: Radicalisation and De-Radicalisation in 15 Countries. The International Centre for the Study of Radicalisation (ICSR) Report. London: ICSR.

Neumann, Peter R. 2009a. Old and New Terrorism: Late Modernity, Globalization and the Transformation of Political Violence. Cambridge, UK, and Malden, MA: Polity.

Neumann, Peter R. 2009b. Personal Communication. London, August 5.

New York Times. 1989. "The Rushdie Affair Lives." April 16. Available at: www.nytimes.com/1989/04/16/opinion/the-rushdie-affair-lives.html

New York Times. 2002. "The Distant Drums of War" June 1. Available at: www.nytimes.com/2002/06/01/nyregion/01JACK.html

New Zealand Herald. 2008. "Protests Erupt in US Over Gaza Attacks." December 31, Section News, World.

Nielsen, Jorgen S. 2004. Muslims in Western Europe, 3rd Edition. Edinburgh, UK: Edinburgh University Press.

Norris, H. T. 1993. Islam in the Balkans: Religion and Society between Europe and the Arab World. Columbia, SC: University of South Carolina Press.

Norton-Taylor, Richard. 2009. "Cabinet Told of Iraq War Risk to UK, Says Ex-MI5 Chief." The Guardian, July 11. Available at: www.theguardian.com/politics/2009/jul/11/mi5-warning-iraq-war-terrorism

Nyiri, Zsolt. 2010. "The Clash of Perceptions: Comparison of Views among Muslims in Paris, London, and Berlin with the General Public." In Managing Ethnic Diversity after 9–11: Integration, Security and Civil Liberties in Transatlantic Perspective, eds. Ariane Chebel d'Appollonia and Simon Reich. New Brunswick, NJ: Rutgers University Press, 98–113.

O'Duffy, Brendan. 2008. "Radical Atmosphere: Explaining Jihadist Radicalization in the UK." PS: Political Science and Politics 41(1): 37–42.

Office of the Deputy Prime Minister. 2006. "Review of the Evidence Base on Faith Communities," London.

Office of the Mayor of London. 2006. "Muslims in London." Report. London: Greater London Authority.

Omaar, Rageh. 2007. "How Heroin Creates Terrorists." New Statesman, 12 November, p. 23.

Open Society Institute. 2004. Aspirations and Reality: British Muslims and the Labour Market. London: Open Society Institute.

Open Society Institute. 2010. "Muslims in Europe: A Report on 11 EU Cities." Report. Available at: www.opensocietyfoundations.org/sites/default/files/a-muslims-europe-20110214_0.pdf

Oswald, Debra L. 2005. "Understanding Anti-Arab Reactions Post-9/11: The Role of Threats, Social Categories, and Personal Ideologies." Journal of Applied Social Psychology 35(9): 1775–1799.

Ottawa Citizen. 2001. "People Worldwide Protest Bombings: Tens of Thousands Demonstrate in European Cities." October 14, pg. A5.

Pape, Robert. 2005. Dying to Win. New York: Random House.

Pargeter, Alison. 2006. "North African Immigrants in Europe and Political Violence." Studies in Conflict and Terrorism 29(8):731–747.

Pargeter, Alison. 2008. The New Frontiers of Jihad: Radical Islam in Europe. Philadelphia, PA: University of Pennsylvania Press.

Pazoles, Matt. 2009. "Stemming the Tide: Evaluating the British Government's Efforts to Counter the Radicalization of British Muslim Youth." University of Delaware Senior Thesis. Available at: http://dspace.udel.edu:8080/dspace/bitstream/handle/19716/5520/Pazoles%2c%20Matthew.pdf?sequence=1

Peach, Ceri. 2006. "Islam, Ethnicity and South Asian Religions in the London 2001 Census." Transactions of the Institute of British Geographers 31(3): 353–370.

Peek, Lori. 2011. Behind the Backlash: Muslim Americans after 9/11. Philadelphia, PA: Temple University Press.

Perelman, Marc. 2009. "Antisemitic Incidents Rise in France as Worry Increases About Ethnic Divisions." The Jewish Daily Forward, January 21. Available at: www.forward.com/articles/15012/

Pero, Saide and John Solomos, eds. 2010. "Migrant Politics and Mobilization: Exclusion, Engagement, Incorporation." Special Issue of Ethnic and Racial Studies 33(January): 1–156.

Petersen, Roger. 2002. Understanding Ethnic Violence. Cambridge, UK: Cambridge University Press.

Pettigrew et al. 2008. "Relative Deprivation and Intergroup Prejudice." Journal of Social Issues 64(2): 385–401.

Pew. 2006. "The Great Divide: How Westerners and Muslims View Each Other." Available at: http://pewglobal.org/2006/06/22/the-great-divide-how-westerners-and-muslims-view-each-other/

Pew. 2007. "Muslim Americans: Middle Class and Mostly Mainstream." Report.

Pew. 2009a. "Mapping the Global Muslim Population." A Report on the Size and Distribution of the World's Muslim Population, October 7. Available at: http://pewforum.org/PublicationPage.aspx?id=1497

Pew. 2009b. "Little Support for Terrorism Among Muslim Americans." Report. Available at: www.pewforum.org/2009/12/17/little-support-for-terrorism-among-muslim-americans/

Pew. 2011. "The Future of the Global Muslim Population: Projections for 2010–2030." January 27. Available at: http://pewresearch.org/pubs/1872/muslim-population-projections-worldwide-fast-growth

Pew. 2011b. "Muslims Americans: No Signs of Growth in Alienation or Support for Extremism." Report. Available at: www.people-press.org/files/legacy-pdf/Muslim%20American%20Report%2010–02–12%20fix.pdf

Pew. 2015. "The Future of World Religions: Population Growth Projections, 2010–2050." Available at: www.pewforum.org/2015/04/02/religious-projections-2010–2050/

Phillips, Melanie. 2006. LONDONISTAN: How Britain is Creating a Terrorist State Within. New York: Encounter Books.

Phillips, Richard. 2008. "Standing Together: the Muslim Association of Britain and the Anti-War Movement." Race & Class 50(2): 101–113.

Phillips, Richard, and Jamil Iqbal. 2008. "Muslims and the Anti-War Movement." In Muslim Spaces of Hope: Geographies of Possibility in Britain and the West, ed. Richard Phillips. New York: Zed,163–178.

Pipes, Daniel. 2002. Militant Islam Reaches America. New York: W.W. Norton and Company.

Pisoiu, Daniela. 2014. "Radicalization." In The Oxford Handbook of European Islam, ed. Jocelyne Cesari. Oxford: University of Oxford Press: 770–801.

Plewa, Piotr. 2007. "The Rise and Fall of Temporary Foreign Worker Policies: Lessons for Poland." International Migration 45(2): 3–36.

Poku, Nana, and David Graham, eds. 1998. Redefining Security. Westport, CT: Praeger.

Price, Matthew E. 2009. Rethinking Asylum: History, Purpose, and Limits. Cambridge, UK: Cambridge University Press.

Pupcenoks, Juris. 2010. Muslim Migrant Impact on the European Security Agenda: Lessons from Germany, France and the UK. Saarbrücken, Germany: VDM Verlag Dr. Müler.

Pupcenoks, Juris. 2012. "Religion or Ethnicity? Middle Eastern Conflicts and American Arab-Muslim Protest Politics." Nationalism and Ethnic Politics 18(2): 170–192.

Pupcenoks, Juris, and Farid Senzai. 2016. "Political Participation of American Muslims in Detroit." In Minority Voting in the United States, eds. Kyle L. Kreider and Thomas J. Baldino. Santa Barbara: Praeger, forthcoming.

Pupcenoks, Juris, and Ryan McCabe. 2013. "The Rise of the Fringe: Right Wing Populists, Islamists, and Politics in the United Kingdom." Journal of Muslim Minority Affairs 33(2): 171–184.

Purdam, Kingsley. 2001. "Democracy in Practice: Muslims and the Labour Party at the Local Level. Politics 21(3): 147–157.

Quinn, Thomas. 2006. "Choosing the Least-Worst Government: The British General Election of 2005." West European Politics 29(1): 169–178.

Ragin, Charles. 1997. "Turning the Tables: How Case-Oriented Research Challenges Variable-Oriented Research." Comparative Social Research 16: 27–42.

Ragin, Charles C., Joane Nagel, and Patricia White. 2004. "Workshop on Scientific Foundations of Qualitative Research." National Science Foundation. Report, Arlington, VA.

Ramadan, Tariq. 2004. Western Muslims and the Future of Freedom. Oxford and New York: Oxford University Press.

Rankin, George T., and Kenneth M. Cowen, eds. 2012. Muslims in Europe: Integration and Counter-Extremism Efforts. New York: Nova.

Reals, Tucker. 2009. "5 Get Life in Prison for U.K. Bomb Plot." CBS Online, April 30. Available at: www.cbsnews.com/stories/2007/04/30/terror/main 2740069.shtml

Regeneration and Renewal Organization Website. 2003. "GLA Group to Tackle Pakistani and Bangladeshi Unemployment." May 2. Available at: www.regen. net/news/415660/

Rehman, Javaid. 2007. "Islam, 'War on Terror' and the Future of Muslim Minorities in the United Kingdom: Dilemmas of Multiculturalism." Human Rights Quarterly 29(4): 831–878.

Reitz, Jeffrey, ed. 2002. "Host Societies and the Reception of Immigrants: Institutions, Markets and Policies." Special Issue of International Migration Review, 36(4): 1005–1083.

Reuters. 2007. "Iraq War Tests Unity among U.S. Muslims." February 25. Available at: www.reuters.com/article/idUSARM55523520070225

Rex, John and Robert Moore. 1967. Race, Community and Conflict. London: Oxford University Press.

Riddley, Yvonne. 2009. Interview with Juris Pupcenoks. London, August 5.

Ripiloski, Sasho. 2011. Conflict in Macedonia: Exploring a Paradox in the Former Yugoslavia. Boulder, CO: Lynne Rienner.

Roberts, Lance W., Rodney A. Clifton, Barry Ferguson, Karen Kampen, and Simon Langlois, eds. 2005. Social Trends in Canada 1960–2000. Montreal, Canada: McGill-Queen's University Press:

Rose, Alexander, 2001. "How Did Muslims Vote in 2000?" The Middle East Quarterly 8(3): 13–27.

Rose Eliot J. B. 1969. Colour and Citizenship. London: Oxford University Press.

Rosenau, James N. 1997. Along the Domestic-Foreign Frontier: Exploring Governance in a Turbulent World. Cambridge, UK: Cambridge University Press.

Rosenberg, Clifford. 2006. Policing Paris: The Origins of Modern Immigration Control between the Wars. Ithaca, NY and London: Cornell University Press.

Rosenblum, Marc R., and Idean Salehyan. 2004. "Norms and Interests in US Asylum Enforcement." Journal of Peace Research 41(6): 677–697.

Ross, Liat Radcliffe. 2013. "Muslim Interest Groups and Foreign Policy in the United States, Canada and the United Kingdom: Identity, Interests, and Action." Foreign Policy Analysis 9: 287–306.

Ross, Mark Howard. 2007. Cultural Contestation in Ethnic Conflict. Cambridge, UK: Cambridge University Press.

Roy, Olivier. 2003. "EuroIslam: The Jihad Within?" The National Interest (Spring): 63–73.

Roy, Olivier. 2005. "Why Do They Hate US? Not Because of Iraq." The New York Times, July 22, pg. A21.

Roy, Olivier. 1998. The Failure of Political Islam. Cambridge, MA: Harvard University Press.

Roy, Olivier. 2004. Globalized Islam: The Search for a New Ummah. New York: Columbia University Press.

Runnymede Trust. 1997. "Islamophobia: A challenge for us all." London: The Runnymede Trust.

Rushdie, Salman. 1989. The Satanic Verses. Viking: London.

Sageman, Marc. 2008. Leaderless Jihad: Terror Networks in the Twenty-First Century. Philadelphia, PA: University of Pennsylvania Press.

Sageman, Mark. 2004. Understanding Terror Networks. Philadelphia, PA: University of Pennsylvania Press.

Saggar, Shamit. 2006. "The One Per Cent World: Managing the Myth of Muslim Religious Extremism." Political Quarterly 77(3): 314–327.

Saggar, Shamit. 2009. Pariah Politics: Understanding Western Radical Islamism and What Should Be Done. Oxford: Oxford University Press.

Salaita, Steven. 2006. Anti-Arab Racism in the USA. London and Ann Arbor, MI: Pluto Press.

Salehyan, Idean, and Kristian S. Gleditsch. 2006. "Refugees and the Spread of Civil War." International Organization Spring, 60(Spring): 335–366.

Salehyan, Idean, and Marc R. Rosenblum. 2008. "International Relations, Domestic Politics, and Asylum Admissions in the United States." Political Science Quarterly 61(1): 104–121.

Salloum, Habeeb. 1998. "Detroit-Arab Capital of North America." Al Jadid, Fall. 4(25). Available at: www.aljadid.com/essays_and_features/Detroit-ArabCapitalofNorthAmerica.html

Samad, Yunas. 2013. "The Pakistani Diaspora: USA and UK." In Routledge Handbook of the South Asian Diaspora. London and New York: Routledge, 295–305.

Sardar, Ziauddin. 2005. "Young, Bright, Muslim, Ignored." The Guardian. October 11, pg. 12.

Schanzer, David, Charles Kurzman, and Ebrahim Moosa. 2010. "Anti-Terror Lessons of Muslim-Americans." Project Supported by the National Institute of Justice. January 6. Available at: www.sanford.duke.edu/news/Schanzer_Kurzman_Moosa_Anti-Terror_Lessons.pdf

Scheuer, Michael. 2008. Marching Toward Hell. New York, London, Toronto, and Sydney: Free Press.

Schmidbauer, B. (1995) "Deutschland im Blickpunkt Extremistischer und Terroristischer Auslaendergruppierungen." Bonn: Federal Intelligence Service and Office for the Protection of the Constitution.

Schuster, Liza, and John Solomos. 2004. "Race, Immigration and Asylum: New Labor's Agenda and Consequences." Ethnicities 4(2): 267–300.

Schwartz, Stephen. 2008. "Scientific Training and Radical Islam." The Middle East Quarterly. (Spring): 3–11.

Sciolino, Elaine, and Don Van Natta Jr. 2005. "2004 British Raid Sounded Alert on Pakistani Militants." The New York Times International, July 14, pg. A12.

Seamark, Michael, and David Wilkes. 2007. "Prophet Cartoon Protest Leader is Found Guilty of Inciting Murder." Daily Mail, January 6, pg. 10.

Segell, Glenn M. 2006. "Terrorism on London Public Transport." Defense & Security Analysis 22(1): 45–59.

Sen, Amartya. 2006. Identity and Violence: The Illusion of Destiny. New York and London: W.W. Norton.

Shain, Yossi. 1999. Marketing the American Creed Abroad. Cambridge, UK: Cambridge University Press.

Shain, Yossi. 2007. Kinship and Diasporas in International Affairs. Ann Arbor, MI: The University of Michigan Press.

Sheffer, Gabriel. 1986. Modern Diasporas in International Politics. New York: St. Martin's Press.

Shibli, Murtaza, ed. 2010. 7/7: Muslim Perspectives. Northolt, UK: Rabita.

Shipman, Tim. 2009. "CIA Warns Barack Obama that British Terrorists are the Biggest Threat to the U.S." The Telegraph, February 7. Available at: www.telegraph.co.uk/news/worldnews/northamerica/usa/barackobama/4550144/CIA-warns-Barack-Obama-that-British-terrorists-are-the-biggest-threat-to-the-US.html

Shryock, Andrew. 2008. "The Moral Analogies of Race: Arab American Identity, Color Politics, and the Limits of Racialized Citizenship." In Race and Arab Americans Before and After 9/11: From Invisible Citizens to Visible Subjects, eds. Amaney Jamal and Nadine Naber. Syracuse, NY: Syracuse University Press, 81–113.

Shryock, Andrew. 2009a. "Finding Islam in Detroit." Presentation during the Opening Symposium. Building Islam in Detroit Exhibit. University of Michigan-Dearborn, Bertkowitz Library. November 14.

Shryock, Andrew. 2009b. Personal Communication. November 23.

Shryock, Andrew, and Ann Chih Lin. 2009. "The Limits of Citizenship." In Citizenship and Crisis: Arab Detroit After 9/11, eds. the Detroit Arab American Study Team. New York: Russell Sage Foundation, 265–286.

Shryock, Andrew, Nabeel Abraham, and Sally Howell. 2011. "The New Order and Its Forgotten Histories." In Arab Detroit 9/11: Life in the Terror Decade, edited by Nabeel Abraham, Sally Howell, and Andrew Shryock. Detroit: Wayne University Press, 381–393.

Siegel, Harry, and Carol E. Lee. 2009. "U.S. Charges Nigerian in Bomb Bid." Politico, December 25. Available at: http://dyn.politico.com/printstory.cfm?uuid=C874339F-18FE-70B2-A893CEDA7EB41098

Silber, Mitchell D., and Arvin Bhatt. 2007. "Radicalization in the West: The Homegrown Threat." The City of New York Police Department Report. Available at: http://hoekstra.house.gov/UploadedFiles/NYPD_Report-Radicalization_in_the_West.pdf

Simmons, Michael. 1988. "Iraqis Held After Brawl." The Guardian. January 19: 3.

Sinno, Abdulkader H., ed. 2009. Muslims in Western Politics. Bloomington and Indianapolis, IN: Indiana University Press.

Sinno, Abdulkader H., and Eren Tatari. 2011. "Towards Electability: Public Office and the Arab Vote." In Arab Detroit 9/11: Life in the Terror Decade, eds. Nabeel Abraham, Sally Howell, and Andrew Shryock. Detroit, MI: Wayne University Press, 315–346.

Sivanandan, Ambalavaner. 1982. A Different Hunger. London: Pluto.

Skerry, Peter. 2003. "Political Islam in the United States and Europe." In Political Islam: Challenges for U.S. Policy, ed. Dick Clark. Washington DC: The Aspen Institute.

Smith, Anthony D. 1991. National Identity. Reno, Las Vegas, and London: University of Nevada Press.

Smith, Anthony D. 2009. Ethno-Symbolism and Nationalism. London and New York: Routledge.

Smith, Graham. 1999. "Transnational Politics and the Politics of the Russian Diaspora." Ethnic and Racial Studies 22(3): 500–523.

Smith, Hazel, and Paul Stares, eds. 2007. Diasporas in Conflict: Peacemakers or Peace Wreckers? Tokyo: United Nations University Press.

Smith, Jackie, and Hank Johnston, eds. 2002. Globalization and Resistance: Transnational Dimensions of Social Movements. Laham, Boulder, New York, and Oxford: Rowman & Littlefield Publishers, Inc.

Smith, Susan. J. 1989. The Politics of 'Race' and Residence. Cambridge, UK: Polity Press.

Sobolewska, Maria. 2010. "Religious Extremism in Britain and British Muslims." In The New Extremism in 21st Century Britain, eds. Roger Eatwel, and Matthew J. Goodwin. London and New York: Routledge: 23–46.

Solomon, John. 2004. "Despite Evidence, Man Deported: Case Demonstrates Legal Difficulties of Terrorism Trial." The Boston Globe, June 3. Available at: www.boston.com/news/nation/articles/2004/06/03/despite_evidence_man_deported/

Solomos, John. 2003. Race and Racism in Britain, 3rd Edition. New York: Palgrave Macmillan.

Spalek, Basia. "British Muslims and Community Safety Post- September 11th." Safer Communities 4(2): 12–20.

Spencer, Robert B. 2003. Onward Muslim Soldiers: How Jihad Still Threatens America and the West. Washington, DC: Regnery Publishing.

Spiegel, Steven L., Elizabeth G. Matthews, Jennifer M. Thaw, and Kristen P. Williams. 2012. World Politics in a New Era, 5th Edition. Oxford and New York: Oxford University Press.

Spiegel, Peter, Jay Solomon, and Margaret Coker. 2009. "Al Qaeda Takes Credit for Plot." The Wall Street Journal. December 29. Available at: http://online.wsj.com/article/SB126203574947307987.html

Stanek, Steven. = 2009. "CIA in Recruitment Pitch to Arab-Americans." The National, November 20. Available at: www.thenational.ae/apps/pbcs.dll/article?AID=/20091121/FOREIGN/711209864/1135

Stern, Jessica. 2010. "Mind Over Martyr." Foreign Affairs. Jan/Feb: 109–118.

Stewart, Catrina. 2010. "Peres Accuses Britain of Anti-Israeli Sentiment." The Independent. Available at: www.independent.co.uk/news/world/middle-east/peres-accuses-britain-of-anti-israeli-sentiment-2041240.html

Stobart, Janet. 2010. "Nine Terrorism Suspects Appear in London Court," Los Angeles Times, December 28. Available at: http://articles.latimes.com/2010/dec/28/world/la-fg-britain-terror-20101228

Stockton, Ronald. 1994. "Ethnic Archetypes and the Arab Image." In The Development of Arab-American Identity, ed. Ernest McCarus. Ann Arbor, MI: The University of Michigan Press, 119–154.

Stockton, Ronald. 2009. "Foreign Policy." In Citizenship and Crisis: Arab Detroit After 9/11, eds. the Detroit Arab American Study Team. New York: Russell Sage Foundation, 227–262.

Strum, Daniel. 2007. "A Difficult Adjustment: Iraqi Refugees in Detroit." Refuge Works, Newsletter 24 (November). Available at: www.refugeeworks.org/downloads/rwnews_24.pdf

Strum, Philippa. 2006. American Arabs and Political Participation. Washington, DC: Woodrow Wilson International Center for Scholars.

Studlar, Donley T. 1978. "Policy Voting in Britain: The Colored Immigration Issue in the 1964, 1966, and the 1970 General Election." American Political Science Review 72(March): 46–64.

Studlar, Donley T., and Zig Layton-Henry. 1990. "Nonwhite Minority Access to the Political Agenda in Britain." Policy Studies Review 9(Winter): 273–93.

Suleiman, Michael, ed. 1999. Arabs in America. Philadelphia, PA: Temple University Press.

Sullivan, Stacy. 2004. Be Not Afraid for You Have Sons in America: How a Brooklyn Roofer Helped Lure the US into the Kosovo War. New York: St. Martin's Press.

Swinford, Steven. 2011. "WikiLeaks: How Britain 'Became a Haven for Migrant Extremists,'" Telegraph, 25 April. Available at: www.telegraph.co.uk/news/worldnews/wikileaks/8472854/WikiLeaks-how-Britain-became-a-haven-for-migrant-extremists.html

Taji-Farouki, Suha. 1996. A Fundamental Quest: Hizb al-Tahrir and the Search for the Islamic Caliphate. London: Grey Seal.

Tarbush, Susannah. 2010. "Number of Elected Representatives of Mideast Origin Increases in Britain." A translation of an article that originally appeared in Arabic in Al-Hayat on June 17, 2010. Available at: http://thetanjara.blogspot.com/2010/06/british-elections-lead-to-increased.html

Tarrow, Sydney. 1994. Power in Movement: Social Movements, Collective Action and Politics. New York: Cambridge University Press.

Taspinar, Omar. 2003. "Europe's Muslim Street." Foreign Policy (March/April). Available at: www.brookings.edu/research/opinions/2003/03/middleeast-taspinar

Taylor Stephanie et al. 2005. "Ethnicity, Socio-economic Status, Overweight and Underweight in East London Adolescents," Ethnicity and Health 10(2): 1130128.

Taylor, Matthew, Jenny Percival, and Vikram Dodd. 2009. "Muslim Group Pledges More Protests against UK Soldiers." The Guardian, March 11. Available at: www.guardian.co.uk/uk/2009/mar/11/muslim-group-anti-war-protests

Teitelbaum, Michael S. 1980. "Right Versus Right: Immigration and Refugee Policy in the United States." Foreign Affairs 59(1): 21–59.

Telegraph. 2010. "US Drone Strike Kills Five 'German Militants' in Pakistan." October 5. Available at: www.telegraph.co.uk/news/worldnews/asia/pakistan/8042774/US-drone-strike-kills-five-German-militants-in-Pakistan.html

Tendler, Stewart. 2006. "Cartoon Protester Stirred Race Hate." The Times. November 10, pg. 29.

Thatcher, David. 2005. "The Local Role in Homeland Security." Law and Society Review 39(3): 635–676.

Thompson, Grahame. 2007 "Religious Fundamentalisms, Territories, and Globalization." Economy and Society 36(1): 19–50.

Tichenor, Daniel. 2002. Dividing Lines: The Politics of Immigration Control. Princeton, NJ and Oxford: Princeton University Press.

Tilly, Charles. 1978. From Mobilization to Revolution. New York: McGraw-Hill Companies.

Tilly, Charles. 1985. "War Making and State Making as Organized Crime." In Bringing the State Back, eds. Peter Evans, Dietrich Rueschemeyer, and Theda Skocpol. Cambridge, UK: Cambridge University Press.

Tilly, Charles. 1986. The Contentious French: Four Centuries of Popular Struggle. Cambridge, MA: Belknup.

Tilly, Charles. 2002. Stories, Identities, and Political Change. Laham, Boulder, New York, and Oxford: Rowman and Littlefield.

Tilly, Charles. 2003. Politics of Collective Violence. Cambridge University Press: Cambridge.

Tilly, Charles. 2005. Identities, Boundaries and Social Ties. Boulder, CO and London: Paradigm Publishers

Tilly, Charles, Louise Tilly, and Richard Tilly. 1975. The Rebellious Century, 1830–1930. Cambridge, MA: Harvard University Press.

Tomlinson, Sally. 2007. "Race and Education in Birmingham: Then and Now." In Immigration and Race Relations: Sociological Theory and John Rex, eds. Tahir Abbas and Frank Reeves. London and New York: I.B. Tauris.

Trades Union Congress. 2006. "TUC General Council Statement Jointly with the Muslim Council of Britain." Press Release. Available at: www.tuc.org.uk/the_tuc/tuc-12388-f0.cfm.

Trask, Kerry 2006. Black Hawk: The Battle for the Heart of America. New York: Henry Holt.

Travis, Alan. 2004. "Muslims Abandon Labour over Iraq War." Guardian, 14 March. Available at: www.theguardian.com/politics/2004/mar/15/uk.iraq

UK Communities and Local Government. 2009. Summary Report: Understanding Muslim Ethnic Communities. Online Publication, April. Available at: www.communities.gov.uk/documents/communities/pdf/1203896.pdf

UK CONTEST. 2011. UK Government Official Website. July. www.gov.uk/government/uploads/system/uploads/attachment_data/file/97994/contest-summary.pdf.

UK Foreign and Commonwealth Office/Home Office. 2004. Young Muslims and Extremism Draft Report. Available at: www.globalsecurity.org/security/library/report/2004/muslimext-uk.htm

UK Home Office. 2012. "The Prevent Strategy." Available at: www.homeoffice.gov.uk/counter-terrorism/review-of-prevent-strategy/

UK Neighborhood Statistics, Office of National Statistics. 2007. "Resident Population Estimates by Ethnic Group, All Persons; City of London (Local Authority). Online Publication, June. Available at: http://neighbourhood.statistics.gov.uk/dissemination/LeadTableView.do?a=3&b=276743&c=London&d=13&e=13&g=325264&i=1001x1003x1004&m=0&r=1&s=1200166746953&enc=1&dsFamilyId=1809

UK Office of National Statistics. 2001. Census 2001. Available at www.statistics. gov.uk/census2001/census2001.asp

UK Office of National Statistics. 2011. www.ons.gov.uk/ons/rel/mro/news-release/ census

UK PREVENT. 2011. Available at: www.gov.uk/government/uploads/system/ uploads/attachment_data/file/97976/prevent-strategy-review.pdf

Undercover Mosque. 2007. Chanel 4 Documentary, UK.

United Nations. 2000. Replacement Migration: Is It a Solution to Declining and Ageing Populations? New York: United Nations Publications.

United Nations General Assembly. 2006. "Report of the Commission of Inquiry on Lebanon pursuant to Human Rights Council resolution S-2/1." November 26. Available at: http://web.archive.org/web/20070630133336/www. ohchr.org/english/bodies/hrcouncil/docs/specialsession/A.HRC.3.2.pdf

US Census Bureau. 2000. Dearborn City, Michigan: Census 2000 Demographic Profile Highlights: Arab. Available at: http://factfinder.census.gov/servlet/SAFFIterated Facts?_event=&geo_id=16000US2621000&_geoContext=01000US|04000US 26|16000US2621000&_street=&_county=dearborn&_cityTown=dearborn&_ state=04000US26&_zip=&_lang=en&_sse=on&ActiveGeoDiv=&_use EV=&pctxt=fph&pgsl=160&_submenuId=factsheet_2&ds_name=DEC_2000_ SAFF&_ci_nbr=504&qr_name=DEC_2000_SAFF_A1160&reg=DEC_2000_ SAFF_A1160%3A504&_keyword=&_industry=

US Committee for Refugees and Immigrants. 1992. Refugee Reports. December 31, 9–13.

US Department of Homeland Security. 2010. Yearbook of Immigration Statistics: 2009. Washington, DC: US Department of Homeland Security, Office of Immigration Statistics.

USA Today. 2008. "Hundreds in U.S. Protest Strikes on Gaza." December 30. Available at: www.usatoday.com/news/nation/2008–12–30-michigan-protest_ N.htm

USA Today. 2008. "Hundreds in U.S. Protest Strikes on Gaza." December 30, Available at: www.usatoday.com/news/nation/2008–12–30-michigan-protest_ N.htm

Vaisse, Justin. 2010. "Eurabian Follies." Foreign Policy (January/February). Available at: www.brookings.edu/research/opinions/2010/01/06-eura bian-follies-vaisse

Varshney, Ashutosh. 2002. Ethnic Conflict and Civic Life: Hindus and Muslims in India. New Haven, CT and London: Yale University Press.

Vaughan, James R. 2015. "'Mayhew's Outcasts': Anti-Zionism and the Arab Lobby in Harold Wilson's Labour Party." Israel Affairs 21(1): 27–47.

Vidino, Lorenzo. 2010. The New Muslim Brotherhood in the West. New York: Columbia University Press.

Voice of America. 2007. "Iraq Sectarian Violence Affects American Muslims." May 10. Available at: www1.voanews.com/english/news/a-13–2007–05–10- voa19–66776267.html

Wæver, Ole, Bary Buzan, Morten Kelstrup, and Pierre Lemaitre. 1993. Identity, Migration and the New Security Agenda in Europe. New York: St. Martin's Press.

Walid, Dawud. 2009a. "5 Years with CAIR in Michigan." A Speech in Building Islam in Detroit Symposium. Mardigan Library, University of Michigan-Dearborn, November 14.

Walid, Dawud. 2009b. Interview with Juris Pupcenoks. Detroit, MI, November 19.

Walker, Clive. 2006. "Clamping Down on Terrorism in the United Kingdom." Journal of International Criminal Justice 4(5): 1137–1151.

Walker, Rowan. 2007. "News Briefing: Protest Thousands Take Part in Anti-War Rallies." The Observer, February 25, p. 10.

Walt, Stephen. 1999. "Rigor or Rigor Mortis? Rational Choice and Security Studies." International Security 23(Spring): 5–48.

Warikoo, Niraj. 2006. "Hundreds in Metro Detroit Protest Israeli Attacks." Arab American Institute, July 14. Available at: www.aaiusa.org/press-room/2260/aainews071406DFP

Warikoo, Niraj. 2013. "Civil Rights Leader Imad Hamad Retired in the Face of Sex Harassment, Assault Allegations," Detroit Free Press, November 22. Available at: http://archive.freep.com/article/20131122/NEWS06/311220120/Civil-rights-leader-Imad-Hamad-retires-face-sex-harassment-assault-allegations

Warikoo, Niraj, Ben Schmitt, and Robin Erb. 2009. "Islamic Leader's Family Urges Investigation into His Death." Detroit Free Press, October 31. Available at: www.freep.com/article/20091031/NEWS02/910310367/1318/Islamic-leaders-family-urges-investigation-into-his-death

Warya Post. 2014. "A Record 9 British-Somali Councillors Elected in UK Local Elections." June 6. Available at: www.waryapost.com/record-9-british-somali-councillors-elected-uk-local-elections/

Weaver, Mary A. 2015. "Her Majesty's Jihadists." New York Times Magazine. April 14. Available at: www.nytimes.com/2015/04/19/magazine/her-majestys-jihadists.html

Weinberg, Leonard, ed. 1992. Political Parties and Terrorist Groups. London: Frank Cass.

Weiner, Myron. 1993. International Migration and Security. Boulder, CO: Westview Press.

Weiner, Myron, and Sharon Russell, eds. 2001. Demography and National Security. New York and Oxford: Berghan Books.

Weiner, Tim. 2007. Legacy of Ashes: The History of the CIA. New York: Doubleday.

Welch, Michael. 2002. Detained: Immigration Laws and Expanding I.N.S. Jail Complex. Philadelphia, PA: Temple University Press.

Weller, Paul. 2006. "Addressing Religious Discriminate and Islamophobia: Muslims and Liberal Democracies. The Case of the United Kingdom." Journal of Islamic Studies 17(3): 295–325.

Werbner, Pnina. 1996. "The Making of Muslim Dissident: Hybridized Discourses, Lay Preachers, and Radical Rhetoric Among British Pakistanis." American Ethnologist 23(1): 102–122.

Westoff, Charles F., and Tomas Frejka. 2007. "Religiousness and Fertility among European Muslims." Population and Development Review 33(4): 785–809.

Whitlock, Craig. 2009. "Western Terror Recruits on the Rise." The Washington Post, October 19. Available at: www.cbsnews.com/stories/2009/10/19/politics/washingtonpost/main5396014.shtml

Wiktorowicz, Quintan. 2005. Radical Islam Rising: Muslim Extremism in the West. Lahan, Boulder, Toronto, Oxford: Rowman and Littlefield.

Wilkinson, Peter. 2010. "UK's 'Broken' Asylum System Remains Battleground." CNN Online, November 21. Available at: www.cnn.com/2010/WORLD/europe/11/18/asylum.seekers/index.html

Wilkinson, Steven. 2004. Votes and Violence: Electoral Competition and Ethnic Riots in India. Cambridge, UK: Cambridge University Press.

Winterdyk, John A., and Kelly W. Sundberg, eds. 2010. Border Security in the Al-Qaeda Era. Boca Raton, London, and New York: CRC Press.

Wintour, Patrick, Kamal Ahmed, Ed Vulliamy, Ian Traynor, and Jabal Saraj. 2001. "It's Time for War, Bush and Blair Tell Taliban." The Guardian, October 7. Available at: www.guardian.co.uk/world/2001/oct/07/politics.september11

Wittgenstein, Ludwig. 1958. Philosophical Investigations. Oxford: Blackwell.

Wright, Laurence. 2006. The Looming Tower: Al-Qaeda and the Road to 9/11. New York: Vintage Books.

Ye'or, Bat. 2005. Eurabia: The Euro-Arab Axis. Madison and Teaneck: Fairleigh Dickinson Press.

Youmans, William. 2011. "Domestic Foreign Policy: Arab Detroit as a Special Place in the War on Terror." In Arab Detroit 9/11: Life in the Terror Decade, eds. Nabeel Abraham, Sally Howell, and Andrew Shryock. Detroit, MI: Wayne University Press, 269–286.

Zagefka, Hanna, and Rupert Brown. 2002. "The Relationship between Acculturation Strategies, Relative Fit and Intergroup Relations: Immigrant-Majority Relations in Germany." European Journal of Social Psychology 32: 171–188.

Ziya-ul-Hasan Faruqi. 1963. The Deoband School and the Demand for Pakistan. Bombay: Asia Publishing House.

Zolberg, Aristide R. 2006a. "International Migration in Political Perspective." In The Migration Reader: Exploring Politics and Policies, eds. Anthony Messina, and Gallya Lahav, Boulder, London: Lynne Rienner, 63–88.

Zolberg, Aristide R. 2006b. A Nation by Design: Immigration Policy in the Fashioning of America. Cambridge, MA and London, UK: Harvard University Press.

Zolberg, Astride R., Astri Suhrke, and Sergio Aguayo. 1989. Escape from Violence: Conflict and the Refugee Crisis in the Developing World. Oxford: Oxford University Press.

Appendix
Muslim Code of Honor—Dearborn

بسم الله الرحمن الرحيم
In The Name of God, The All Merciful, Bestower of Mercy

Council of Islamic Organizations of Michigan

Preamble

Reports of sectarian tension overseas, particularly in aftermath of the American invasion of Iraq, have prompted the Muslim American leadership to speak out against communal divisions and all sectarian violence. Such expressions of sectarianism, if unchecked, may add fuel to the fire, engulfing the Community in historical grievances that magnify theological differences and minimize the common 'Pillars of Faith' on which all Muslims agree, irrespective of their school of thought (madhhab).

As Muslim Americans who live and struggle for a dignified existence for Islam and Muslims in a spirit of peaceful coexistence and respect for all, we believe that the practical challenges of the future supersede the ideological differences of the past. Moreover, in recognition of our communal duty to promote goodness and peace, we remain eager to offer any help we can and to join hands with all those who wish well for the Family of Believers (Ummah) in stopping the senseless, inhumane violence in Iraq and elsewhere in the world.

In our view, we must begin by preventing such tragic sectarianism from spilling over into our Muslim communities in the United States. As a first step toward this goal, we agree to live in peace and respect each other in accordance with a 'Muslim Code of Honor.' We remain committed to this Muslim Code of Honor not only during times of agreement and ease but, more importantly, when faced with contentious issues and in times of mutual disagreement.

Muslim Code of Honor

❖ No group or individual should use, spread or tolerate the rhetoric of takfir (branding others nonbelievers) against anyone who believes in the oneness and supremacy of God, the prophethood of Muhammad Ibn 'Abd Allah, peace be upon him, as the last of God's messengers, and in the reality of the Last Day, agreeing on the authenticity of the Holy Qur'an and facing Mecca (qibla) in daily prayers.

❖ Muslims should respect one another and the people, places and events that any Muslim group or individual holds in esteem, even when they disagree about the relative importance of such people and events. Such disagreements, moreover, should only be expressed in a respectful manner, avoiding inflammatory language and insulting verbiage.

❖ As to differences in the performance of worship ('ibādāt), we agree to respect the rules in effect and the authority of the leadership that endorses them in the particular mosque or religious institution where they are the norm.

❖ We agree that steps should be taken to protect the general Muslim population in America from the distribution of divisive, inflammatory or irrelevant literature, primarily from overseas, in order to maintain the integrity and protect the future of Islam in America and curb the spread of harmful and misleading propaganda.

❖ We support the establishment of objective, scholarly study groups (halaqas) to examine Muslim history, creed and law, in an effort to increase our knowledge and understanding of one another and to aid in mutual reconciliation. In the event, however, that problems should arise in this regard, a joint body of Muslim scholars from both Shia and Sunni traditions should be consulted in order to prevent schism.

❖ Finally, we encourage all Muslims in the United States to work to emphasize their commonality, in accordance with God's statement:

"And hold fast, all together, to the rope of God, and be not divided among yourselves. And remember with gratitude God's favor upon you, when you were enemies and He joined your hearts in love. Thus by His grace you became brethren. And you were on the brink of the Fire, and He saved you from it. Thus doth God make His Signs clear to you, that you may be guided. So let there arise out of you a band of people inviting to all that is good, enjoining what is right and forbidding what is wrong. They are the ones to attain felicity. And be not like those who are divided amongst themselves and fall into disputations after receiving clear signs. For them is a dreadful penalty." (3:103-05)

We, the undersigned, on 10 May, 2007 (22 Rabi'll, 1428), endorse the contents of this Code of Honor and commit ourselves to upholding it. We encourage, moreover, all Muslims to honor the terms set forth herein to the best of their ability. We ask God the Exalted to aid us in this and all our efforts to conduct ourselves in a manner that is most pleasing to Him (in alphabetical order).

Imam Jowad Al-Ansari
As-Sojood Muslim Hospice

Sheikh Ali Suleiman Ali
Muslim Community of Western-Suburbs, Canton

Imam Husham Al-Husainy
Karbala Islamic Educational Center, Dearborn

Imam Hassan Al-Qazwini
Islamic Center of America, Dearborn

Dr. Main Al-Qudah
Islamic American University, Southfield

Imam Abdullatif Azom
Masjid Alfalah, Detroit

Hajj Ghalib V. Begg
Chair, Council of Islamic Organizations of Michigan

Imam Abdul Latif Berry
Islamic Institute of Knowledge, Dearborn

Imam Kassem Baydoun
Islamic House of Wisdom

Imam Baker Berry
Islamic Institute of Knowledge, Dearborn

Imam Abdullah Bey El-Amin
Muslim Center of Detroit

Imam Mohammad Ali Elahi
Islamic House of Wisdom, Dearborn Heights

Imam Mustapha Elturk
Islamic Organization of North America, Warren

Imam Shuaib Gerguri
Albanian Islamic Center, Harper Woods

Arif Huskic
Bosnian Islamic Center Gazihusrevbeg, Hamtramck

Dr. S. Abd al-Hakim Jackson
University of Michigan, Ann Arbor

Imam Aly Mohammad Lela
Islamic Association of Greater Detroit, Rochester Hills

Imam Mohamad Mardini
American Muslim Center, Dearborn

Malek Menad
Muslim American Society, Detroit

Imam Muhammad Musa
Muslim Unity Center, Bloomfield Hills

Imam Achmat Salie
American Muslim Diversity Association

Imam Omar Soubani
Islamic Society of Greater Lansing

Sheikh Mostafa Tolba
MAS Quran Institute, Southfield

Muhammad M. Uddin
Imam Mohammad Muyeen Uddin
Al-Islah Islamic Center, Hamtramck

Hajj Dawud Walid
Executive Director, Council of American Islamic Relations
Michigan Chapter

Index

For Product Safety Concerns and Information please contact our EU
representative GPSR@taylorandfrancis.com
Taylor & Francis Verlag GmbH, Kaufingerstraße 24, 80331 München, Germany

www.ingramcontent.com/pod-product-compliance
Lightning Source LLC
Chambersburg PA
CBHW050424280326
41932CB00013BA/1987